THE BOOT HILL COFFEE CLUB
VOLUME I
WAR TIME MEMORIES OF WORLD WAR I AND WORLD WAR II

By

Ernest C. Frazier

© 2003 by Ernie Frazier All rights reserved.

No part of this book may be reproduced, stored in a retrieval system, or transmitted by any means, electronic, mechanical, photocopying, recording, or otherwise, without written permission from the author.

ISBN: 1-4107-5997-0 (e-book)
ISBN: 1-4107-5995-4 (Paperback)
ISBN: 1-4107-5996-2 (Hardcover)

This book is printed on acid free paper.

Front Cover Photo is from the US Army Chaplin Museum.

1stBooks – rev. 07/01/03

CONTENTS

ABOUT THE BOOTHILL COFFEE CLUB v

WORLD WAR I vii

    CHAPTER 1 JESSE EDMISTEN 1
    CHAPTER 2 CHER AMI & MAJOR WHITTLESEY 15
    CHAPTER 3 FRANK SHRIWISE & ALFRED E. SWEET 20

WORLD WAR II 27

    CHAPTER 4 WILLIAM C. (SANDY) SANFORD 29
    CHAPTER 5 W. R. (BILL) BRENNER 35
    CHAPTER 6 WILFRED BILLEY 53
    CHAPTER 7 ROBERT (BOB) ICHIGI KASHIWAGI 66
    CHAPTER 8 GENE STEGMAN 83
    CHAPTER 9 BOB DOLE 88
    CHAPTER 10 KENT ROSS 96
    CHAPTER 11 JOHN SCHLICHTING 105
    CHAPTER 12 FLOYD KIRBY 122
    CHAPTER 13 MERL BEEMER 132
    CHAPTER 14 VERNON V. SCHRAEDER 137
    CHAPTER 15 WILBUR T. HAUGEN 144
    CHAPTER 16 GENE EASTIN 162
    CHAPTER 17 WILLARD DAVIS 167
    CHAPTER 18 MARVIN CLARK 173
    CHAPTER 19 EDGAR FRANK COMBS 181
    CHAPTER 20 ARNOLD (GABBY) HARTNETT 190
    CHAPTER 21 DON SMITH 197
    CHAPTER 22 ORVILLE BREHM 204
    CHAPTER 23 ALBERT ROTMAN 212

CHAPTER 24	WENDELL SWANK	218
CHAPTER 25	ORVILLE BERGER	228
CHAPTER 26	BERT EARLS	240
CHAPTER 27	STAN SUTTON	248
CHAPTER 28	M. J. COMBEST	253
CHAPTER 29	GEORGE QUASENBARTH	267
CHAPTER 30	CARL KURT ZACHARIAS	276
CHAPTER 31	RUBY BRADLEY	297
CHAPTER 32	WILLIAM W. (BILL) CARLIN	300
CHAPTER 33	HARRY FUKUHARA	312
CHAPTER 34	CLAY DECKER	335
CHAPTER 35	HENRY FORD	366
CHAPTER 36	RUSSELL MONICAL	379

ACKNOWLEDGEMENTS 388

Every morning the coffee shops in the towns and cities of America come alive. Aging men and women shuffle in and sit down to visit with their friends. They discuss politics, sports, health, and their families. The subjects of war, sacrifice or heroism seldom come up. If so it's usually a brief reference to a long-ago military experience.

A passer-by would be amazed to discover that he was in the presence of heroes—men and women who fought the wars that now guarantee his right to drop into a coffee shop or do anything else he wishes.

The Boot Hill Coffee Club, mostly military veterans, meets daily in Dodge City, Kansas. They are only a few of the thousands of unsung heroes who gather daily in coffee shops all over America. The term "Boot Hill Coffee Club," as used here, is symbolic of all coffee clubs where veterans gather every day. You may belong to a "Boot Hill Coffee Club" in your town. If you do, this book is dedicated to you.

These are their stories.

PAT ROBERTS
KANSAS

WASHINGTON, DC 20510-1605
(202) 224-4774

United States Senate
WASHINGTON, DC 20510-1605

COMMITTEES
ARMED SERVICES
AGRICULTURE
ETHICS
HEALTH, EDUCATION,
LABOR, AND PENSIONS
CHAIRMAN
INTELLIGENCE

Dear friends,

This is a book written about military service and combat experiences. Every soldier from every branch has important stories to tell about their service to their country. Ernie's book is a collection of some of those vivid stories, told in the words of those who experienced them.

These stories also reveal the growth of our military which parallels our cultural growth in accepting all Americans as part of our cultural and military brotherhood, regardless of race or gender. Every American should understand the feelings of segregated African, Indian, and Japanese Americans, as they volunteered for their country, but were treated shamefully while taking a far larger percentage of the risks in battle.

Robert Kashiwagi was interned with his family in Colorado but ultimately helped save the Lost Battalion from the Germans, amidst hunger, unsanitary and of course deadly conditions.

Wilfred Billey's Navajo heritage brought him to one of two all-Navajo Marine Units. His descriptions of the confusion and fast-pace of battle should be appreciated by anyone who has criticized the military from their safe, warm homes and offices.

My own experience with the US Marine Corps from 1958 to 1962 has provided me a strong foundation for everything within my life's experiences, from newspaper publishing, to teaching to legislative work to becoming a member of the US House of Representatives and now US Senator. I work on a daily basis to ensure that our armed forces have the resources they need to continue to protect our freedoms, that they and their quality of life are protected as they serve in dozens of overseas stations, and that our veterans are taken care of in a spirit of appreciation for their sacrifices and service.

I urge you to read this book and try to imagine what our world would be like if the heroes in it had not fought for us in Germany, Italy, France, Japan, Hawaii, the South Pacific, Korea, Vietnam, the Middle East, and dozens of other dangerous places around the globe. Then, say a prayer of thanks to these men and all their male and female brethren who fought and died or fought and lived to tell their tales.

United States Senator

WORLD WAR I

A century will soon have passed since World War I. Major John McRae was a surgeon attached to the British 1st Artillery Brigade that was in battle in the Ypres Salient in the spring of 1915. He wrote the poem, <u>In Flanders Fields</u>, a haunting piece that captured the hearts of Americans and British alike and set the tone of the times. It has endured to this day, symbolic of all men who were there.

<u>In Flanders Fields</u>
By: John McCrae 1915
In Flanders fields the poppies blow
Between the crosses, row on row,
That mark our place; and in the sky
The larks, still bravely singing, fly
scarce heard amid the guns below
We are the Dead. Short days ago
We lived, felt dawn, saw sunset glow,
Loved, and were loved, and now we lie
In Flanders fields
Take up our quarrel with the foe:
To you from failing hands we throw
The torch; be yours to hold it high
If ye break faith with us who die
We shall not sleep, though poppies grow
In Flanders fields

CHAPTER 1

JESSE EDMISTEN

"The shell exploded in the ground and the concussion threw me up in the air."

I knew that an interview with a World War I combat veteran would make for a great opening chapter for this book. Locating a healthy, articulate veteran from that era that had distinguished himself in combat proved to be a problem. Luckily, I was introduced to Jesse Edmisten, of Lexington, Nebraska on December 28th, 2001.

Jesse, an uncommon man, fought in France in WWI. He earned a Purple Heart when wounded on the battlefield in a heroic effort to save his men. He turned down The National order of the Legion of Honor that was offered to him by the French government as he felt undeserving. Eighty years later, the French government dispatched an envoy to Lexington and he finally accepted the decoration.

The war ended in 1918. His story will be one of the last memories of WWI, if not the last, to be recorded in a personal interview and published in both a book and in condensed version in a magazine article. Most WWI soldiers were born before 1900.

Jesse celebrated his 109th birthday on January 16, 2003. That fact alone makes his story most unique. But, that's only one part of his story.

Named after Jesse James

My date of birth was January 16th, 1894. My name, Jesse, comes from Jesse James. My grandparents lived in Southwest Missouri.

Ernie Frazier

That's the area where the James boys lived. The local people liked the boys and helped them out. My dad was only six or seven years old and didn't know anything about it. But his dad, my Granddad, had a barn hidden in a grove way up in the hills. Dad's older brothers used to take care of the James' horses when they showed up. They said that some days they'd go up to the barn and find a bunch of old, rode down horses that looked like they were almost dead. They'd feed 'em and take care of them, sometimes for months. Sometime later they'd go back to check on the horses; they'd be gone and there'd be a different set in there.

A rich family history

    Grandmother was a cousin to the Younger boys that rode with the James'. After they pulled a job, they'd come riding back home, one at a time. No two ever came in together. The law couldn't catch 'em because the whole community was all for them. Nobody would turn 'em in.

    Years later, after Granddad developed a nice farm up here by Oconto, he traded his good level land off—it had a real nice pasture for a hill place back down in Missouri. I was old enough to remember it but I never knew why he did that. He died down there. After I grew up, I went down to see whether he died naturally or somebody killed him. I never found out, either. They wouldn't tell me anything.

    My dad's brother, Abe Edmisten, was in the cavalry during the Civil War, around that time, and knew a lot about the James and Younger boys. I saw him and he told me all about our family's involvement with them. He told me a couple of other interesting things: When the Civil War ended, his unit was told that there wasn't any money left to pay them, so they could just take their horses and saddles and walk away. Some just walked out. They didn't even want the horses.

Abe 'borrowed' about seven horses. He didn't have any feed but started working his way north; trading some horses for feed for the ones he kept. That's the way he came home from the Civil War.

Raised a cowboy

I grew up on my father's ranch at Oconto, Nebraska, a little town about 25 miles north of Lexington. We raised cattle and I grew up being a cowboy. Dad said I was a damned good one, but I don't know whether I was or not. I could ride and rope, that much I know.

First battle: the great flu epidemic

World War 1 broke out and on June 4th, 1917, I went to register for the draft. I was the 19th draw in the county and was drafted in the fall of 1917. I was single then and didn't get married until I was 26. We were called over to Broken Bow and they had a big doings for us boys there. The next morning, we were loaded on a train and taken to Camp Funston, Kansas, between Ft. Riley and Manhattan. My old doctor from Oconto had joined up in the medics and he was at Ft. Riley. He came to see me one day. That is when the flu was so bad that thousands of people, especially soldiers, died from it. He came over on a Sunday and brought a pint of whiskey. We had just gone dry the year before. He said, 'Now, Jesse, I know you don't drink whiskey, you ain't a whiskey drinker, but I've got a pint for you. You take it. Every night, after the lights are out, you take the cork out and take two swallows, then put it back until the next night. If you get the flu, it won't hurt you very much. That's all we use down here.'

I took it like he said. A guy from Texas was bunking next to me. Come to find out, he was drinking whiskey, too. He'd brought in a pint from outside. He and I were the only two that could take care of the men in our barracks who were all down with the flu. We took care of the whole damn barracks and we never did get the flu. I remember all of that very well.

We took all of our training at Camp Funston, mostly with a rifle. They wanted to send me down to the re-mount station where they kept the horses. We didn't have many trucks in those days—just horses and wagons. I didn't want to go down there and shoe horses and do all of that kind of stuff and my company didn't want me to, either.

I didn't go home for Christmas and Thanksgiving but stayed around my company, doing all kinds of duties. One night, I was getting ready to go to bed and a fellow we called Old Tar came in and asked, 'What are you doin' here?' I said, 'Getting ready for bed. What are you doin' here?'

He said, 'You've got a ticket over at the office to go home.' I said, 'What?' He said, 'Yeah, and you'd better get out of here before taps blow because you're headed for home.'

I thought that was mighty strange because I hadn't even asked to go home. You know, those devils sent me home purposely to keep me from having to go down and work the horses. So, I got ten days leave. When I came back, I was still assigned to my infantry unit.

They trained the hell out of us for about a month, and then picked out the fellows that couldn't take it, guys with bad legs or something—and sent them to the medics or the band or wherever they could do some good.

We shipped out in the spring from New York. We were in Coney Island for two weeks until 16 shiploads of men were ready to go. They wanted a bunch of us to travel together for protection. We had fighter ships as escorts. They circled around all the time to keep the German subs away. If they got to us, it would have been all over.

They took us clear up to the North Sea, and then brought us down between England and Ireland, which we could see on either side of the ship. They had a big port at Liverpool and that's where we unloaded.

From Nebraska to the Towers of London

We were marched to the east until we could see the Towers of London and then we headed south. We walked for miles and miles on roads made of big, old rocks. The hike lasted two weeks. Lots of the rocks weren't smooth so your feet and ankles and legs were being twisted all the time. It was really hard on us. I have no idea how many miles we covered, but it was a lot. We walked clear down to a fort, and then crossed the English Channel on a ship. That's how we got to France.

We were out east of Paris and did about a week of training. We had a few of the old time trucks that had solid wheels. They didn't amount to much. Most of our equipment was drawn by horses or mules. They pulled all of the big artillery and hauled our grub.

To Chateau Thierry

We were sent to Chateau Thierry. The Germans were going to take Paris and we had to defend the river and bridge. That was our first battle and we were never very far away from the war after that.

The Germans were just coming in hordes, coming down through there. I was a rifleman—the 2nd Sergeant—and was third in command of our platoon. We had a lieutenant, two sergeants and six squads of men.

On the first day of the battle, the lieutenant got hit pretty hard in the leg and went down. Gates was the Top Sergeant. He took over and the next day he got hit. So, I was then in charge of the First Platoon. Two different lieutenants were sent in. They were good boys that were well educated but didn't have much military training. One got scared so bad that he about shook himself to death and I had to send him to the doctor. They made a lot of mistakes and didn't do well with us old birds that had been doing the fighting.

Night patrols

I had to go out on a lot of night patrols. They were really dangerous. One night, the Captain told me, 'Get your men ready. You're taking out a patrol.'

I said, 'Captain, why don't you send some of these other birds out. I've been going out every night.'

He told me, 'Yeah, I know you have but you're the only one that's been bringing any results back. But, I tell you what. You take your men out tonight and I'll see about sending somebody else out tomorrow night.'

Ernie Frazier

<u>Gas!</u>

I took five men out on patrol that night. There were a lot of wires around our trenches and the German's trenches and we had to cut them to get out into No-Man's Land. We didn't much more than get there until the Germans laid down a barrage of poisonous gas on our battalion, the 89th Division, 355th Infantry, which numbered about a thousand men. They gassed us for seven hours and it killed half of our men.

My patrol was very fortunate. We were flat on our bellies all night in No-Man's Land. The gas drifted over and away from us. We could hear the shells coming over. They made kind of a soft whispering sound. It was estimated that the Germans fired 6,400 shells at our outfit. Companies A, B, and C, were decimated. I was in Company D. A lot of our men that weren't killed came out blind and had their lungs burned. We had to help pick up the bodies in the morning. It was horrible!

Gas floats on water. So, we couldn't drink from any rivers or streams. It'd kill you.

We were in and out of trenches a lot. The Germans had their lines established up on the high ground, maybe up a mile or two away; down lower they might be dug in just a quarter of a mile or so from us.

We'd hit one bunch and knock 'em back. They'd move out to someplace else. If you sent new men in to fight, it was tough. They might be educated but they didn't know how to fight.

I was firing a rifle and a .45 caliber automatic pistol. Sometimes we got within 30 feet of the Germans. The river was only about 12 or 14 feet across, probably waist deep at the most, and they'd come to the river, trying to get across. Our machine guns would open up and they'd try to run through the fire. The Germans didn't blow the bridge because they wanted to cross it to get to Paris. They never made it. Our orders were, 'Don't let them cross the river.' I saw one man make it across. He didn't make it back.

The battle lasted three days. We'd get a little sleep at night if we weren't too scared and excited.

Mud and lice

We had a lot of mud to deal with in France. It dried up in the summertime and wasn't so bad, but it was terrible in the spring. We'd get taken to the rear to get cleaned up and get a change of clothes once in a while, but it wasn't very often. Lice were a big problem. We shaved our heads. I remember that after several days in the trenches, everyone got infested and they took us back and de-loused us. We had a barber from Denver named Barnett. He shaved a lot of heads but we didn't have to shave our faces. We carried razors but most of the time we didn't have the decent water or soap. Back then everyone used straight razors.

We slept wherever we could find a place and even lay right down in the mud. A lot of time, in the fall of the year, two of us would go together and dig a drainage ditch around a spot to take care of the rainwater. We'd join our raincoats together so one would cover our heads and the other our feet. You think about home a lot when you lay down in the mud without any supper because we were out of rations and nothing to look forward to the next day except more of the war. I never thought I'd get out alive. I kind of went hog-wild and decided I'd take as many Germans out as I could before they got me. I shot a lot of them, using my .45 at close range.

We'd move at night so the Germans couldn't see us.

Our medical care was pretty good. If you got wounded, they took you back to an aid station. If the wound was minor, they doctored you up and sent you back to your outfit. You didn't go to the hospital unless it was really necessary.

Food was in short supply. Hot coffee was the biggest part of our rations, at least it seemed that way. We had hardtack that we carried. It was sort of a biscuit that had meat and other stuff in it, kind of like a real hard potpie. It was so hard that you couldn't bite through it. You had to take your gun barrel and smash it or dig into it with your knife to get it to pop open. We'd soak it in our coffee or water. We never got much to eat.

Ernie Frazier

Sergeant York came by

Sergeant York got a lot of medals for the soldiers he killed and captured. We by-passed his outfit at Mount Sac the big mountain that we took in the south of France. It was about 11 miles wide. They had trenches on both sides of the mountain. Our forces took 39,000 prisoners off that mountain. They had big caves dug in the mountains, so big you could get a whole regiment in there, and they used it as a place to rest their soldiers. They'd been there for four years and could control a lot of territory from there. The French and English tried to go up and take it, but couldn't do it. We spent two days getting around that thing. We came up on the east corner and they told our outfit to hit that corner and bust in. Another outfit was to follow up on the inside and others were coming on the outside. We hit the trench at four minutes 'till five that morning. York and his boys were following in through there. Lots of the Germans were trapped. Thousands would have been killed if we'd thrown grenades into the caves. We by passed them and let the other troops take care of 'em. We went on through for five or six miles until we met up with the fellows coming from the west. I had pictures of the caves, the huge rooms, where the Germans were. After we busted through, we didn't meet a lot of resistance. We went through pretty fast. I did lose one man when we went in. He got shot, but it didn't kill him.

We didn't get into any hand-to-hand fighting because the Germans wouldn't stay with us. They were giving ground all the time.

That's how York wound up capturing so many men. I think it was kind of a worked deal. He could have captured thousands if he wanted to. We could have done the same thing, but we were told to keep going.

After Mt. Sac, we were straightening out some lines and got into another battle. We had eight new men that came in the day I got hit. I sat up until 10:00 that night, telling them what not to do. I said, 'Whatever you do, remember, we go by objectives.' We'll just go so far, and then wait until our artillery and machine guns catch up with us. We couldn't just run a bunch of infantry up there and blast the Germans back. Our artillery would come in and tear 'em up, you know, getting them to come up out of the trenches. Then the machine guns would blast 'em. Finally, they'd let us infantrymen go through. That's the way it worked.

I told the new kids, 'Whatever you do, two of you are never to take cover in a shell hole together. If a bunch of you dive in together, they'll drop a shell on you just as sure as the world.' Another thing I told them was to be cautious. If they weren't sure of things, use a hand grenade.'

Balloons overhead

The Germans had men in reconnaissance balloons flying high in the sky. They could spot us down below and see what we were doing. They wouldn't drop a shell on just one person, but, if they saw a bunch of men going in a hole together, they'd drop a big one. After you were around a while, you learned about them shells. We could tell by their whine whether they were going to drop in or were going to fly over us.

That morning, the German's machine guns stopped us. I had one fellow take two other men and go west while I took a couple and went east so we could surround them. We came up from two different sides. There were three or four mounds and the Germans had machine guns hidden behind them. One of them was holding us up pretty bad. We were going to have to cross some open ground before we got to his mound. I told my men, 'I'll start across. If I make it, and don't get hit, you boys follow me.'

Caught red handed!

I started out and made it across. Just as I was ready to lie down, here came four Germans, charging over the top of the mound. I didn't know they were there. I should have taken the advice I gave my men, 'When in doubt use the hand grenade.' But, I hadn't thrown one; that was my mistake. I was caught red-handed. I fired my rifle and took care of three of 'em. The fourth one kept coming. He was out of ammunition so he pitched his rifle at me. I seen it coming and I hit his gun with mine, knocking it down. The point of his bayonet hit my leg. It dug out a little moon-shaped hole out of the inside of my leg. Leroy Farmer, a buddy of mine, finished him off right there.

The French and English had observers with glasses way up behind us. They wrote it up that I had charged a machine-gun single-handed and wiped it out. Actually, I hadn't. I got into it by mistake by not using a hand grenade. My boys knew that, so I wasn't going to take any medals for what I did. I refused a medal, but they kept a record of it.

Four or five of our men ran into one of the shell holes all together.

My Captain crawled up behind me. The Germans were just giving us hell. He said, 'Sarge, you're going to lose that whole bunch of new men. They all went into that hole together.' I told him, 'I seen 'em, Captain. I'll try to get over to them as soon as I can.' I couldn't move out right then. I'd have gotten hit for sure.

Jesse airborne!

I waited and waited. When I thought the time was right, I started over to where they were. Evidently, I waited a little too long and I heard the shell coming in. I threw myself down and threw my arm out to protect the men. The shell exploded in the ground and the concussion threw me up in the air. I don't know how high. One of the boys said later, 'The last I ever seen of you, you were up in the air.'

I was knocked silly. It tore up my right arm up and I can't straighten these fingers. It cut the leaders in my arm, tore the muscle up and broke my shoulder. The good Lord took care of me. It's a wonder I wasn't blown to pieces.

They sent me into the hospital and the war ended two days later. I remember waking up and a Red Cross woman with some gray in her hair was sitting talking to me. Evidently she got me to talking while I was unconscious and she knew everything in the world about me! She told me the name of my saddle horse and everything about my family.

Our outfit was sent into Germany as part of the Army of Occupation, but I wasn't able to go. A young attorney bunked next to me that was in Army Intelligence. When I got up and around, he told me, 'We need some drivers in our outfit.' A lot of guys couldn't drive anything but horses back then, but I was 23 years old when I left home and had my own car. I said, 'Hell, I can drive anything.' So he said, 'Well, maybe you're the guy we're looking for. You won't have to go back up to Germany where it's cold. It's a lot warmer here. You have to stay six months.'

I decided I wanted to try it. He took me down to headquarters. They questioned me and called my Captain in Germany. After that, they told me, 'You're just the guy we're looking for. You'll be here for the next six months.'

As soon as I signed the papers, I was no longer in the infantry. I was in intelligence. It was interesting and a lot easier than the infantry. We traveled all over, even to Florence, Italy.

A lot of our soldiers had deserted and got into stealing carloads of sugar off the supply trains and selling it to the British. It was the Intelligence Service's job to nab those guys. When we did, the army was really tough on 'em. Some got life in prison.

Back to the ranch

When the six months were up, I was ready to go home to our ranch. They asked me if I wanted to stay in the reserves and I said I would. It paid $15 a month. I drew it all the way through the dirty thirties and it helped a lot. By then I had a family."

Jesse's story about WWI ends here, but his adventurous life was far from over. He told about serving as a U. S. Deputy Marshal during WWI1, and about his grandparent's involvement with the outlaw, Jesse James after whom Jesse was named.

I stayed with the cattle business, mostly. When World War II broke out, they took my two oldest sons. The oldest one went with Patton and his tanks for four years. After he came home, he was killed out here on the highway. The other boy went to the Navy right out of high school.

The Japanese were thick in California. After they blew up Pearl Harbor, our government was worried about the ones that might be loyal to Japan and sabotage our defense plants. The FBI tried to sort them out but there weren't enough to handle the job.

Ernie Frazier

Working for the FBI in WWII

So they hired several of us as United States Deputy Marshals to work for them and sent me to the Douglas Airplane Factory in Santa Monica, California. I stayed with an old army buddy and his wife. They both worked. She told me I could stay there for $30 a month if I would help out with the washing and other chores. I had one day off every week and did a lot of housekeeping for them.

There were 42,000 people working in the Douglas factory. They had people coming and going all the time and wanted us to pick out suspicious people. If we spotted a suspect, we'd call the police in his hometown and find out all about his past. I'd go out to their houses and find out if they were drinking and carousing around or chasing women or whatever else. We'd go down and work around with them on the job to see what kind of work they were doing. If we thought someone needed to be arrested, we just picked up the phone and called the local police.

Sorting out the Japanese was about impossible and we didn't have much luck. Finally, the government gave up so we loaded all the Japanese onto several train cars and sent them to Cheyenne, Wyoming. The government started a town out north in the mountains. They sent me out on one of the trains and I was in charge of one carload.

Later, headquarters in Omaha called me and wondered if I had time to go over to Holdrege, which wasn't far from Lexington. They had a big carnival going on and some pickpockets were cleaning out people's pocketbooks. So, I went. I put on a mustache and sort of a beard because half of Lexington was over there and I knew most of them. They had no idea I was that deep in with the F. B. I. I went out and looked around and spotted three people. I took a good look and knew I'd seen their pictures. They were pushing a baby buggy. I went down to the police station and told the chief that I wanted two of his big boys. I told him we'd take off their badges and put them in their pockets.

A little after dinner, we went back to the carnival. There was a set-up where you'd pull on a weight and try to ring a bell on the top. It took a real man, but there was a trick and I knew how to do it. I went over and told the people that I used to ring that bell. A crowd began gathering. That's what I wanted—a crowd. I said, 'Some people think that I hire someone to fire a shot into the bell to ring it, but I don't do that. You people just watch the bell and see if you can catch anyone shooting at it.'

I stooped over and pulled the two handles right up over my knees. When I straightened up, the weight went straight up and rang the bell. Well, the pickpockets had come up and were right there in the crowd. I showed the policemen the pictures and told them I'd get the man and for them to get the woman. There was a crying doll in the carriage. We moved on them and one guy jumped ahead of me and turned around and butted into me, shoving me back. The guy behind me got my billfold, which didn't have anything in it. One of my policemen grabbed the woman and I grabbed the guy that was trying to butt me around. We cleaned that mess up in a hurry. That was one of the fairly exciting things I got involved in.

I served as a U. S. Deputy Marshal for about a year.

Farming and ranching

I really went to town with my farm in 1945 and 1946. My youngest son was still at home. I needed more help and there were a bunch of German P. O. W's locked up down by the creek. I got a hold of four of them at 75 cents a day per man. One could speak a little English. I raised hogs and we farmed the whole damn country down there.

My first wife and I had two children. She died in childbirth after we'd been married for five years. I remarried and we had three children. My second wife's health began to fail a few years ago; she had heart surgery, a triple-bypass. Before she passed away, we decided to start getting our estate in order. Two of my daughters are still living and I have 19 grandchildren. I was 90 years old back then and was sure I'd never live to be 100.

Jesse at age 108 during the interview

TAPS FOR JESSE

Just a cowboy

Jesse and I met again on December 27th 2002, one year after our interview. At the care home, they told me he'd been sick but was still able to sit up and talk. My daughter, Shelli Rehmert, and I went into his room. He looked tired. He told us in a matter-of-fact voice that he was dying. His throat was sore and he was very weak, but was able to talk and we took a few pictures. After a few minutes, we grasped his hand and said our final goodbye. He said, "Well, I was raised a cowboy and I was always a cowboy. That's about all I ever wanted to do."

He was admitted to a hospital the next day. He lived until January 16th, his 109th birthday, and died the following day: January 17th, 2003.

Military honors

A soft snow was falling on Lexington, Nebraska at 11:00 a. m. January 21, 2003. Shelli, her son Seth, and I attended Jesse's funeral at Reynolds-Love Funeral Home and then accompanied the hearse to Greenwood Cemetery. His burial, of course, was with full military honors. We stood at attention, humbly, as an honor guard of local veterans, Jesse's comrades, raised their rifles and offered the final salute to one of the nation's last WWI heroes. The sound of gunfire, reminiscent of Jesse's days at Chauteau Thierry, cracked sharply through the frozen air, and then was softly muted by Taps wafting over his resting place. The old cowboy/soldier had finally gone home.

CHAPTER 2

CHER AMI & MAJOR WHITTLESEY

Few people of the 21st century, raised in the world of high-tech warfare, would have dreamed that many of the greatest heroes of World War I weren't human at all; they were pigeons. It was a time when telegraph lines were vulnerable to sabotage and signaling by heliograph and signal flags was difficult under combat conditions. In desperate need of a practical vehicle to carry vital messages to and from the battlefield, the military turned back the clock, remembering the Iraq and Syria war of the 12th century when pigeons were used to transport news between the enemy lines.

During World War I, about 20,000 homing pigeons from both sides were killed in combat. Their job: Fly dangerous missions through enemy fire with a little message capsule wrapped to one of their legs. The U. S. Army Signal Corps used about 600 of them in France.

No story about World War I is more poignant than that of the last flight of the stout hearted little bird named Cher Ami (dear friend).

WW1 Carrier Pigeon

Ernie Frazier

Major Whittlesey

Two soon-to-be heroes would meet between October 2 and October 7, 1918 in the Argonne Forest of France: John Whittlesey and Cher Ami. Major John Whittlesey, a lawyer from New England, commanded a battalion of the New York 77th Infantry Regiment, a rag-tag group of street-wise kids from New York City. Wearing glasses and looking more like a scholar than a warrior, he was decried by the regular army officers he served with as a "New York Lawyer" and bore the nickname "Galloping Charlie" that came from his slender build and thin legs.

Major Whittlesey (Galloping Charlie)

Ambush in the Argonne Forest

Whittlesey feared an ambush when ordered to attack vastly superior German forces in the Argonne Forest on October 2, 1918. He argued against the mission but was reassured by his superiors who erroneously (perhaps knowingly) told him that French units were supporting his flank. Against his better judgment, he obeyed orders and led a battalion of the 307th Infantry into immortality. His unit was the only one that made it to their destination, arriving to find no support on either flank, neither French nor American. The Germans quickly surrounded them, cut their lines of communication, and concentrated withering fire into their ranks. Besieged, the battalion dug in, watched their buddies being blown to pieces, and fought for their lives.

Cher Ami

Cher Ami, a registered Black Check Cock carrier pigeon, had flown 11 news-bearing missions but his most important flight was coming up.

For five days, Whittlesey and his men fought a battle of desperation against the Germans. Soon their supply of food and water and medicine was exhausted and they were running out of ammunition. On the fourth day of the battle, Whittlesey was offered a chance to surrender the battalion. The Germans knew they were doomed. Incredibly, though half of his unit was either dead or wounded, Whittlesey scorned the offer.

Friendly fire!

In the meantime, an American artillery unit came on line. Thinking they'd spotted the Germans, they began lobbing shells...directly onto the battalion!

Whittlesey had to get a message out to stop the shelling!

Three pigeons were standing by...awaiting orders. One of them flew out with a plea for help in his message capsule. He was shot down.

A second pigeon was dispatched. He too was felled.

It was then that Cher Ami, a veteran flyer who represented the last hope for what became immortalized as "The Lost Battalion" was dispatched. His message read, "Our artillery is dropping a barrage on us. For heaven's sake, stop it!"

Cher Ami's heroic flight

The Germans, ever alert to the tiny messengers wheeling across the sky, fired at the fleeing Cher Ami. Undaunted, darting and dodging, he raced through a blizzard of shot, smoke, and fire.

No one could know the terror the littlest hero faced in his wild flight, but evidence of his narrow escapes with death marked him for the rest of his life. Upon reaching the friendly confines of his loft, the wounded, exhausted bird collapsed into the hands of his handlers. He had been hit with shot in the breast and the leg. Dangling from the ligaments of his leg was his message capsule. Carefully, they extracted the message, read it, and raced to headquarters. Without delay, an order was forwarded to the artillery units. "Cease firing!"

Ernie Frazier

Rescue!

Relief units were sent out. Within a few hours, 194 survivors of the "Lost Battalion" were safe behind American lines!

Awards

Cher Ami was awarded the French "Croix de Guerre" with Palm for his heroic service. After the war, he and some 40 other pigeons were sent back to the United States and honored for their brave service. He died in 1919 from his wounds. His preserved body can be seen in Washington, D. C. at the Smithsonian Institution.

Major Charles White Whittlesey, Cher Ami's comrade-in-arms, was awarded the Medal of Honor for his actions in the Argonne Forest.

He was also recognized by General Pershing as one of the "three outstanding heroes of the Allied Expeditionary Force.

He was a pallbearer for the opening of the "Tomb of the Unknown Soldier."

He was also named Chairman of Red Cross Roll Call.

Sadly, his story ended in tragedy. He committed suicide on 11/29/21.

The Boothill Coffee Club Volume I

The President of the United States
in the name of The Congress
takes pleasure in presenting the

Medal of Honor

to

WHITTLESEY, CHARLES W.

Rank and Organization: Major, U.S. Army, 308th Infantry, 77th Division. *Place and Date:* Northeast of Binarville, in the forest of Argonne France, 2-7 October 1918. *Entered Service At:* Pittsfield, Mass. *Birth:* Florence, Wis. *G. O. No.:* 118, W.D., 1918.

Citation:

Although cut off for 5 days from the remainder of his division, Maj. Whittlesey maintained his position, which he had reached under orders received for an advance, and held his command, consisting originally of 46 officers and men of the 308th Infantry and of Company K of the 307th Infantry, together in the face of superior numbers of the enemy during the 5 days. Maj. Whittlesey and his command were thus cut off, and no rations or other supplies reached him, in spite of determined efforts which were made by his division. On the 4th day Maj. Whittlesey received from the enemy a written proposition to surrender, which he treated with contempt, although he was at the time out of rations and had suffered a loss of about 50 percent in killed and wounded of his command and was surrounded by the enemy.

CHAPTER 3

FRANK SHRIWISE & ALFRED E. SWEET

World War I, like most events where men were thrown together under adverse, if not hellish conditions, created bonds of friendship that can only be forged in the crucible of shared dangers. One such friendship between two American soldiers, Frank Shriwise and Alfred E. Sweet, is revealed in a long-forgotten letter dated February 22, 1919. It was written by Alfred E. Sweet to Mr. George Schriwise, the father of Frank Shriwise. In WWI, Germans were sometimes referred to as "Boche" or "Fritz" or "Jerry". American soldiers were known as "Doughboys".

This letter is presented in its entirety.

Dear Mr. Shriwise:

I never have had the pleasure of meeting you as yet, but I certainly hope the day is not far off when I can shake hands with Frank's father. Your boy and I have had some interesting experiences and some good times together and I am sorry to say they are going to come to an end soon due to the fact that I am going to be transferred to Army headquarters in Coblenz. More than ever I have regretted that Frank and I were not thrown together earlier in this game involving the destinies of the world but I am thankful for the times we have been together which dates back to the first of September. And our hardest work has been since then.

You see, transportation has been quite a problem over here and during the first part of our time we had none at all and whenever we moved we had to rely on what we could borrow either from our own supply train or from the French. We got our first taste of war in the great offensive at Chauteau Thierry and we all thought we were seeing and doing such a lot but as we look back at the whole, that first part seems very trivial. What an impression the first shell hole made, but when there was nothing in sight but holes and ruins, we hardly noticed it unless the hole appeared with a deafening roar only a few feet away. Then it was passed off with such sour remarks as, "Gee, that was pretty damn close."

The first German steel trench helmets we saw we thought they were wonderful souvenirs, but after a while they were common as dirt.

The first time we heard a motor in the air, everybody was outside breaking their necks to see the "bird", but later, a couple of dozen could pass over the house and nobody would even bat an eyelid. That shows how we passed from the "rookie" class into the being of veterans. We will always remember our days at Chauteau Thierry for it was there that we, the Fourth Division, had a larger part to play in teaching the "Boche" the meaning of the term "To the rear, march!"

The hospitals were all busy and did their share in the work. I was busy in the supply department of the field hospital section keeping the outfits supplied with food and clothing and other equipment necessary for the successful operation of a hospital. We never saw all of the equipment that we so carefully packed and marked and shipped from the states. God knows where it went.

From the fifteenth of July 'till the signing of the Armistice in November, there were just ten days when the sanitary train was in a rest camp that we were far enough back to be safe from shellfire and air raids. Every other minute of our time we were likely to be in the path of some piece of lead or steel. Some came damn close but fortunately Frank and I were born under a "lucky star".

Right after we left the rest camp the last of August, we succeeded in getting three trucks (we should have had thirty-three) such as they were, and your boy was assigned to one as driver and it was then that we began an acquaintance that I hope will be life long.

The trucks that we did get formerly belonged to the supply train and they surely had seen service. Orders came in for one of the vehicles to report to the medical supply officer and Frank was elected. We were then camped in some heavy woods out of sight from enemy planes. It had rained for two days and nights and was still coming down heavily. The wind was awful but at half past five we started; and having gotten a load of medical supplies, we set out in the rain and absolute darkness for the front.

When we neared our destination, the M. P. ordered gas masks at alert position. We had forgotten ours so we trusted in God and kept going. The road was jammed with artillery and ammunition and it sure was tough traveling. The night was inky black save from the flashing of the guns. As long as we had no masks they put us down in a gas proof cellar because "Fritz" was throwing gas. At daylight, we got rid of our load and set out for Vavincourt where we were camped.

We were going down a hill and a damn old Frenchman came out and Frank put on the brakes and being muddy the rear end tried to catch up with the front and there we were, criss-cross of the road and only two skid chains. Well, we got busy and built a road ahead of the wheels and behind and in two hours we were out and on our way again. So much for that trip.

On September 9th we got our three trucks loaded in preparation for a move. We got out of the woods and on the road and waited for the other trucks to arrive to move the companies. Well, some damned fool had gummed the works and we sat there two days and a night with it raining like "Sam Hill" and all we had to eat was some cheese, bread, and "corned will" (army corned beef).

About 10:00 pm on the tenth, we set out for Handeville and when we arrived at five the next morning, we were a pretty tired, hungry, cranky, lot. But after we got rid of our load, we turned in for some sleep. We were within easy walking distance of Verdun and we walked over one moonlight night. Well, "Fritz" had his "birds" out looking for prey and they found us. That night, and for several other nights, we made several trips to the "cave" as the shells were coming pretty close. Some of them were gas shells and one of the officers went nosing around and found a piece of a mustard gas shell. He thought it would make a good souvenir so he put it in his pants pocket. Well, he got "burned" around the "foul sector". It was quite a joke on him.

While we were in this place, we saw the most spectacular air battle. A "Boche" was lurking around about three in the afternoon and all of a sudden three American planes dropped out of the heavens and took after him. Ours was a fast little scout plane and was leading the rest. Jerry tried to escape by going into a cloud but our boy was close after him. In a few seconds, out he came with the Yank close on his heels. For the next six minutes there were all sorts of spiral dips, back somersaults, and double bumps and all the actions known to aviators. But the "Boche" was licked and down to earth he came for the last time, he and his observer being killed and the machine was a mass of ruin.

On the nineteenth of September we moved to Lemmes for a two-day stay only to go on to Sury la Perclie (sp?) on the 21st, Frank's birthday.

Our first question on arriving at a new place was, "Do they shell this place, much?" Well, we asked it here and the M. P. said he hadn't heard a shot in ten days. Hardly had he said it than "whizzzzz" and over came one. Well, we got several more between then and the next morning and it is a wonder we didn't get a few bombs because it was those dreaded moonlight nights.

From that first night until the 25th, everything was fairly quiet. One night we started for rations right after supper in a pouring rain. We got to the "dump" which was in a wood at eight o'clock. We got stuck in the mud and by the time we got out of that trouble and loaded ready to start back to Sury, it was after two in the morning and it was four-thirty when we got to our billet.

We were coming back with rations at midnight on the night of the 25th of September and that was (although we did not know it at the time) the beginning of the end. Hell sure broke loose that night! That was the opening of the Allies big offensive on a 175-kilometer front. All that you could see for miles was just our continual blaze of fire. From the top of the hill behind our town we could see the fire coming from the muzzles of the German artillery and the ground just shook underneath you. The concussion was terrific and our ears felt as though the drums would burst.

The next morning the hospitals got orders to move up. So, we loaded and started before dinner. The trip took nearly twenty-four hours one way and the destination was ten miles away. The spot where the hospital set up had been in German hands when the drive started--not thirty- six hours before.

The engineers were building the road ahead of us as we went across "no-man's land." And it had been "no-man's land" for four years. That night, still on the road, the word was passed back, "Artillery falling short. Pass it back."

The communications had been broken so we were in danger from our own heavies as well as from "Fritz". Well, after one hell of a trip, we reached the site for the hospital, which was up ahead of our own light artillery and not far behind the infantry. After unloading, we got orders to go up to the advance dressing station for a load of the wounded. Well, up we went, and where we got our patients was less than a mile from the German front lines and the enemy machine gun bullets were playing the tune, "Keep your head down, Yankee soldier" and we did, too.

From the edge of the woods behind the dressing station, you could see the enemy if their heads weren't down. It was up in this region that our "Doughboys" found potatoes and coffee still warm in evacuated German dugouts. That shows how we took them by surprise and how hastily they left.

Well, we got our load and started back and the trip back took us just fifty-four hours and nothing to eat. It is a wonder that all the patients didn't die. That was not all. "Fritz" evidently had seen us for shells seemed to follow us for nearly two miles, but he was a damn poor shot. The worst that happened was a piece of shrapnel hitting the rear wheel. This will give you a little idea of what we went through in the Argonne. If Hell is anything like that, I am going to an awful good boy from now on. We had this kind of work practically every day until October 26th when we moved back a little way. But the hospitals were busy with the sick. Perhaps it wasn't a relief when we got the word that the Armistice was signed and hostilities had ceased.

Then rumors began to float around. Some had us going home soon and others had us going into Germany. Well, here we are! On November 20th we set out. Frank's truck had the office equipment of the headquarters of the field hospital section and the supply officer on (board) and at 12:30 p.m. the lieutenant said to me, "Are you all ready?" I replied, "Yes sir." All right, go ahead," he said. "Where to?" was my question. "I don't know," was his reply. So, with this send off, we set out for the march of victory into enemy country.

Several trucks had pulled out so we followed them in hopes that that was right. We moved from twenty to forty kilometers a day and had a different cover every night. We slept in everything from barns to abandoned German officer's quarters. One night Frank and I were abed and asleep at six o'clock and we never got up 'till seven the next morning.

From the 25th of November 'till the second of December, we stopped in Uchtenhagen for a rest. After we had moved headquarters up to Kaltenhofen, we had to go back for a load of wood. It was six o'clock when we came by 19th Field Hospital so we went in for some supper--and what luck! They were having their Thanksgiving dinner that night: roast duck, potato, dressing, jelly, salad, macaroni, cake, pie, and coffee. We felt in luck and as it late when we got through, we stayed with Frank's old company all night. One of the companies brought a great big fat sow for Thanksgiving. One morning, they went out to kill it for dressing and there were six little pigs. Not a bad deal after all.

As we got into Germany, the roads grew more hilly and finally they became mountains. In one place we were fifty-two hundred feet above sea level. But we came through without any mishaps with the exception of burning out our brakes several times.

To be sure, we enlisted to fight these people, not to live with them. But we have no cause for complaint. Frank and I have a nice bed to sleep in and his helper on the truck has a cot in the same room. Downstairs we have a nice warm room in which to spend our spare time. It surely is very comfortable and I hate to leave it and Frank as I expect I will most any day for Coblenz.

Ernie Frazier

When I started in I did not intend to do anything but write you a note but this is more of a short story. And you have probably heard it all from Frank. But I hope you won't get sick of it and throw it at the cat. I am going to miss your boy an awful lot when I go but I hope that, before long, I will see both of you together in the good old USA.

Very sincerely yours,

Alfred E. Sweet

Acknowledgement: Letter contributed by Clare Shriwise, son of Frank Shriwise.

WORLD WAR II

World War I proved nothing. It only set the stage for the next Great War, World War II, that began for the United States in the early dawn of December 7, 1941 when the Empire of Japan launched a savage air raid on the slumbering naval fleet at Pearl Harbor, Hawaii.

That Sunday morning, Japanese pilots soared in on the rays of a brilliant sunrise and were greeted by the sight of one of the greatest military blunders of all time. The pride of the Navy, consisting of six great battleships and more than two thousand men, was helplessly moored in a bottlenecked harbor with no way to escape.

Japanese bombs fell and machine guns blazed away in a merciless onslaught. With no hope for escape, five out of eight great battleships sunk to the depths of the harbor leaving their crewmen entombed for eternity. Other boats in the area were sunk or badly crippled. Japanese planes swarmed on to bomb and strafe Hickam Field. Crewmen and planes were blown apart, leaving the Army Air Corps with only sixteen serviceable bombers. The death toll was astounding: 2,400 Americans dead. Few allied airmen were able to get their planes into the air.

The news of the attack was broadcast by radio; a stunned nation was outraged and President Roosevelt declared war on Japan.

Millions of America's youth rushed to answer the call to arms. It was a "popular" war in the sense that our enemy was clearly defined. Almost every family in the nation had a relative or loved one in the war, creating a camaraderie that bound the people together in a common cause.

Ernie Frazier

The music of the day: *White Christmas, I'll Be Seeing You, In The Mood, Sentimental Journey,* and dozens more, promised better times ahead and helped keep up the spirits of our fighting men.

These are the stories of many of those gallant men and women who fought on battlefields all over the world and emerged as unwilling heroes.

CHAPTER 4

WILLIAM C. (SANDY) SANFORD

"I saw that the pilot's eyes were focused on the ships at Pearl"

The ranks of Pearl Harbor survivors are thinning. I was fortunate to hear of Sandy while traveling in New Mexico. He vividly recalls that day that will live in infamy.

Hickam Field

My brother and I were living in Standish, Michigan when we joined the Army Air Corp on December 5th, 1939. We took our training at Hickam Field, which was adjacent to Pearl Harbor, Hawaii. They needed truck drivers and I was assigned to drive for a Lieutenant Colonel. Before long, I wound up driving for Brigadier General Jacob H. Rudolph. He was the commanding general of the Air Force when the Japanese attacked us on Sunday morning, December 7th, 1941.

When the attack started, I was at Hickam Field, cleaning up at the motor pool and getting ready to go into town for the day. At about 7:50 a. m., my plans all went up in smoke.

Other guys were in the area, getting ready to go to town, and they ran in yelling that the Japs had just attacked Pearl Harbor. We were very close because there was only a fence separating the airfield from Pearl.

Ernie Frazier

Battleships explode in a holocaust!

We ran out and saw the Zeroes coming over. I swear they weren't 50 feet above us, swooping down to torpedo our ships moored at Pearl. We saw and heard the tremendous explosions as they hit our battleships. It was totally unreal. They swooped in across a civilian airport and then passed right over us. They were looking for the carriers, which they couldn't find. Our carriers weren't there because Admiral Halsey had orders to stay away and was out about 300 miles.

So, they went for the battleships. They got down low real quick because the channel wasn't very wide and they had to get their torpedoes into the water to hit the ships.

The Jap's eyes

I could see the pilot's eyes, they were that close. They weren't after personnel at that point. They were staring straight ahead at their targets.

The main worry at that time centered on sabotage so all of our ships were trapped in a bottleneck harbor. The consensus of opinion was that the Japanese couldn't hurt us. Their bombsights weren't any good and their fleet was a thousand miles away, on maneuvers.

Strafed by machine gun fire

Another wave came in. They opened up with machine guns and strafed our runway. We tore out, running for our lives. I ran toward the civilian airport and wound up heading straight into some Jap planes that were coming in low and fast. Their machine guns were fixed in position so the only way to lower their fire was to drop the nose of the plane. When I saw they were close enough to open fire, I hit the dirt and the bullets flew over my head.

No weapons!

During our training, we were issued .45's with live ammunition. Then, they changed their mind and took our guns away. A typical military screw-up.

We were helpless because we didn't have time to grab weapons. If we would have had rifles or machine guns, we could have downed some of the planes. They were that close.

They machine-gunned our planes on the ground and dropped a few bombs on them, pretty well wiping out our air force. They blew up some of our buildings and bombed the hell out of our baseball diamond because the old plans showed it as the aqua system. It had been relocated, but they didn't know that.

Our mess hall took the most casualties. It was the showplace of the Air Force. It was a big hall attached to the barracks and could feed 5,000 people. I don't know how many were killed. But it was around breakfast time when a torpedo hit it.

2,200 Americans are lost

We lost a total of 2,200 people in the attack and 1,200 were on one battleship. That was terrible but it was amazing that we didn't lose a lot more.

Another guy and I found some brush to hide in and we laid low for a while.

Out in the harbor, our ships were on fire. Ammunition, fuel, and oil were on fire and the smoke was terrific.

When things slowed down, I got to the staff car and drove up the hill to a command post. The General had already driven his own car up there. From then on, another guy named Sergeant Meyers and I were armed with a machine gun and .45's. Our job was to haul documents from the base up to the command post. We delivered messages and papers all night long.

I remember driving by the hospital later. A long row of sheets was strung out beside the building, covering the dead.

The attack took about an hour and a half. We had our planes all lined up on our hanger row.

Ernie Frazier

Our troops had plenty of guns and ammo. I drove around and saw that our coastal and field artillery units were operational. Scholfield Barracks housed our Army troops, two divisions of infantry. It hadn't been hit and they had ambulances available.

Everyone was shooting at anything that came flying in. A couple of our B. A. T.s were coming back from a recon patrol at dusk and our people fired on it. Meyer and I jumped into a ditch when they opened up. I tell you, there was plenty of lead in the air.

No crying, no hiding

Believe it or not, there was no crying or hiding. Everybody just went to work, doing what he or she could to clean up and make the best of the disaster. You really didn't see a lot of panic or hysteria. The mess hall stayed open all night. I didn't sleep in a bed for three days; we just kept working.

Another interesting thing; the government had to blame someone so all of the top command staff were relieved of their duties. Complacency was our biggest enemy.

The Japs came in at 7:55 a.m. We had a squadron of bombers, unarmed, coming to Hickam Field and they got caught up in the attack. They were flying in to get armed and for more training.

There were a lot of rumors about the Japanese launching an invasion against us but it would have been pretty tough. We had our two infantry divisions, coastal and field artillery batteries, and a Marine division. I don't think they could have taken us.

The general volunteered my services to a lieutenant colonel. He told me he had a job that he wanted me to volunteer for. I was to pick out any 12 men I wanted, regardless of their job or rank. So, I picked the men, even got a couple out of the jug. We flew down to a place called Ellis Island. I didn't know what our mission was. He said we'd get our orders when we were airborne.

A job at Tarawa

We got into an LST and crossed the equator over to the Gilbert Islands and landed on D-day plus three at Tarawa. Our job was to work with the Seabees and the Marines to repair the Marston Mat, a steel mat used to make an airstrip and to sort and stack bombs and gasoline supplies and other stuff that the Japs had left. Tarawa was where a Jap commander had 5,000 troops and said that there was no way anyone could take the island. They had spent years digging in and fortifying the place. He was almost right. Our troops pounded the island with 2,000-pound bombs and 16-inch guns. Not a palm tree was left standing but many of the bunkers were still intact when our Marines attacked.

The 14th Street Rescue

After we got the clean up done, I was sent back to Honolulu. The Colonel made me the Sergeant in charge of the "14th Street Rescue". That's a round-the-clock eat, drink, and fun place where pilots and crewmen came in for R & R. They'd get drunk and tear things up and the Colonel thought, that since I'd been there on December 7th, they would respect me.

When the new crews started coming in, I'd get a couple of M. P.'s and we'd call a meeting and tell them that they could have all they wanted to eat and drink but they were going to stay in the perimeter and were not going to tear anything up.

That was good duty and I finished my time there.

I wound up being in the military 5 years, 5 months, and 18 days. I'd have gotten out a lot earlier except for Pearl Harbor."

Sixty years after the attack on Pearl Harbor, Sandy is retired from his dirt contracting business. He lives with his wife in Hobbs, New Mexico, a town that boasts two Pearl Harbor survivors: Sandy Sanford and Jim Sturgill. On Memorial Day, May 28, 2001 he was presented with a certificate of appreciation by the city of Hobbs.

CHAPTER 5

W. R. (BILL) BRENNER

"We lined up and started out on what came to be known as The Bataan Death March"

Almost every American knows that the Empire of Japan bombed Pearl Harbor on December 7th 1941. What isn't so well known is that they bombed the Philippines the next day. That set off a series of events that plunged thousands of Americans, Filipinos, British defenders, and civilians into a man-made hell that lasted three and one half years.

Faced with overcrowding problems and dependent on outside countries for most of their raw materials, the Japanese set out in 1931 on a well-planned and bloody conquest to expand their empire. They had overrun Manchuria and by 1937 were deep into China, committing unspeakable atrocities. In the Rape of Nanking, an estimated 300,000 people were murdered and 80,000 women raped. Films were smuggled out that showed young Chinese men tied to poles while still alive; then blindfolded and bayoneted by merciless Japanese soldiers.

In July 1940, the United States warned them to cease their conquests. When they refused, President Roosevelt froze all Japanese assets and soon imposed a commercial blockade on Japan. Infuriated at the loss of critical fuel and other supplies, the Japanese, in quick succession, attacked Pearl Harbor, The Philippines, Thailand, Burma, Singapore, Malaysia, and the Dutch East Indies Archipelago. Their plan was to achieve an impenetrable position before the Americans could strike back.

Ernie Frazier

The United States had a long business and military relationship with the Philippines. Officials knew how critical those islands were to the Japanese expansion so they maintained airfields, hospitals, and coastal defenses there. Unfortunately, many of the tactical blunders that led to the carnage at Pearl Harbor were repeated in the Philippines. The Japanese succeeded in destroying 18 of the 36 Flying Fortresses at Clark Field in addition to 56 fighters and 25 other airplanes.

Bill Brenner, a newly minted doctor with a promising future, suddenly found himself an unwilling participant thrust into one of the greatest tragedies of World War II.

Major W.R. (Bill) Brenner
Survivor of the Bataan Death March & Death Camps

Getting rid of recruiters

"I was in my senior year at Creighton University Medical School in Omaha. Suddenly military recruiters started coming in and taking up our time. That caused us to be late for our jobs at a local restaurant and made our boss mad. So we signed some papers just to get rid of the recruiters, not realizing that we had signed up for two weeks of training at Ft. Leavenworth. When we got down there, we were a very unhappy group of men, me included

A great number of my classmates, along with others from different schools, took a week to learn how to do a column right and a column left. On the weekend, a lot of the guys that had money, which I didn't, went out on pass and got soaked to the gills. The next morning, we were to pass in review before a general. They got us lined up in a column of fours and we started marching. They gave a command to turn the column and our group split like a covey of quail. We were pulled off the line and never did pass in review. They were glad to get rid of us and sent us back home.

I finished my hospital work in San Francisco on July 1, 1940. My fiancée and I were married August 6, 1940 after I was called to active duty with the Army Air Corps at Hamilton Field.

I learned the ropes there, then went to Randolph Field for the Flight Surgeon's course, and then returned to Hamilton Field where I was assigned to the 35th training group and to the hospital staff where I worked in surgery. I told the colonel that I could remove tonsils and do appendectomies if they were in the right place. He said, 'You're the man I want—somebody who knows what he can do and can't do.' So, they put me in charge of surgery. In a matter of a couple of weeks or so, we got a surgeon. I still carried the assignment but he did the first surgery. After that, he walked over to the assistant's side and I did the surgeries.

Shipping out in style

They told me I wasn't going to be moved. I requested a transfer to the 20th, an active group, because I thought they would be sent overseas. However, it worked in reverse and the 35th was sent over instead of the 20th. We didn't know where we were going but they sent us down and we had to buy heavy winter clothes. That caused a real financial burden on me and some of the others. It was a total waste of money because we were sent to the Philippines—a tropical climate. We sailed out on the Coolidge, a luxury liner. We had five men to a stateroom and some of the boys rang the bell and got room service. That was quite a thrill.

It was an uneventful trip except that some men got seasick and we had to give them shots. A cruiser escorted us from Guam on to Manila. They insisted we observe 'lights out' at night. I couldn't see the sense in that because I wasn't really indoctrinated to the fact that we were about to go to war ourselves.

Easy duty—for awhile

We landed on Nichols Field in Manila on November $20^{th,}$ 1940, just before the U.S. got involved in the war. The troops there were on strictly peacetime duty. Offices were only open from 8 to 12, and then closed for the rest of the day. That went on until about three days before the bombing.

Our group got in new P-40 fighter planes. But that didn't solve many problems. They
didn't have the supplies to clean the cosmoline off their guns. Gasoline was in short supply. The engines had to be slow-timed and flown several hours before they could be opened up to perform properly. When the Japs attacked, the planes hadn't been adequately slow-timed and a couple of them hadn't been off the ground at all. I lost a lot of good friends there. They were just sitting ducks. The guns weren't free of the cosmoline, so at about 4,000 feet, their guns froze and they couldn't fire. Since they weren't slow-timed properly, the plane's engines would burn up when they tried to out run the Japs.

We were bombed and strafed; a new and unpleasant experience.

Another portion of our Air Force was at Clark Field. I think the command there stunk from the word go. Remember, the Philippines were a dumping ground for incompetent officers. They'd serve one year and get two years of credit for doing foreign duty.

They sent up all of our bombers and fighter groups from Clark Field to bomb Formosa, which was an assembly point for the Japanese.

The P-40's went up to protect them. However, they didn't get permission to proceed to the target and they had to be brought back in for refueling. Our bombers and fighters landed and lined up in rows, just like the ships did at Pearl Harbor, and the pilots decided to go to lunch. The Japanese struck. The planes were lined up perfectly for them so they just went down the line, firing away. That attack destroyed most of the Air Force at Clark Field.

Doctors dig foxholes

At Nichol Field, we were put out at the edge of a field and told to dig foxholes. I wasn't too enthused about digging because I'd been raised on a farm and had dug many, many post holes. But, fortunately, I did and it got deeper as the bombing went on.

We had some men wounded and I had to go to work. I think that saved the day for me, having something to keep me busy.

A couple of sergeants came running up, wondering what to do. I pointed up at a mess tent and told them it was wrecked and for them to go see if they could fix it up, and then go down the line and see what else they could find to do. That satisfied them and soon they had everyone at work instead of just standing around. It helped ease the tension and excitement a little bit.

Our executive officers disappeared. In fact, there were two of them that I never did see again. A lot of situations came up that would cause people to become separated.

Our surviving planes were sent to little fields, mostly dirt, around the area. When they'd come in to land or would take off, they kicked up a lot of dust and it became another turkey shoot for the Japanese. So we lost a number of excellent planes and pilots.

We became dependent on each other and a lot of the downed pilots had become good friends of mine.

Before we left Manila, some of us stopped in at the cathedral there to pray. Father met us and took us back for a good breakfast of bacon and eggs, a real improvement over what we got in the field.

On to Bataan

The Japs began landing troops in the Philippines so we were sent over to Bataan, to a little landing strip. The Japs began bombing us there. The airfield didn't amount to much. It was pretty much a decoy to divert the Japs away from other camouflaged fields that hid some of our P-40's. Honest to God, there was only one little observation plane that flew out of our strip. I think it was a two-seat Stearman. I talked the pilot into taking me for a short ride. We circled around for a short time, and then came back at dusk and landed on the strip, which was lit up by one small string of lights.

Almost all of the ammunition had been shot up. Men at the front had no bullets left. We had a couple of bombs left. The Japs were unloading a huge amount of men and supplies across the bay from us. Our plane, a P-40 piloted by Captain Ed Dyess, flew three sorties over there. He caught a large number of men working on ramps and strafed them twice. On another run, he dropped one of the bombs down the smoke stack of a Jap ship and blew it up. He made it back safely. He was flying that old, patched up P-40. He was an excellent pilot that knew what he was doing but he didn't give a damn and was taking big chances when he made those runs.

Eating dogs and snakes

Our hospitals on Bataan were tents set up out among the trees. I wasn't involved with the hospital at that time but was out in the field. You'd dig a foxhole and a while later you'd dig another because the first one had gotten too deep and you weren't sure you could climb out of it. We got hit several times and took casualties. We were there about 90 days before we were captured. In the meantime, we only had supplies for 20,000 people. When the collapse came the Filipinos and Americans numbered about 120,000. In a month, we were on half rations. After another week or so, the rations were cut to one quarter. So the men in the fields and those that were doing anything at all were going through a period of starvation. We scrounged for fruit, bananas especially, and anything that walked or crawled. We ate dogs and snakes or anything else we could catch.

Malaria

We were in a malarial infested area and didn't have enough quinine. Many began to die of cerebral malaria and others of just plain malaria and fever. Others died of dysentery and malnutrition. As a result of the malnutrition, they developed beriberi; both wet and dry, which caused great swelling clear up to their bellies. The dry malaria was a neuritis-neuralgia affliction that caused great pain that the patient had to live with 24 hours per day.

No hope

There were all kinds of rumors that we were going to be rescued, but when MacArthur left the area, we knew we were through. There was no question about it. The Japs controlled all of the waters around us, flying whenever and wherever they desired. We were causing them very little trouble with our remaining planes that were only able go up and reconnoiter or survey our position.

We were exhausted, starved, and in terrible physical shape. Our men at the front had either no ammunition or a few rounds at the most. Our food was gone and we had no way to hold out.

I wasn't too alarmed when General King surrendered us to the Japanese We were prisoners of war and expected to be treated as such according to the rules of the Geneva Convention. Our fear wasn't what it should have been. We didn't know what was coming. The next day we were lined up.

The Bataan Death March

We got only a little bit of rice and one canteen of water, and then started what became known as the Bataan Death March. I was in one of the earlier groups and was apparently treated better than some of the others. Most of the group had dysentery. We were only issued one canteen of water per day. If you were too sick to get it and your buddy didn't get the water for you, you just went without. I was fortunate, as I had not contracted either malaria or severe dysentery at that point.

We were in the tropics, marching on hot black top. Lots of the prisoners had fevers of 103-104 degrees and they began to collapse. There were artesian wells running; we passed by three or four of them. They were probably three-inch wells that produced a good-sized flow of water. Some men were crazed with thirst and weren't even sane at that point. They'd break ranks and go tearing over to the wells. The Japs wouldn't tolerate that and the prisoners were immediately shot or bayoneted. The same procedure occurred at each well.

Drinking from a buffalo wallow

We did stop close to a carabao (water buffalo) wallow. A carabao came out of the wallow, defecating as he came. The men were so thirsty that they made a break for the water, scooped the defecation aside, filled their canteens and drank heartily. If you tried to stop them, it was at the risk of your own life because they wouldn't stop for anything. Most of them that drank the polluted water died from fulminating diarrhea.

Colonel Dyess, our squadron commander, who was a Captain at that time, followed behind with another troop. We wondered what happened to our men that dropped out along the way. He said a squad came by and you could see a flash from a muzzle here and there as the Japs shot them down.

We were in groups of 100—some groups had gotten there ahead of us. When we arrived at San Fernando we were herded into a small pen with one latrine. Our rations consisted of a small bit of watery rice cooked in a pan. It was almost impossible to find a place to sleep with all those men jammed in there, vomiting and suffering from diarrhea.

Horrors of the railroad cars

The next morning we were put into small, metal grain cars on a train that ran on a narrow gauge railroad; a hundred men to a car. They locked the door and closed the vents at the top. It was about two hours before the train moved. In the hot tropics, that turned into a real bake job. Men with dysentery and vomiting couldn't control themselves and many of them passed away. Others fainted. It was so crowded that a lot of them didn't even hit the floor. When they opened the door about four hours later at Tarlac, we were really a foul smelling mess. We had about four kilometers left to go to get to Camp O'Donnell.

I helped one man in on the latter part of the walk. We had a different set of guards. I looked at one of them and pointed at the sick man. He nodded so I helped the fellow on in. It didn't make much difference because he died two days later.

Enslaved

At Camp O'Donnell, they put us in barracks. If you got a blanket, you were lucky. Some had them. Many had none. That was the extent of the bedding we were issued. The bed in this case was the wooden floor. The barracks were made of woven grass and were called nepa shacks. The windows amounted to a cut in the grass. We were exposed to the mosquitoes and there were plenty of them. We had one little spigot of water and there were any number of men lined up at a given time trying to get to it. The Jap commander was real short, so he addressed the prisoners by getting up on a table. He told us that Japan had not signed the Geneva Convention and that we were their slaves.

I woke up one morning but couldn't see anything. I rubbed my eyes. They were all puffed up so I massaged them until the eyelids opened. Then I realized that my eyes were all right. However my body was puffed up like a balloon. I'd developed fulminating diarrhea and when that ran its course, I was nothing but skin and bones. I was weaker than a cat but I survived it.

Many a day our rations for the day consisted of nothing more than a mess kit of soupy rice, one in the morning and one at night. They had a green, pipe stem vegetable that had all kinds of fiber in it so you couldn't chew it up and swallow it. All we did was chew it a while then spit it out. We continued to starve. Prisoners couldn't escape because they were too weak to get very far. I think that was part of the Jap's plan; keep us weak.

One sick doctor

Up until then, I'd had a mosquito net but it had been left behind. Consequently, I developed malaria. I had a friend, Dr. V. V. Anderson, a New Mexico National Guardsman from Del Norte, Colorado. We teamed up and he tried to help me. I was out for about 24 hours. A couple of the sergeants that were in my group came around to see why I hadn't been around to look after them and found out I was sick. They went out and rounded up enough quinine to get me through the malaria. Quinine is normally a nice, white tablet. The ones they found for me were shiny and black. They were single tablets, acquired from individuals that had been carrying them in their sweaty pockets while on the march. But, they served my needs and while I was relieved, I was not cured.

Ernie Frazier

Unbearable misery

I made the rounds of the hospital. The only good thing about it was that it had a thatched roof and a wooden floor. Some patients had blankets. Others didn't. It was a place to go to die. The men had vomitus and their blankets were soaked with urine and diarrhea and they were covered with a quantity of flies like you've never seen in your life. It was horrible.

I heard someone call my name. I couldn't figure out who it was. He called me again. I looked down and here was a young man who'd been a fine physical specimen, originally. He'd been pulled out of the line on the march and put on work detail. They worked him down with nothing to eat and he came back just skin and bones. His blanket was soaked just like I'd been describing. His condition was terrible and there was nothing I could do for him. The fellow died the next morning. He was just a fine man in every manner I could name. It really hurt to see someone like him die in the manner that he did. The memory of that incident stayed with me for a long time.

We had no medication. We'd started out with bags of medicine but used them up on the march.

They pulled work details out of there, selecting men that were so weak and sick they couldn't work. They were put to work anyway and died on the job. Others, who made it back to camp, just came back to die.

Counting the corpses

One day I counted 40 corpses that were taken out of our group. Up on the hill there was a Filipino camp. I counted 100 being carried out of there one day, and I wasn't there all day. They just kept carrying them out. I asked one of the Filipino Scouts at San Francisco how many had died per day. He said, for a while it was 500 a day. Many of the men who buried them died in the process.

Escaping was almost impossible; if you tried, you didn't have enough energy to go very far. A few tried. Of course they were caught and examples were made of them, a process that ultimately killed them. While I didn't witness this punishment, I heard that if a man escaped out of a group of ten men, the Japanese would behead the remaining nine.

<u>At Cabanatuan #1 & #3</u>

After O'Donnell, we were moved up north to Cabanatuan 1. I looked at Anderson, the man I'd been with, and told him, 'This looks like another O'Donnell to me.' 'It sure does,' he said. I said, 'Why don't we just volunteer for the first detail out and see what happens.'

So, we did. We were sent up Cabanatuan 3 that was holding a group of prisoners from Corregidor: Navy, Marines, and Army that were able to get over to the area. There was also a group of American and other civilian men that the Japs didn't like or trust. That was interesting because some of them were well connected on the outside and were somehow able to get stuff brought in. I didn't know for sure if they were bribing the guards, but I surmised as much. A couple of them lived quite well but they didn't share anything with the rest of us.

One of them was Ted Lewin. I remember him real well. In the United States, he'd operated a gambling ship outside of Los Angeles. The I. R. S. was after him so, before the war, he moved his operation to the Philippines. It didn't take long until he had things under control there. He had his own casino and ran jai lai and other games. He happened to wind up in my group so we got well acquainted; however, he and his friends weren't about to divulge any of their connections.

There were work details going out every day and we met some of the Filipinos. I got some blank paper and made up checks, a $100 at a time, and sent them out with the work detail to buy us some medicine. About two weeks later, I'd get some medicine from them. Later I found out that the Bank of America had received one of my checks and called my wife to verify my signature. She told them to go ahead and cash it.

I made my purchases without any problems. However, after I moved on, another officer and some enlisted personnel began writing checks for medicine. When the Japs found out about it, they shot the enlisted men and beat the devil out of the officer

Ernie Frazier

The compound was divided into three groups. Two were Army and the other was Navy and Marines. Each had its own medical dispensary. Of course, all they had to dispense was advice until we started writing checks, which the suppliers—probably Chinese merchants operating in the Philippines—accepted.

The Japanese cure: Lydia Pinkham Vegetable Compound!

One thing the Japanese did was to go out and raid all of the local drugstores. About all they came in with was a big batch of Lydia Pinkham Vegetable Compound, which was supposed to increase fertility in females. It had a slight bit of alcohol, but, since it was old stuff, the alcohol had probably evaporated. They brought in case after case of it and some innocuous cough medicine. Also, the Japanese had given us rice polishings, which we didn't know how to utilize. We didn't want to dump it in the men's food because the first thing you'd get was a fist in your face. I don't know where he found it, but Anderson got hold of a bowl. We dumped in a couple of bottles of the Lydia Pinkham Vegetable Compound along with a little of the cough medicine and some of the rice polishings. We let the word out that we had some medicine in stock and that resulted in a real run on the stuff. We'd measure out a one-ounce dose at a time, changing the color of the mixture every day or so, and had a real line-up to get it when the men came in after work. That's the way we got rid of the rice polishings.

We even had men crawling the fence from down at the other compound; wanting some of our medicine. They weren't supposed to go from one compound to another. It was the first thing we could dispense that gave the men any hope at all. It was just a little bit of something to help them out. It wasn't true medical quackery, but was pretty close. However, it paid off in dividends because the men needed hope.

The people that came in from Corregidor were in better shape than the Bataan survivors. They were immediately pulled out and put on work details so their numbers were diminished. I was with the Navy and Marine group. There were 1,800 men in the camp for just two of us to try to care for and listen to. They were suffering terribly *from beriberi and neuritis. They'd get any kind of container they could and soak their feet and hands in water all night long—anything to help stop the pain.*

As a doctor, I was fortunate because they issued us an armband to wear and we didn't have to go out on work details.

Escapees beaten to death and beheaded

The men were mostly sent out to raise gardens. Fortunately, the heavy punishment, such as being shot, brutally beaten or bayoneted for trifle offenses had ceased. Most all of that went on during the Bataan Death March. There were three of our officers—stupid individuals—who tried to escape from Cabanatuan. They waited until it was dark, and then crawled out under a fence. The guards spotted them with their searchlights and actually let them go for a short time. Then they brought them back in and strung them up to be beaten by everyone who went by. Finally, they died and one of the men's head was cut off and stuck up on a post at the camp.

Andy and I decided to volunteer to go out to Japan as prisoners of war, figuring it wouldn't be any worse than where we were. By then, we'd been in the Philippines for a year and a half. We rode a train out to a prison in Manila where we spent a night. It was a different kind of ride since we weren't packed so tightly into the boxcars and they left the vents open in the top.

Degradation

On the second day, we were marched out to board a ship. I don't know how many men were on board but we were packed so tight down in the hold that there was barely enough room for us to lie down to sleep. There were two five-gallon cans to use as a toilet. In a very short time, they were overflowing and were only emptied twice a day. So we were sloshing around in feces, urine, and vomit day and night. We had one stairway. The Japs closed the hatch and stood two guards with Tommy guns on either side. Anyone trying to escape would have been shot down. The only way we got more space was when a prisoner died, a lot of them did, and the body was thrown overboard.

There was a prisoner named Quintero on another ship. I think he was from New Mexico. En route, he developed an acute appendix. A doctor told him, "I can take your appendix out. We have no anesthetic. However, without the operation, you are probably going to die." Quintero said, "Take it out."

No anesthetic for Quintero

The captain sent down some thread and a razor blade. Four men held Quintero down and the doctor took out his appendix. He survived. When he got up into the north part of Japan, he still had a draining abscess so he was put to work in the infirmary. He got some Mercurochrome and gauze and fashioned it into an American flag, which he concealed because he would have been killed if the Japs saw it. At the time of the Jap surrender, our planes were flying over his camp but didn't know that it was full of Prisoners of war. Quintero ran out and signaled the planes by waving his homemade flag. So, they dipped their wings in recognition and dropped some supplies. A little later, they came in to rescue them.

We went into Formosa and could buy some food—one can for two prisoners. It was so many pesos for a can of fruit. We scraped up the money and Andy and I shared one can.

We continued on to Japan. When we unloaded, I was pulled out of the American contingent—I didn't know what was going on—and was stuck in a British P. O. W. camp on the Japanese island of Kyushu. There were a hundred men with no doctor; that was why I was sent there.

Getting sent to the British camp was a good break for me because only American planes were bombing the area. The treatment the American prisoners got depended on the severity of the bombing. Since the British weren't doing any bombing, we didn't have to suffer as much as the Americans.

My treatment remained about the same as it had been and I wasn't singled out for any special punishments. Of course, we were still starving but we had a much better commander than we'd had before. We still had discipline with the guards barking at you and some prisoners were beaten, but not vigorously or to the extremes that it happened in other camps.

Dining with a Jap commander

Strange things happened sometimes. Mr. Williamson, a General Motors salesman from Johannesburg, South Africa, had the responsibility of acting as our commanding "I" officer. One day a Jap commander got a couple of guards and took Williamson and me, up the side of a mountain. When he stopped, he sent the guards several yards away where they couldn't hear us and then addressed us in perfect English. He had been educated at Washington University in horticulture and gave us the names off all the pines and other plants. We visited quite a while before he called the guards and we went back down to the camp. He did that on two different occasions. Also, he had us over for dinner twice, which was quite unusual. He was the only one of the Japanese that was humane to us, as far as I was concerned.

While our treatment at the camp was not brutal, we did have to bow and salute because the Japs demanded it all the time, wherever you were. One time I was sent to town with two guards for some reason that I've forgotten, and there were a couple of civilians on the street who did not salute them. The Japs pushed me back and proceeded to beat the devil out of them—their own people. It made me wonder; in their eyes just how badly were we treated.

Atomic bomb explosion

They dropped the "A" bomb on Nagasaki, which was just across the bay, some thirty miles from us. We heard the explosion and knew something really big had happened because the guards ran all of the prisoners on work details back to camp instead of marching them. They made us each grab a blanket and go to the air raid shelter.

A couple of the people actually saw the explosion and the huge clouds of dust and smoke but didn't know what it was.

Ernie Frazier

Factories were built around the town where the workers lived. Just prior to the Japanese surrender to the allies, our planes firebombed the area on two occasions. The people had dug holes in the floors of the buildings to shelter them from bombs. On the first run, the wind died and very little damage ensued. On the second bombing, firebombs hit the town and in seconds the whole city was ablaze. I don't know how many died, but there were a lot, not from the bombing but from asphyxiation when the oxygen burned out of the air.

The guards disappear

By the time of the surrender, our guards had all disappeared. There was a little building that was kept locked and we knocked the lock off. It was packed full of Red Cross medicine and food. The Japs had orders to save it for themselves and we'd gotten none of it.

I went up to a little guardhouse that overlooked the burned factory and heard a big plane coming in overhead. It had a star on the side. It was the biggest plane I'd ever seen. I found out that it was a B-29. It went down on a 90-degree turn and I was hypnotized just watching it. About the time they made their second turn, the Bomb bay doors started opening and I thought, "Oh, for God's sake!"

There was nothing for me to do so I just stayed put. They were dropping 50 gallon drums, welded together end-to-end to make up a container that held a lot of food. A small parachute opened and jerked them upright, then tore away so they'd free fall to the ground. One crashed through one end of the barracks and another came through the other end. I was in the middle, watching, and didn't get hit. The Good Lord was looking after me.

Liberated!

We opened up the containers. They were full of food and clothing. This was after the surrender of the Japanese to the allies. U. S. ground troops were on the ground in Kyushu, but at that time none had reached us. It was four or five days until our troops arrived to liberate us. I'd been a prisoner in Japan for two years. My treatment there hadn't been too bad because I was in a British camp.

The first thing that needed to be done was to rebuild the railroad in Nagasaki so we could get through there. A dry dock area was constructed and that's where we showered and got clothing. They brought us in around the bay. It was beautiful territory until we got up toward Nagasaki where things started looking brown and soon there was nothing to see. We saw huge trees that had been totally shattered and stripped of all their limbs and bark. We came to a warehouse where the steel girders had been melted and twisted into pretzels. We were unloaded and that's where we got clothing, showered and disinfected with DDT One group, I don't know which one, was sent to Nagasaki to rebuild the railroad. That was right in the heart of the radiation. The men that put us on the dock to shower us had been right in the middle of the radiation. Fortunately, we came through it all right because we weren't there long enough to be affected.

We walked around the area for a while and then were put on the destroyer USS Scott. We skirted a storm, and then made it into port at Okinawa.

They were going to fly us to Nichol Field, south of Manila. We had to wait over a day for a plane and I really got bored. I saw a sentry standing out about 30 yards away so I decided to go out and visit with him. I got about half way to him and said something. He spun around in a split second and his gun was pointed straight at me. He said, "For God's sake, Major, don't ever do anything like that again!" He was a nervous wreck.

I found out that he was one of the original companies that made nine landings on Japanese occupied islands. On Okinawa, his unit had been undergoing training for the invasion of Japan. We talked for quite some time and he brought me up to date on what had been going on while we were in prison.

MacArthur

As far as my opinion about General Douglas MacArthur, he had to be one of the most egotistical people on earth. He had to be in complete charge at all times. We heard that one time headquarters called when he was out so they talked to his second-in-command. Headquarters wanted to make a landing on Cebu. MacArthur's aide saw no reason not to. So, the landing was made based on that conversation. From then on, the aide was alienated from MacArthur because he hadn't waited to consult with him. He acted like a king and everyone else were the serfs in his kingdom. The only good thing I can say about him is that he knew how to deal with the Japanese, which he had to do after the war. One time, after Truman became president, MacArthur even kept him waiting for ten minutes after Truman's plane landed before he went to greet him.

I had three brothers that were in the military: Leo was a bombardier that was shot down over Romania and spent a year in a German P. O. W. camp; Ed flew out of Okinawa; Harold was in the Navy during the Korean War.

Meeting Quintero again

After the war, my former wife and I went to Las Vegas for a veterans' convention and sat at a table with a veteran and his wife. She was very talkative. He didn't say much but other vets came by and spoke to him like he was someone special. I wondered what the hell was going on. I corralled one of guys later and he told me the man was Quintero and told me the story of his homemade flag. We'd been sitting with a dignitary and didn't know it

The speaker was a general in charge of the Washington National Guard. Previously, he commanded the New Mexico National Guard. He came over and visited with us a few moments prior to going to the podium for his speech. We learned that the flag Quintero had made as a P. O. W. was now hanging on the general's office wall in Washington, D. C."

CHAPTER 6

WILFRED BILLEY

"At Camp Elliott, they told us Navajos that we were going to become code talkers."

    The Navajo country of Arizona and New Mexico is an enchanted land of painted deserts, flat-top buttes, conical peaks, gnarled trees, plunging canyons, spectacular sunsets and awe inspiring rock formations.
    The story of Wilfred Billey helped answer some of the questions that arose during my numerous travels through the region. I'd always been drawn to the haunting beauty of the sprawling reservations. I'd seen the isolated Indian squaws covered in layers of multi-hued dresses, tending their tiny bands of sheep many miles from any sign of civilization. I wondered what type of people these Native Americans really were. But, throughout the years, I never had a meaningful talk with a Navajo Indian—until I met Wilfred Billey.
    In Wilfred I met an American patriot. His incredible journey through Word War II was made even more remarkable when one considers that he was fighting a war for a government that had conquered his forefathers, forced them off their property and made them bend under that cruel yoke of the white man, the unforgiving and barren reservation. He and his fellow Indians answered the call to battle as second-class citizens. Many died but those that made it back came home as war heroes. It begs the question, "Why did they bother to fight at all?" Maybe the answer lies in Wilfred's story.

Ernie Frazier

The Navajo reservation

I was born right on the reservation over close to the mountains. I didn't know one single word of English. My first language was Navajo. I was very close to my grandparents, especially my grandfather. He taught me a lot of things and we lived a very simple life. We didn't have running water and no electricity. We had to carry water in. We lived in a Hogan. The life was so simple. My grandmother prepared two sheep skins to sleep on in the Hogan and during the day she would air it out. We were happy living a real simple life. My grandfather had a little farm up in the mountains and he planted potatoes and wheat and that kind of stuff. It was about 12 miles up in the mountains from where we lived. He taught me how to plow, you know, when you lift it up it goes in, when you push it down it comes up.

One day my grandfather brought two horses back and he said, 'Son, I'm taking you to school.' I was to ride one horse and he was to ride the other one. So, we saddled up and took off. He took me to the Bureau of Indian Affairs Boarding School. It was the Twilena Boarding School, about 20 or 25 miles on horseback. I stayed there nine months. A lot of kids who were there ran away and went back home. I didn't run away because I had respect for my grandparents. I didn't want to embarrass them, so I stayed there nine months. Then after that I went to Shiprock Boarding School in Arizona for another couple of years. So, my time spent in the government schools was about three years. The rest of the time I went to public school. I graduated. That's the way it was in those days.

A raw Marine

These young men enlisted in the Marine Corps from the Navajo Methodist Mission High School. This photo was taken before they left for Santa Fe New Mexico for physical exams. Wilfred Billey is third from the right.

When the war started in 1941 when the Japanese bombed Pearl Harbor. I didn't even know where that was. I had no idea. In 1943 I enlisted in the Marine Corps. I was about 17 or 18. I was in school here in Farmington, New Mexico. I wasn't the only one enlisting. There were recruiters on the reservation at that time and they visited different boarding schools on the reservation and recruited.

I joined the Marines because I guess I just followed the crowd so to speak. From our school there were about eight or nine of us and we learned that we were going to be together. This was of course untrue. Yeah, in the boot camp we were together, but after that we were split up in different directions.

When I enlisted in the Marine Corps, we got our physicals in Santa Fe, New Mexico. When we got our physicals, some didn't make it, but most of them did. When we went out to San Diego, I had never been on a train. It was a completely new environment. The food was different; the regimentation was unbelievable in the boot camp. We had about 12 to 13 weeks of basic training indoctrination. We learned how to march and how to say yes sir and no sir. I didn't have any problem physically because of my background. I had my share of chores in the family.

It was a completely new experience for me. I had never been to the ocean, and that kind of stuff. We learned how to shoot rifles in the rifle range. We learned how to swim. Of course most of the guys in our platoon knew how to swim. The officer was surprised. They were teasing us, saying, 'You guys are from New Mexico. There's no water there. How did you know how to swim?'

The Marines wanted radiomen—code talkers

After that was over, we went to a place called Camp Elliot, not too far from San Diego. That's where the training was to take place, for the code talkers. When I went in I did not know I was going to be a code talker. All we were told was that we were to be together in some kind of a communication area.

A lot of people don't know the name, Navajo Code Talkers. During WWII, from 1942 to 1945 when the war ended, we weren't called code talkers. We were called radiomen.

I might tell you that one of the reasons why they had to code in the Navajo language were because there were many English words that they didn't have in Navajo. That's why they had to code the language, especially the military words. There was no word for artillery, no word for machine guns or mortars. That's why they had to improvise. The Marine Corps demanded if a message was sent from one point to another, it had to come out exactly the way it was written, so just plain interpreting was not enough. There was always a mess-up.

Only two all Navajo platoons went to basic training

My particular platoon in March of 1943 was platoon 297. Three were 58 of us. Prior to us, there was another platoon, all Navajo. You have to remember, a lot of people don't know that there were only two all Navajo platoons that went to basic training. One was in 1942 and another one, my platoon, was in 1943. The first group called themselves the Original 29. There were 29 who went to San Diego. They were the ones responsible for coming up with the Navajo Code back in 1942.

The Boothill Coffee Club Volume I

They gave us 10 days leave after boot camp and we came back to the reservation. After our leave we assembled in Gallup, New Mexico and they shipped us back to San Diego to go to school. This is where we learned the code that had been developed by Platoon 382, the original 29 Navajos that came before us. They did that back in the early part of 1942. They retained two of them to be instructors for the incoming future marine code talkers. The rest of them were shipped over.

Philip Johnson

The idea to use the Navajo language came from an Anglo-person by the name of Philip Johnson. I'm sure you heard of him. I understand that his mom and dad were doing some missionary work on the Arizona portion of the Navajo Reservation when he was just a little boy. The family moved back to California. He grew up, got a college education, and in the early part of 1942 was working for the city of Los Angeles as an engineer. He heard about how the Japanese were breaking codes left and right, disrupting our shipments and troop movements. In the back of his mind, he remembered when he was a young boy playing with the Navajo kids on the reservation that he learned some Navajo words. He decided to go to San Diego and discuss it with someone in the higher echelon in the Marine Corps. He met with General Clayton B. Vogel and Major J. E. Jones, a communications person. He approached them on the idea of the military using the Navajo language for classified messages. The Marine Corps was kind of reluctant to accept his idea but finally did so and it turned out to be a very profound decision.

About 400 became code talkers

When it was all said and done, I understand there were over 400 who have served as code talkers but only two platoons were made up of all Navajo. The others went to Anglo platoons in twos or maybe threes. Navajo arriving at the base in San Diego were soon directed to the code school. A lot of them were drafted in the later part of 1944 and the early part of 1945. Of the actual ones who really saw all these battles, I would say probably there were 120.

We were trained as radiomen. When we were learning the code we were simultaneously exposed to learn how to use the radio. Not so much theory stuff, but the prismatic stuff, the practical use of the radio. There were different types of radios that we were exposed to; one was called the TBY, a navy walkie-talkie that you carry on your back; A TBX was a much bigger radio that had a transistor receiver unit with a cable running in it. It takes two persons to operate the TBX. One has to crank the generator to put juice into it. It had a distance of 60 or 75 miles, depending on terrain and the weather. We used that as a voice communication and also they taught us CWO, Morse code.

On a battalion level they usually have a radio chief with a much bigger radio and transistor receiver with a range of 400 or 500 miles. In a battle situation the unit is too clumsy to have on the front lines, so they had to use a code talker.

You have to know something about the organizational structure of a division. A division has approximately 20,000 troops consisting of three regiments that are composed of three battalions for each regiment. You just don't go out and join the Marine Corps and start *fighting. You have to be organized.* A communications section was made up of radiomen, messengers and telephone operators as a group.

Some of the code talkers were assigned to division level, some on the regimental level. *Unfortunately, I was the unlucky one and was assigned to Headquarters Company First Battalion, Second Regiment in a communications section.*

Code talkers were in every major battle in the Pacific

When the Japanese occupied Guadalcanal, they were there with the First Division and the Second Marine Division in August of 1942. Code talkers, or radiomen, have been in every battle that the Marine Corps were engaged in: Odenville, Palau, Tarawa, Saipan, Guam, Tinian, Iwo Jima. They were in every one of those engagements with the Marine Corps. In 1944 when I was on Saipan, they came up with another radio called the SER300. It is a signal corps radio. I really liked that one for a walkie-talkie. It is much better. You carried it on your back and it weighed about 36 to 38 pounds.

At the battalion level they assign an actual combat radioman to each company on the line, so I was right there, especially during the Saipan and Tinian operations.

First landing: Tarawa

The first landing I was on was Tarawa. Then I went to Saipan, Tinian and Okinawa.

We invaded Tarawa in December 20, 1943. I joined the Second Marine Division down in Wellington, New Zealand. They were ready to leave when I arrived on the scene. The guys were really nice to me. They accepted me as one of the radiomen. We arrived at Tarawa and were there 76 hours. Tarawa is about 2,000 miles southwest of Hawaii. It is a little bitty island, about a mile long and less than a mile wide. All we wanted was the airstrip. It is right on the equator. When we arrived there the temperature was about 120 degrees.

I was assigned to the executive officer of the battalion. My commanding officer was Colonel Kyle. No matter how elaborate the plans were there was always a screw up. That's what happened on Tarawa. In fact, the first day we got there, we got a little too close. The Japanese started shelling us and our ships had to move back. Finally, at about 9 o'clock, the first wave went in. Our landing crafts, the Higgins boats, couldn't get to the beach but the Amtrak's could. An Amtrak is a boat that goes on the water with a propeller and then, when beached, can travel on land. That was the first time Amtrak's were used. Unfortunately, the Japanese had learned a lot and were well dug in. They knocked out every Amtrak and I guess most of our guys were killed. Somehow Colonel Kyle made it in and landed on the beach.

There was a pier made of coral rock. It came out several yards and that's where the Japanese unloaded their ships. The first night, we probably gained about 100 yards of the island. It was a good thing the Japanese didn't attack that night. They had a wall along the shore made out of pine trees and we had to go over them. They had pillboxes or machine gun nests all along that.

The first word we got from Colonel Kyle was a message for Major Andrews, the executive officer I was assigned to, telling us not to come in. So, we just stayed out there in the water all the rest of that day and into the night. They finally called us back to the ship and we got some hot lunch. The next day, about noon, they finally gave us the green light to come in but our boat couldn't make it in to the beach. They dropped us off way out by the pier. I was carrying the TBX antenna and canvas and wading in water up to my neck. You had to be there to believe what happened.

Huddled on the beach

They had 4,700 elite Japanese soldiers defending that little island. In 76 hours, we had approximately 3,000 casualties. About 100 of our officers—the company commanders, mostly second and first lieutenants—lost their lives on that island. But, we took the island. As far as me using my specialty as a code talker, I didn't have a chance. So, I transmitted in English, the radio watch and that kind of stuff. Everything went so fast it was unbelievable. We set up a battalion command post, if you want to call it that. We had no cover at all, no building, no foxhole, nothing. We just huddled there together.

I got to know some of these officers, like Colonel Kyle, and because of my position, I got acquainted with those guys. They were officers and I was just a PFC, but still I got to know them. Colonel Kyle was a good commanding Officer, who'd graduated from Texas A & M. His first name was Wood.

I didn't have to fire a weapon. My job was strictly communications. Major Andrews would tell me what to say and I would say it to the company or to the regimental headquarters. Sometimes we'd get a message from regimental headquarters telling us what to do. On a small island like that it is unbelievable how fast everything moved. We were catching fire, mortars and machine guns, real close to our position. They didn't have any planes come over, except for the first night when one lonely plane came by. I don't know what island he was coming from, but it was a Japanese plane. In the middle of the night they called a condition red and he flew over. I guess he used the psychological stuff, you know. He just flew around and finally dropped a bomb on the water. He missed everything.

Only 17 Japanese surrendered

We didn't have troops around our perimeter to guard us. We were alone, right behind the line. Our riflemen were in front of us. Some of them encountered hand-to-hand fighting. I never saw so many people dead, both the Japanese and the American Marines. Out of the 4,700 Japanese who were there, only 17 surrendered, the rest either escaped or were dead. That was my first combat experience. We took the island and then went back to Hawaii, the big island.

We had specialists trained in the use of flamethrowers and our troops used them on Tarawa, Saipan and Tinian. There were a lot of caves on the islands of Saipan and Tinian. The Japanese were entrenched in those caves and our men used flamethrowers to flush them. I saw them used. It's just a jelly gas that they would shoot right into the caves. It burned the Japs alive if they didn't get out fast enough.

Ernie Frazier

<u>Saipan & Tinian</u>

The Saipan operation was different, although the fighting was about the same. The Japanese kind of modified their operation. Instead of meeting us right at the beach, they wanted to fight inland. They held back. The first night on Saipan they shelled us from the jungle. Saipan is about 50 to 75 square miles, much bigger than Tarawa. It is a big, big island with lots of jungle. The Marine Corps wanted to get to the highest point of the island. When you get on top of that you can see the whole island and you could see Tinian on the other side. They called that mountain Matapache. There was really thick jungle. Also on Saipan they had a huge sugar cane field that the Japanese had developed. Of course they had to burn all that stuff down and fight right out in the field. We took the island of Saipan. This is where I really became a regular radioman.

<u>Wilfred replaces a Mission Indian</u>

About the second or third week of the operation, we were on the west side of Saipan Island, along the coast. I had a friend named Levi that I met in Wellington, New Zealand. He'd gone into the service in 1942, before I did. He was a member of a tribe from California and was a Mission Indian. I don't know if you ever heard of Mission Indians. They had a little reservation not too far from San Diego. He was from that tribe. He was kind of a heavyset, dark looking guy. He was a regular radioman, very articulate and he knew his stuff. During the operation at Saipan, he got shot. The bullet passed right through the radio. They brought him back and we thought he would live, but we received word that night that he died. This is when the radio chief of this gang that I belonged to asked me to take over Levi's job. I carried the radio for the company during the rest of the operations on Saipan and Tinian.

I have a friend (still alive) who lives in Forty Pines, Arizona. He was assigned to regimental headquarters. When a message in Navajo came from him, we'd communicate in Navajo. When the company would call me back, I'd get the message and copy and send it back to the battalion headquarters. That was my job. I was on Saipan for almost two years.

In 1944 we regrouped for training on the big island of Hawaii. My battalion was specially trained to go in a few days before the actual invasion of Saipan. We were supposed to go on top of the mountains and establish defense. We practiced landings on many of those islands in Hawaii.

At the last minute, just as we arrived as Saipan, they called it off. We didn't have to do the mission we'd trained for and I was really glad of that.

Japanese suicides

After we had secured both islands, Saipan and Tinian, there were still a lot of Japanese running around in the jungles. At night they would come around through the commissary and steal stuff, so my outfit had to go out into the jungle early in the morning and look for these guys. I would carry the radio for the company. Everyone else was armed and we would kill a lot of Japanese. You know, the Japanese were really good fighters. On Saipan, and especially on Tinian, there were quite a few prisoners taken. Of course a lot of them committed suicide, jumping off a cliff. You've heard of the suicide cliff where a whole family would jump off. We had a boat out there with a loud speaker telling them not to do it, but they still did it. Of course a lot of them came through and surrendered.

When I was with the company I met a lot of guys, riflemen and machine gunners. They called me chief and I used to tease them saying, 'Don't call me chief, If I was your chief we wouldn't be in this mess,' or something like that.

A lot of guys would ask me, 'How are we doing? Are we winning the war?' because I carried a radio and talked to the company commander all the time. They asked me lots of questions.

To me, looking back in retrospect, I really have high respect for some of those guys. They were good fighters. I remember one time about two in the morning when the Japanese started to come over the barbed wire. They didn't make it. Our men just mowed them down. This is one of the reasons why I really have respect for those riflemen

Ernie Frazier

that did their job. Of course a lot of them were wounded and got killed, but still, they did their job. When I talk to the groups, (I work with Salmon College here) there will be some old WWII veterans. I ask them, 'How many regulars do we have?' They raise their hands and I tell them, 'I really have high respect for you guys. You did your job and I salute each one of you for doing a tremendous job. I agree with Tom Brokaw that you're the greatest generation. I belong to your generation.'

I was in the Marine Corps from 1943 to 1946. I got discharged in January of 1946. Most of my time was overseas, a little over 30 months. The Marine Corps in WWII was very stingy with rank and the highest rank I got was corporal. There's an old saying in the Marine Corps; it's not what you know, it's who you know. Some of that stuff goes on even in the military.

An educator

For 13 years, I was the principal in the high school in Shiprock, Arizona. In fact I was in education for almost 40 years. When I talk to Indian students at the high school level, I tell them that ever since the white man came to this country from Europe 400 years ago, they've been telling us directly or indirectly, 'If you want to be successful in this world, you must leave your culture and your language behind.' I tell them, 'That's a bunch of bologna, don't you believe it. You can be successful and still maintain your language and your culture.' I give an example of this guy that I know, Fred Begay, a scientist at Los Alamos. He is a physicist and he works with atomic energy and hydrogen bombs and all that kind of stuff.

Navajo code talkers played a significant role in the war. I tell the Navajo people, "We took part. WWII was a united effort. It was not just one group. We were all working together to end the war. There were Negro pilots, women pilots and the Nisei, (Japanese Americans), who went to Europe to make a name for themselves. Everybody had to help. I could see it with my own eyes when I would land on some of those islands. Sure, code talkers were there, but you must remember there were Navy who took the Marines to shore."

We heard about how the Germans treated the Jews, many thousands of them were killed. The Japanese were just as mean. On the island of Tinian, there is a little town called San Jose. Just beyond that there's a monument that was established by Koreans. I was there in 1995 and they had two ovens. This is where the Japanese burned over 5,000 Koreans. This is one of the reasons why the Japanese and Koreans don't like each other. The Koreans were used to defend some of those islands. They were used as slaves.

<u>Why I tell these stories</u>

One thing I might say too, you know some people ask me, 'Why are you telling these stories?' I tell them that I am doing it for all Americans now and for historical and educational purposes for future generations. They need to know what the code talkers did during WWII.

Then, too, a lot of people, especially kids, ask me, 'What is it like to be a Marine?' You know in an actual combat situation it becomes very personal. You are there fighting. You might say you live minute-to-minute or day-to-day and you keep thinking, 'When is this going to end?' Then when it's all over with you read about it in newspapers and magazines and relive what happened. It's really personal.

In 1995, I went back to the islands of Saipan and Tinian and it is unbelievable what I saw. Guess who is fueling the economy there? The Japanese and Koreans. I also had a chance to go to Korea and Japan and spent about three weeks over there. It is unbelievable. I tell you, there are just too many people over there. They have to live in crowded apartments. They can't really be out in the country, where it's free.

CHAPTER 7

ROBERT (BOB) ICHIGI KASHIWAGI

"Companies K and L were ordered in to rescue the Lost Battalion."

Robert Kashiwagi recipient of two
Purple Hearts

Thousands of Japanese had migrated to the United States during the 1800's and early 1900's but were not able to earn citizenship until 1952 when the law changed. Much has been written about the unjust and incredible hardships they were forced to endure when the United States government, fearing that they might become spies or saboteurs in support of the Japanese Empire, uprooted entire families and confined them in isolated, desolate camps, known as internment camps, across several western states. These United States citizens, who had committed no crimes against the government, faced the humiliation of being forced from their homes and businesses and being confined, at great financial loss, for the duration of the war.

It seemed improbable that a group of young Japanese-Americans would answer the call to arms when recruiters came to the internment camps, and volunteer to serve as front line infantry combat troops, intelligence personnel and interpreters for the United States military. But, many did exactly that.

In battle, they were ordered into near suicide missions, primarily in Europe, suffered horrendous casualties and won many, if not the most, battlefield decorations of any combat units in the United States Army.

They were the Nisei, the first generation of children born to immigrant Japanese parents in America.

Bob Kashiwagi was one of them.

Prior to his enlistment, he was interred at camp Amache, near Granada, Colorado, a tiny town about 125 miles from my hometown. I passed by the sign pointing to its location many times over the years, but didn't stop. I wish I had. Like most Americans, I had no idea of the shameful, dark chapter of American history that was being forged in those dreary camps. Now, only the foundations of the buildings remain.

The term Nikkei describes the four generations of people of Japanese ancestry in America.

The Issei are the immigrant generation from Japan.

The Nisei are the first generation born in the United States.

The Kibei are the Niseis who returned to Japan for education.

The Sansei are children of the Nisei and are the second generation born here.

The Yonsei are children of the Sansei and are the third generation born here

A family comes to America

My father, Frank, was born in Japan in 1876 near Yokohama. He heard of the wonders of America and, in 1896, came here to establish a business. He worked two years in northern California, buying and felling redwood timber for fence posts and grape stakes. He shipped

Ernie Frazier

them out by the trainload. He then went into fruit farming at Borden, California. In 1906 he married T. Shinomia. She died in 1916, leaving three children: Joseph, Susan, and Miwako. His second marriage took place in Japan in 1916 to Tatsu Furusawa. They returned to live in Hayward, California. All of their six children were born there.

My father worked for a while as a foreman for the Meeks Ranch in Hayward. When it sold, we moved to Knight's Landing. I was in the third grade.

As far as my siblings, Chiyo was my oldest sister. She was born July 29, 1917

I was born in Hayward, California on February 11, 1919. George, Iseko, Kimiko, and Tommy followed.

Chiyo was placed to rest on September 25, 1990. She was the valedictorian of her high school graduating class, received a B. S. degree from the University of California at Berkeley. Her diploma was mailed to her while she was interred at the Amache relocation camp. After her release, she moved to Chicago, was married, raised a family and joined Dr. I. Davidson in a research team that helped develop spot tests for mononucleosis and tests for sickle cell anemia. She retired as manager of the West Lake Community Hospital Lab with over 25 years of service.

George was born December 8, 1921. He became the first U. S. Army volunteer from the Amache relocation camp and was assigned as forward observer for the 522nd Field Artillery, which was part of the 442nd Regimental Combat Team. His unit opened the gates to liberate the inmates at the Dachau extermination camp. He retired from the U.S. Army after 20 years of service and died in January 1994.

June Iseko Yokota was born June 25th, 1922 and died in December of 1996. She was the valedictorian of her high school graduating class, received a B. A. degree from the College of Holy Names in Oakland, California, a M. A. degree from San Francisco State University, and was awarded the Professor Emeritus designation from Contra Casa College. She was also married and raised a family.

Kimi Kashiwagi was born in 1923, was interred in Amache, and then moved to Chicago during the war where she worked as a receptionist in a dental office. She married, had no children, and died on September 11, 1987.

Tom was born December 29, 1925. He married and raised a family and retired from the City Corporation Yard as a foreman after 38 years of service.

Our home was in an isolated area two miles from town. Consequently, I had no playmates. Family chores kept us occupied and we had no outside activities except for school.

I spoke English, not Japanese

After grammar school, I attended Woodland High School. I had little contact with Japanese families so I mixed with the Caucasian boys. This did not help me to pal around with Japanese children, as I was unable to converse in Japanese. However, since I could speak English without an accent, my teacher in math and English favored me to lead the classes. I took part in several class activities, such as astronomy, and even served as the president of the Japanese Student Club. I graduated in the top 10% of the class in 1937. I hoped to attend the University of California at Berkley but I was needed to work on our farm to help support our large family.

I worked many long hours, without any allowance, for full-time work. My father kept pressuring me to work harder so as to not hold back the Filipino workers that he employed.

The world situation was getting serious. In preparation for war, the United States initiated the draft system. I had joined the YMCA and was the president of the Japanese club they sponsored. I arranged send-off parties for each of the Nisei that received a draft notice. To make it more meaningful, I would invite many of the school and city officials to those parties. Eventually, my number came up and I was drafted in November 1941, just prior to the December 7th invasion of Pearl Harbor.

Ernie Frazier

Working 18 to 20 hours a day, six days a week

Having just completed the harvest of our tomato crop, which required my working 18 to 20 hours, six days a week, my weight was down to 105 lbs. The minimum weight requirement for service in the United States Army was 115 pounds.

I talked the examiner to record me at 115 pounds and he did so. That didn't help any because the doctor rejected me for an abnormal lung x-ray.

After being rejected, I went to Pescadero with our Filipino friends to harvest brussel sprouts. Brussel sprouts had to be picked every day, rain or shine. That became my first experience in working in drenching rain, which would go on all day long. It was during that time that Pearl Harbor was attacked. I was walking the seashore that day to find anything I could to supplement my boiled broccoli and rice, which I would have for dinner.

Back at my hut, many of the Filipino workers were listening to the radio. Lots of them were crying as the Philippines were attacked just a few hours after Pearl Harbor. The news got progressively worse so my Filipino friend, Ciriaco, suggested that we leave the others and return to Woodland.

We encountered difficulty when we tried to cross the Carquinez Bridge as U. S. troops were guarding it, and were stopping any Japanese. To make matters worse, we had a flat tire. Because I was traveling with a Filipino, the guard finally allowed us to continue on our trip.

The county health department caught up with me because of my abnormal x-ray and advised me to enter the Colfax Tuberculosis Sanitarium.

Executive Order 9066 sent us to internment camps

President Franklin Roosevelt signed Executive Order 9066 on February 19, 1942. It provided for the internment of Japanese-Americans. That created a problem for my doctor because I was the only Japanese in the hospital and he didn't know what to do with me. It was determined that I didn't have tuberculosis. My condition was *coccidio mio coccus, a fungus disease known as San Joaquin Valley fever. At that point I was bed-ridden. I voluntarily left the hospital and re-joined my family so I could evacuate with them. When I boarded the train at Woodland en route to Merced Assembly Center, the only person who came to see me off was my YMCA director.*

Our entire family had to go there together and remained intact as a family unit. I remember when we arrived at the center, which was at the fairgrounds: the army issued each of us a body bag and some hay to stuff into it to make a mattress. Our living quarters were a long horse shed. Nothing separated the many families that were coming in, except for sheets that we hung for privacy.

The community latrine was like a horse trough. It was sloped a little and had a water receptacle on top of the wall that flushed down into the trough. A board with holes cut every two or three feet accommodated six or eight occupants who sat side by side. We had no warning as to when it would flush and you'd get a shower whether you wanted it or not. Soon, we found that you never wanted to sit on the end. That's where the biggest splashes occurred. Mischievous boys would roll up a newspaper and set it afloat down the trough, forcing everyone to stand up.

At Camp Amache, Colorado

We were transferred to the Amache camp in Colorado, about two miles from the little town of Granada. I was still bedridden and was very bored. I met another inmate, Ichiro Kato from Broderick, California. He loved to play cards, so that's what we did.

His sympathies were to Japan and mine to the U. S. and we had a lot of heated discussions about our divided loyalties.

While I was loyal to America, I was very vociferous about our Government's treatment of U. S. citizens and wrote many letters to the Denver Post newspaper. About a year later, in late winter or early spring of 1943, a U. S. military recruiting team came to Amache to recruit volunteers for a combat infantry unit.

Those of us that were interested completed a loyalty questionnaire. I felt that question number 27 was unfair, not because of the wording but because of the recruiters explanation to us. They

Ernie Frazier

said the U. S. Army was only ready to accept volunteers for a segregated combat infantry unit slated for front line duty and no other branch of the military was open for us.

Front line combat duty for the NISEI

I felt that this was a suicide unit subject to grave consequences. I was correct. In combat, we suffered over 300% casualties in only two and a half years.

Surprisingly, even after all the debate about it, Ichiro and my brother George were the very first volunteers from Amache for the 442nd Regimental Combat Team.

Ichiro was wounded very early in combat and was sent back to the States for treatment. George was a forward observer for the 522nd Field Artillery Battalion, fought into Germany and was there to help open the gates at the Dachau extermination camp.

The U. S. military set a goal of 3,000 volunteers to be recruited from 10 relocation camps and 1,500 to be recruited from the territory of Hawaii. They were very disappointed to get only 1,300 from the 10 camps but got over 10,000 from Hawaii.

The No-No Boys

The 1,300, along with their families, received a lot of harsh abuse from the No-No Boys (Japanese internees that sympathized with Japan) and other die-hard groups. They called us very derogatory names and more or less turned their backs on us. We tried to keep away from them. In fact, most of us volunteers left for camp soon to get away from the hostile atmosphere.

Our first 1,300 volunteers should have received more recognition in the war than they got. They were sincere in what they were doing but were lumped into the same category as the No-No Boys, many of whom were draftees that had tried to evade the draft. That upset me because I knew many of the No-No's very well and knew that they were not sincere.

After examining other options that might be available to us, rather than accept the take-it-or-leave-it proposal from the recruiters, I finally volunteered knowing full well that I was in for some difficult times.

A look into the future would have revealed that the 442nd Regimental Combat Team, my unit, would fight in seven major campaigns in 2 ½ years, sustain 311% casualties, and earn 9,486 Purple Hearts.

We rescued the Lost Battalion in a campaign considered to be one of the ten most significant battles fought by the American ground forces.

Since I'd been sick in bed for a year, I went into the army in a very weak condition. I was sent to Camp Shelby, Mississippi for basic training. I remember that every afternoon, after we finished training in the field, we'd wind up four or five miles from camp and would have to go on a forced march back to our barracks. We had 45 minutes and were loaded down with our packs. I would come in so exhausted that I would lie down on my bunk, too drained out to go to the mess hall for supper. When I got enough strength, I'd go over to the USO, since the mess hall was closed, and get some junk food.

In the South, black soldiers rode in separate cars

We got a rude awakening to the resentment that black people were experiencing in the south. There were two doors to the theatre, one for blacks and one for whites. The same was true for drinking fountains. Blacks sat at the back of the bus and whites in the front. We didn't know just where we would fit in. I remember the time when I headed south on a train from Chicago. I was in uniform, sitting with a black soldier. At Birmingham, Alabama they removed us all from the train. When they re-loaded us, they separated the blacks from the whites. I didn't know which way to go so I went with the blacks. A soldier stopped me and said, 'No, you go with the whites.' That was very embarrassing to see that fellow who came all the way from Chicago with me now have to separate because he was black.

Our state of health didn't seem to make a difference as many under-sized and over-aged recruits were in training. The commanding officer had us keep an eye on the older ones when we were sent out on long, strenuous hikes. After basic training, the military wanted to see how we Orientals would react to a group of German prisoners that were captured, mostly by the British, in North Africa. They were part of Rommel's army and were considered the cream of the crop, more or less equal to SS Troopers. We were sent to Troy, Alabama to guard some of them that were helping the local farmers harvest peanuts. We got along with them because they were tired of fighting. We practically became their buddies.

We had a few fights with Caucasian soldiers that resented our dancing with white girls at the USO clubs. Also, some of our Hawaiian buddies fatally injured a prejudiced bus driver that gave them the same treatment as black people.

A free-for-all before the real war

We climaxed our last few days in the U. S. with a free-for-all at our port of embarkation. Fortunately, our boys were unable to secure guns and ammunition from a locked ordinance room. Otherwise, there might have been a different ending to the 442nd story.

To North Africa, Gibraltar, and Naples

The majority of the 442nd boarded a Victory freighter at Newport News, Virginia and joined a 250-ship convoy sailing for North Africa. We traveled a zigzag route at about four knots per hour and the worst part of the trip for me was being seasick for 29 days.

Sailing through the Straits of Gibraltar was quite a sight with all ships passing through, single file. A huge barrage balloon was tethered to each ship and flew overhead to discourage German planes from strafing us.

I was in Company K, 3rd Platoon, 442nd Regimental Combat Team. As the 34th Red Bull Division that we were assigned to was fighting in Italy, we headed for the bombed out harbor at Naples and passed through some spectacular scenery between the toe of Italy and the island of Sicily. The Sicilians came alongside in boats stocked with blood red oranges. They wanted to trade them for our cigarettes so we'd pitch them some and they'd throw oranges up to us. The oranges looked beautiful but they were blood red in color inside.

Little kids crawled all over us when we docked. To our surprise, we found out that they were very proficient in stealing our K-rations from our backpacks with no demonstration of affection intended.

We soon boarded an infantry landing craft and proceeded to the Anzio beachhead. We were a reserve unit, ready for battle. The 5th Army had just broken out of the Anzio stalemate and was heading for Rome. We crossed the Rapido River at Monte Cassino, where bitter fighting occurred a few months earlier. This was in mid-June 1944, just prior to the Normandy Invasion.

The Germans decided not to defend Rome—so as not to have it destroyed.

Draft animals were used to haul our supplies up into the mountains. It was a strange sight to see our unit following the many mules and packhorses that were winding their way along through the famous sights of Rome.

The 100th Infantry, another Nisei outfit, joined us just outside Rome where we replaced the 417th Parachute Division in leading the 5th Army in pursuit of the enemy.

Some of my combat memories were later included in the book, <u>Unlikely Liberators, The Men of the 100th and 442nd</u>, *by a Japanese author*, *Masio Umezzawa Duus, copyright 1987.*

In the combat zones, there was a great amount of confusion and our situation and conditions were changing all the time. Consequently, we developed very few buddy-buddy relationships. Many new recruits became casualties, even before we got to know their names.

I respected and was willing to co-operate with Tech Sergeant Sakamoto who was drafted in the first Nisei draft. He did not smoke or drink and set a fine example as a non-typical platoon sergeant. He played no favorites and assumed his share of exposure to danger.

<u>Walking half the night across no-man's land</u>

I recall one of my most anxious and frightening tasks. I served as his support while we walked half the night in no-man's land, trying to make contact with our supply unit.

Ernie Frazier

Even though I was first scout when we moved into Luciano, Sergeant Sakamoto assumed the lead point. It was standard procedure for the ranking person to take the lead when enemy contact was made.

As was feared, a sniper shot hit Sakamoto. I noticed him clutching his chest as he jumped into a nearby ditch. We immediately pulled back and ducked into a wine cellar. A German tank was hidden in a courtyard a few hundred yards away. He fired at me as I stood in the entrance of the cellar, wasting his 88 shell that missed me. But it knocked a lot of bricks onto my helmet. We eventually got even when the 522nd Field Artillery blasted the building on top of the tank, putting it out of action.

We were unable to reach Sergeant Sakamoto until dark. The medics and our chaplain, holding up a Red Cross flag, retrieved his body and confirmed his death as instantaneous. It is unfortunate that he didn't receive greater recognition than he did for the example he displayed.

I was assigned the first scout position and a good buddy of mine, Bill Kochiyama was my second scout. This put us at the front of the 5th Army every time it was our unit's turn to take the lead.

Hit by an artillery barrage

On July 17, 1944, our company was caught in an artillery barrage at a crossroad. It was terrifying. Bill and I literally dug our foxholes with our noses; trying to get deep enough to escape the artillery blasts.

That's when I received my first wound. Bill got a large shrapnel hole in his helmet but miraculously escaped injury. People that saw it couldn't figure out why he was still alive.

Amidst the exploding shells, I was hit with shrapnel in the buttocks and legs. Things were terribly disorganized. I considered my wounds minor and waited until the aid station was set up the next day before I went in for medical attention.

The wounds I received on November 1944 were a bit more extensive. We had just survived a near suicide mission. Two other American units had been thrown back in their efforts to rescue what came to be known as the Lost Battalion: a battalion of U. S. soldiers that found themselves surrounded by overwhelming German forces and facing annihilation in the Vosges Mountains near Biffontaine, France.

The order came to send in the Nisei. We went in, knowing our chances of survival were very slim. Our fears were well founded.

The Lost Battalion episode

The period of October 25 to 30, 1944, was referred to as the Lost Battalion episode. It was a truly a very bloody, painful, and frightening period; a most miserable and uncomfortable experience. Ours was an infantry unit, supported primarily by artillery. The terrain restricted our tank's mobility, limiting their support. We assaulted the German positions in attack formation and with fixed bayonets. For two weeks we were in continual combat, living on K-rations and dried, raw onions. It was cold and rainy. We were soaked and chilled and never got warm. We dove into shell craters to escape the terrifying tree-burst mortar and artillery shells that exploded all over and around us. The craters were full of muddy water, which compounded our misery.

An artillery shell hit our rest area, killing and wounding several of our buddies and destroying our field shower. We then moved on to more demoralizing events, all of which etched a permanent scar on my mind.

I went from performing the docile chore of butchering and cooking live rabbits, because our Hawaiians were reluctant to kill them, to killing humans. That was really a mind-blowing experience.

Because of the urgency to make contact with the Lost Battalion, we received many, many orders that were quickly changed. Our battles were fought in constant confusion.

The cold, wet rain, along with the grime and filth, soaked into our clothing. We were unable to change our undergarments for several weeks and suffered greatly as our skin was badly chapped.

Our intended showers and clothing change were halted when the artillery shell destroyed our shower.

Ernie Frazier

To take care of my feet, I washed them in a puddle of icy rainwater and put on a pair of damp socks. I always carried a pair under my helmet. Lots of the fellows that didn't take care of their feet wound up with trench foot. In one ward I was in, 15 of the 35 patients were suffering from it. Many had developed gangrene and were going to lose their feet.

When we came into contact with the enemy, we were grimy, cold, wet, miserable, scared and mad. We attacked recklessly, often totally exposed to enemy fire. A lot of heroism was displayed but only a fortunate few were recognized and cited for their achievements because few survived to tell the story. It is really mind-boggling to come upon a bloody, gruesome corpse, whether enemy or comrade, and have to step over the body or move it so we could pull our shift on guard duty.

The conditions we faced battling the Germans were almost beyond description. We experienced seeing a comrade's head blown open by a shell and had his brains splash all over us. It makes one very disgusted with war.

Diarrhea amid exploding artillery

What little humor we experienced was not very funny at the time. I was afflicted with severe stomach cramps and diarrhea. That resulted in my relieving the pain in my stomach at the risk of exposing my vanity to the cold elements and hot, flying metal that the Germans were exploding all around us. We found lots of raw, dried onions while foraging for food. We ate them and that brought on much of our stomach problems.

I was the assistant squad leader and delegated to handle the hand grenade launcher. Staff Sergeant Yoshida was my squad leader. Later, he received a battlefield commission and became the commander of K Company.

The enemy was well dug in. I got in as close to them as I could, and blew up several of their positions with my grenade launcher. I'd see the enemy running away from their cover but I was unable to fire on them because I didn't have the proper weapons. It was very frustrating.

The Germans had kept supply vehicles from reaching the Lost Battalion. Airplane supply tanks full of goods littered the roadways. The situation was getting desperate.

800 Nisei died rescuing 211 of the Lost Battalion

Our opponent commanded the high ground and pounded us to pieces. Our men were falling, some killed, others maimed, but we had to keep going. We finally reached the Lost Battalion and got them out of there, but it was a disaster for us who fought the battles. We suffered approximately 800 dead and wounded while rescuing 211 men that were waiting to be slaughtered. But, our mission was considered a success because we had saved the Lost Battalion.

Wounded and evacuated

We had just completed the mission and were trying to secure our position against a counter-attack when I was wounded two different times. A tree-burst mortar shell struck my right hand, amputating the tip of one finger and splitting one finger open. I recognized it as a mortar shell because a large mortar fin landed near my feet.

I was surprised that the Germans were lobbing in shells that close to their own troops. We had just destroyed a hastily set-up machine gun nest, killing the gunners and shooting several of their riflemen. Since my hands were bleeding profusely, I told my comrades that I was going to the aid station for first aid. I was making my way back when another barrage of tree bursts came in. This time shrapnel from an 88 shell tore into my left foot. The hot shrapnel and pain numbed my leg and I jumped into a foxhole, joining a member of my company. I don't remember his name but he assured me that my foot was still attached and he wrapped it with a bandage. I was cold, apprehensive, and miserable but the misery and wetness kept it numb. Even so, I couldn't walk. A litter bearing team eventually found me and took me to an evacuation area. Ironically, as we were driving out with four casualties on this Jeep, another artillery barrage came in and blew out one of the tires. Flat tire or not, there was no time to dilly-dally and we hot-rodded out of there, post haste.

Ernie Frazier

I was evacuated to the 27th Field Hospital, and then sent on to the general hospital at Dejon, France. Eventually, fifteen of us litter bound patients were put in a hospital plane on a miserably cold and rainy day, for transfer to Whittington Barracks hospital in Kichfield, England. As we proceeded down the runway, a tire blew and we ran off the runway. No one was injured but one patient that had extensive wounds to his abdomen had a difficult time. We loaded onto another plane. A storm was on and we began vomiting with airsickness while flying over the English Channel.

While I was waiting transfer back home, in the spring of 1945, I was assigned to a port Marine maintenance detachment in Le Harve, France and was put in charge of a motor pool. I was assigned over Fifteen German prisoners of war and three enlisted men. We were to maintain and repair vehicles. One of the enlisted men was a tall Polak, Al Witkowski, who spoke Polish. He could interpret for me with a German who spoke Polish. Al and I became known as Mutt and Jeff. We were a comic sight around the motor pool. He was 6'3" and I was 5'4".

Both VE and VJ days happened while I was at Le Harve and those were my most pleasant experiences in Europe.

We were quartered in the old bombed out Normandy dry dock. We enjoyed ourselves fishing for bonita and mackerel and had many delicious fish fries. However, the thousands of huge rats that infested the docks really bothered us.

Eventually, my discharge points added up and I was moved to a staging area to wait for transportation back home. There, I ran into my brother Tom who was coming over with the army of occupation. Since two of his brothers were in the 442nd, the military felt he shouldn't be in the same unit. He wound up in a tank unit in Belgium, rounding up German officers to stand trial for war crimes. He met with some misfortune when he ran into a land mine that exploded. It broke his leg and jaw and he had to go around with his mouth wired together. Unfortunately, the war was already over so he received neither a Purple Heart nor any veteran's benefits for those injuries.

I sailed home on a heavy cruiser, the S. S. Savannah. For seven days I was hopelessly seasick and couldn't eat.

Back home to find his parents

I was discharged upon arrival in New York on New Year's Eve, 1945 and returned to Sacramento. When I got there, I found out that my parents had no place to go. While they had to pay a fee to stay there, they remained in Walerga camp, which was no longer an internment camp and was now known as Camp Kohler.

I joined them there for a month until I could locate a home to move them into.

The first place I applied for work was the U. S. Engineers in Sacramento. I was offered, and I accepted, a position working in the motor pool. I became the first Japanese to be hired in the motor pool. The engineers have a warm spot in my heart because they were the first to hire me. That gave me quite a boost and built my confidence in this country. I later took a test and was hired by the Sate of California.

A guy said he'd quit if a Jap worked with him

However, my first day on the job wasn't exactly friendly. One of the mechanics approached his foreman and threatened to quit, 'If this Jap is going to work here!'

I felt that I'd served my time in Europe while he had been at home sleeping in a warm bed and making money. I stood my ground and he quit his job.

I stayed with the department until I ultimately retired after 32 years of service.

Lillian Asoo and I were married on Nov 2, 1947. We raised a family and are now grandparents. Our home is in California.

Over the years, I volunteered my services to a multitude of community, church, and charitable causes and served as Scout Master for various Boy Scout troops.

My legacy

Having suffered first hand the pain of racial prejudice, I wish to leave my descendents a legacy of tolerance to others, especially to

Ernie Frazier

people of a different heritage, and want them to support their communities and honor their commitments.

Author's acknowledgements: I thank the <u>Florin Jacl Oral History Project</u> for allowing me to utilize excerpts from Christine Umeda's May 24, 1988 interview with Robert Kashiwagi and the <u>Go For Broke Educational Foundation</u> for their valuable assistance to me.

CHAPTER 8

GENE STEGMAN

"As a kid, I sang on a western radio show. As a young man, I fought at Iwo Jima."

Any American with even a casual interest in World War II has heard of Iwo Jima and seen the stirring picture of a small band of battle-weary Marines raising the American flag in victory atop Mt. Suribachi, the photo that became the most publicized photograph of the war.

The battle for Iwo Jima stands in stark contrast to the massive air, naval, and land victories won by the allies on dozens of European and Asian battlefields. While many of those great battles covered hundreds or thousands of square miles, the battle for Iwo Jima was immortalized in a special way: The tiny, miserable chunk of barren volcanic rock and sand only covered eight square miles but that desperate battle became the Marine Corps' bloodiest battle of the war.

The stark, photographic images of the horror that was the everyday life for young U. S. Marines, Seabees, and Sailors for five weeks in 1945 became an unforgettable part of the folklore of America

The island had three airstrips that were vital to the Allied cause. Capturing Iwo Jima would stop Kamikaze pilots from flying out of there. And it would provide a base for American fighter planes that escorted B-29s on their bombing missions. Because it was located half way between the Mariana Islands and Japan, it would provide an emergency landing strip for the allies.

The Japanese had no intention of surrendering the island. They built some 800 pillboxes and dug over three miles of tunnels into the tiny island.

The bombardment to soften up the Japanese was carried out for 10 weeks by carrier based planes and medium bombers. It was the heaviest preliminary bombing undertaken by the United States to that date.

Seventy thousand Marines were committed to battle on February 19th, 1945. They began landing on the beaches at 8:59 A. M.

The Japanese defenders numbered about 27,000. They survived the bombardment and emerged en massse from their pillboxes and tunnels to meet the attacking Marines. They occupied the high ground. From Mt. Suribachi, they could fire on any position.

Marines and Seabees, some carrying 100 pounds of equipment, hit the beaches. Those who made it to shore found themselves quickly mired in volcanic ash; the curse of Iwo Jima.

At 9:15 A. M. the Japanese laid down a mortar barrage.

The carnage that began that day and lasted until March 26th is a testament to tenacity on the part of both forces. Most of all, it reveals the fighting spirit and unyielding determination of a corps of young men—some barely 17—who were molded into fighting men in a matter of minutes and became heroes just as fast. The stark numbers tell the story:

Personnel: Killed; 6, 821; Wounded; 19,217; Combat fatigue; 2,648

The Boothill Coffee Club Volume I

Japanese Casualties: Killed; 20,000 (est.) PRISONERS OF WAR, 1,083

The following is the story of one young Marine's five weeks in hell. Gene Stegman spent most of his life forgetting what he saw and did at Iwo Jima. But, his fading memory could still dredge up some of the horrors he witnessed. He showed me a picture of himself and his little brother dressed up in cowboy suits. They had their own western show on KGNO radio in Dodge City, Kansas, during the Great Depression. For them, it was a time of fleeting innocence.

Then he produced a photo taken only a few years later with other fresh-faced, eager young Marines who, unknowingly, were getting ready to sail away and create for themselves a special place in history.

He produced a jar full of the volcanic sand taken from the island. We examined it quietly, remembering that the blood of thousands had been soaked up on the sands of Iwo Jima.

Training for Iwo Jima

I was 21 and going to college when I decided to enlist in the Marines. The training at the San Diego Recruit Depot was good as far I was concerned. I'd worked hard all my life so I was able to handle whatever they threw at me. We got  *a short leave after boot camp. Soon after that, we were on a ship headed for Hawaii. Our time there was spent training for one mission—to hit Iwo Jima. We also did a training mission at Saipan. The plan was to take Iwo, then attack Japan.*

I was a PFC in the 28th Marines, 5th Marine Division.

Ernie Frazier

We assaulted Iwo Jima

Our landing craft was one of the first in the assault and were called assault troops. Our boat didn't make it up to the beach so we had to drop into the water and wade in. It was fairly shallow and I don't think that any of our men drowned.

The Japanese really opened up on us. We started taking heavy fire right away. I can't say that I was really scared to death. I just took it as it came, figured I'd do what I had to do. A lot of guys got hit right away. My first assignment was on an 81-mm mortar. Our job was to fire over the top of our advancing infantry. They were charging straight into the Jap's fortifications and were cut down without mercy. We barely had time to set up our mortar until we had to stop everything and become litter bearers.

Marines became litter bearers

Our guys were getting blown to pieces. The Japs had the high ground and could hit just about anything on the island. Seabees and Marines were falling everywhere—dead, dying, and wounded. We'd grab a litter and run through the shelling—right up to the front lines to pick up anyone we could. We'd be carrying a man and he'd get shot again while we were trying to get to the aid station. Also, the Japs would cut down the stretcher-bearers. Some of my buddies died right in my arms. We were dragging one guy out on a stretcher and everyone went down but me. I was the only one left to drag the stretcher back.

We'd fire rounds for a while, sometimes I was firing a heavy machine gun, then run out to pick up more guys. The slaughter was unimaginable. Our gun positions regularly came under mortar, artillery, and small arms fire and more of my friends fell dead or wounded beside me.

I'd been lying in the sand and bullets were blowing sand right up into my face. But, I never got hit. We saw a lot of heroic things, but no one thought he was a hero. As the saying goes, "Uncommon valor was a common virtue."

At night we had to keep flares and illumination going all the time because the Japs were masters at infiltrating our positions. We had trip flares set up all around. It was hard to go to sleep. You knew that you might not wake up.

Burning the Japs alive

We couldn't root the Japs out of the caves--they had tunneled everywhere--so we had guys come up with flame-throwers to burn them out. We'd yell, "Fire in the hole!" Our man would fire in a stream of napalm and a Jap or two would come running out--on fire. Some guys would shoot 'em down.

I was down around the base of Mt. Suribachi when the famous photos were taken of our flag being planted.

Gene Stegman after Iwo Jima

I could have been one of them.

It was tough but most of our guys kept their sanity. It was a miracle that I ever got out of there alive.

They sent me back to the states after the battle and I was discharged in April.

By his own admission, all Gene ever did was work. He was very good at everything he did. He built and operated a large, custom harvesting company and constructed three beautiful homes—including building the cabinetry. He now lives alone in one of them. His first wife died. He and his second wife divorced. His son-in-law recently took over the operation of the harvesting business.

While I was interviewing him, he agonized that ankle pain—from a fall 50 years ago—was causing him to re-think a house-painting project he had planned. When we parted he said, "Well, I think I'll go ahead and try it. I can't just sit around here all day."

CHAPTER 9

BOB DOLE

The man who couldn't quit

I knew very little about Bob Dole in the late 1960's when he came to Liberal, Kansas, campaigning for the office of United States Senator. He was a small-town boy that went to war, returned home badly wounded, entered public service, moved up quickly and was elected to the United States House of Representatives. At his reception, I was impressed with his flashing eyes and quick wit. I'm sure the women thought him very handsome. I reached out with my right hand to shake his and was taken off-guard when he extended his left hand. I quickly stammered an apology when I realized he could not shake with his right hand. Thoughts of his battlefield injuries flashed through my head. He smiled and made a wise crack to put me at ease.

Such is the way of the quick-witted Bob Dole. From then on, I watched with great interest as he won his senatorial seat and rose to prominence on the national, and then the international stage.

Most of his adult life was spent in the House or the Senate, fighting and winning many political victories that are well documented. But Bob had a prior life far from the glamour of the Senate's chambers. A defining moment in that life started one day in 1945 on a battlefield in Italy. Bob agreed to my writing this story for inclusion in this book.

April 12 & 14

President Franklin D. Roosevelt died on April 12, 1945, the day that "Operation Craftsman", an allied assault on a German stronghold in northern Italy, was to begin. The attack was re-scheduled for April 14.

If the attack would have proceeded as originally planned, the story of Bob Dole may have taken a dramatically different course. But, it didn't.

For the past year, more than 200,000 men of the U. S. Fifth Army and the British Eighth Army battled their way up the jagged mountains of Italy, paying a tremendous price in human lives as they were blown apart in mine fields, machine gun fire, bombs, and artillery barrages. It was a bloody, hill-by-hill, ridge-by-ridge campaign to oust the Germans from Italy and the Allies were winning. Hill 913 was one of the last major obstacles in their path. Nobody knew that the war in Europe was about to end. The Germans would surrender to the Allies on May 7 1945, only three weeks away. One of the great tragedies of war is in the numbers of fighters that are killed or wounded in the final days of battle. If they could of only survived for a few more days...

Lt. Dole was fresh out of Officer Candidate School. Less than two months earlier, he'd been assigned to take the place of a fallen officer in the Army's U. S. 10th Infantry Mountain Division, a crack outfit trained in the high mountains of Colorado to ski and fight. He would be leading a platoon of battle-hardened soldiers on the assault of Hill 913.

The young lieutenant was well suited to the job. A star athlete in high school, he was now 21 years old, stood 6'2 and weighed over 185 pounds. But, more important, was the fact that he had great charisma and was a natural leader, qualities that caught the eye of his superiors and the men under his command. He knew all about hard times, being a child of the Great Depression and raised in a family that was desperately pressed for cash much of the time. On this day, his life was about to get even harder…a lot harder.

A split second on April14 1945 would become a defining moment in the life of Bob Dole.

The attack!

Lt. Dole and his platoon of 40 men anxiously awaited the order that would release them from the intolerable bondage created by waiting…waiting…waiting. Nerves were frayed, breakfast was gulped, and weapons were checked. They stood by, waiting for the order to move out. They'd seen death before. They knew that the assault against the battle hardened German Wermacht would end the lives and maim many of them. But, combat veterans are a fatalistic group. They would fight. They would die. A dense fog allowed only brief glimpses of the rock-hard, heavily armed fortification that loomed high on the hill ahead.

At 0830, the tension broke. The troops heard the unmistakable drone of heavy bombers as formation after formation appeared high in the sky overhead. They watched, and then bellowed with glee as billowing clouds of smoke puffed up from the stronghold, followed by the deafening concussion of thousands of tons of exploding bombs. Then medium and light bombers swooped in to strafe and bomb individual strong points.

The Fifth Army had amassed some 2,000 artillery pieces on the front. They opened up with all their guns and the Germans suffered another 30 minutes of a savage bombardment. The hill practically disappeared from view under the pall of dust and smoke.

The Germans 334th Grenadier Division, though badly mauled, were well dug in and held firm. They waited. In addition to their fortifications on the hill, they had buried hundreds of deadly mines in the valley below. Unseen until stepped on, they were one of the G. I.'s worst nightmares.

By 1000 hours, the bombardment stopped. The men of the 10th Mountain Division took a deep breath. Dole's orders were to take his men the half-mile across the valley and attack the stronghold. They moved out with Dole leading his platoon, single file, into the valley…

A fanatical defense

The Germans, their backs to the wall, filled the valley with lead and steel and high explosives, creating a virtual wall of hell to greet the advancing troops.

Burp guns fire bursts of ammunition, usually hitting the target with a hail of bullets. Machine guns do similar damage. Either can cut a man in half. Mortar rounds, lobbed from a tube, land on the target and explode, usually killing anyone nearby. Land mines are planted just under the soil. Some explode with enough force to blow a man to bits or disable a tank. Others are only meant to disable by blowing off a foot or other extremities. Since it requires the immediate services of five to seven people to remove and care for the wounded soldier, the effect of the blast is compounded.

This description of firepower is impersonal. It's something altogether different for the men trying desperately to escape its lethal wounds.

Dole raged at seeing his men shot down around him. Mines exploded, transforming healthy young men into amputees in an instant. Shrapnel whistled through the air slicing men apart. The shock to the advancing soldiers was overwhelming and the attack took on a secondary mission: survival. They fell down on their bellies, crawling from one shell hole to another, but found little relief. The withering barrage continued from the hill and tough soldiers screamed and cried as they saw their buddies torn to pieces.

The machine gun

A heavy machine gun, positioned in a farmhouse, fired on Dole's platoon, halting their advance. It had to be silenced. Dole called in mortar fire and began moving toward the building. He was within 15 yards when the machine gunner fired at him. He threw a grenade that fell short of its mark. Then one of his men was shot as he rose to throw a grenade.

When his radioman was hit, Dole crawled over, grabbed the disabled man, and began dragging him to a shell crater. This was to be his last action on the field of battle.

Ernie Frazier

Shrapnel

Shrapnel—hunks of metal from an exploding shell—whistles through the air aimlessly, aimed at nothing in general. Its purpose is to maim, kill, disrupt, and demoralize. It's only by chance that it strikes someone. When it does, the results can be horrific.

As he struggled to help his fellow soldier, an errant piece of flying shrapnel ripped into Dole's body, striking his right shoulder and back, packing the destruction of a blow from an axe. His men saw him lunge up, and then fall headlong in the dirt. Those that could reach him were horrified to see their lieutenant near death, pale, soaked in blood and unconscious. However, this was war. The assault had to continue. The company was under orders to leave the wounded and continue their attack but one of Dole's squad leaders, Sergeant Carafa, who was much smaller than Dole, paused. Exhausted and sobbing, he struggled mightily to push and shove the helpless body to a safer place. Another soldier appeared and administered a dose of morphine. Another, who suffered lesser wounds, stayed behind to watch over the fallen lieutenant as the others continued on.

Dole was hovering between life and death when the medics got to him. They ministered to him the best they could, and then put him on a stretcher and carried him away. Nine long hours had passed from the time he was hit to his arrival at the Fifteenth Evacuation Hospital. Dole's right arm was hopelessly shattered, he was as good as dead, but the greatest battle of his life was just beginning. His blood remained on the battlefield, but his spirit moved on.

Dr. Kelikian

Dole spent three agonizing years, much in despair and near death, in military hospitals in Italy and the United States, undergoing the surgery and therapy he needed to return him to "normal" life. But, his right arm remained useless. When his military doctors were unable to fix it, he contacted Dr. Hampar Kelikian, a civilian doctor, a refugee from Armenia, who agreed to do his best—for no fee. Seven operations later, the arm's mobility was restored to about 40% of its prior use.

The hell he endured during those years is indescribable. So I won't attempt it. Thousands of wounded soldiers experienced some of the same treatment. But, what makes Bob's story so remarkable is what he did after he returned to "normal" life. Of course, his life was anything but normal!

No challenge too great

Most men's achievements pale alongside his. A *few* of the highlights of his civilian career are:

1950s: Law degree; Kansas State Legislature: U. S. House of Representatives
1969: U. S. Senator-Longest serving Republican Leader in the U. S. Senate.
1976: V. P. running mate with President Gerald Ford
1990: Instrumental in Congress passing Americans with Disabilities Act
1996: Loses Presidential race to President Bill Clinton

US Senator Bob Dole

A really tough loss

Losing to Bill Clinton was a bitter pill to swallow. "Where's the outrage?" was the question Dole posed to the American people who had seen sexual, political, and financial scandals on an unprecedented scale erupt and engulf the President; scandals that were swept aside by the charismatic leader and an apathetic government. A rising stock market became the barometer that ruled the hearts and minds of the people. The sacred ideals that Dole paid an unfathomable price to defend had been forgotten; or had never been taught to a new generation of Americans that was drifting into a malaise of indifference and amorality.

But only Dole could toss off the defeat with a quip, a one liner he fired off when President Clinton unveiled plans for the WWII memorial and awarded Bob the nation's highest civilian award: The Presidential Medal of Freedom. Bob said that he originally hoped to be there to accept the key to the front door of the White House.

Mrs.(Senator) Dole

Along the way, in 1975, he married the extraordinarily talented and beautiful Elizabeth Hanford of North Carolina. One of the most admired women in the United States, she may be the perfect match for the chronic over-achiever. Her brilliant career, a book in itself, includes these high points:
>Degrees in Law and Government, Harvard
>Served with President Lyndon B. Johnson's Health, Education and Welfare Department
>Served as Deputy assistant to President Nixon for Consumer Affairs
>Appointed Secretary of Transportation by President Reagan
>Appointed Secretary of Labor by President George H. Bush
>Served as President of the American Red Cross
>Elected U. S. Senator from North Carolina

Together, they present a united front that makes Americans proud. They made it to the top the old fashioned ways: with *integrity* and *class*.

A $100,000,000 challenge

Bob is retired from the senate…but not from life. While most men of his age rest on their laurels or dream of opportunities lost, he accepted another challenge in life; one he believes in most fervently. He heads the campaign to construct a permanent WWII commemorative monument in Washington, DC. As usual, he didn't seek out a small job. It's a $100,000,000 project! (Bob notified me on April 1, 2003 that **$191,000,000** had been raised!)

The honored shoe box

Besides the great doctors and nurses that played such a role in his journey Bob got more than a little help along the way in his early struggles, during his darkest hours, from the folks at home. He recalls with emotion when the financially hard-pressed people in his hometown of Russell, Kansas collected $1,800 (a lot of money in the 1940s) in a shoebox marked "Bob Dole Fund." to help out when a hospital needed paid. The box found a place of honor in his home. It rests beside his Purple Hearts and Bronze Star.

CHAPTER 10

KENT ROSS

"Hermann Goring got excited. I laid my club on his shoulder."

Kent was an unassuming farm boy, barely a year out of high school, when he was drafted in June, 1944. Until then, he led an uneventful life, seldom traveled more than a few miles from home, and would have never believed the astounding events that would soon engulf him. By November 20, 1945, barely seventeen months after entering the army, he won a Bronze Star on a foreign battlefield and came face to face with former Reich Marshal Hermann Goring and all the other surviving leaders of Nazi Germany.

Battle of The Bulge coming up

Our fifteen weeks of basic training in Camp Ft. Walters, Texas, was shortened by a couple of weeks. It was just prior to the Battle of The Bulge and they needed replacements quick. We shipped over on a small ship that we called a banana boat. It took eleven days to get to Marseille, France because we had to zigzag a lot to avoid German subs.
We went through more training and did some target shooting. Then we were loaded on a train to ride in '40 & 8' cars (40 men or 8 horses). We were heading for Belgium to cross the Rhine River. I came down with the mumps, landed in a hospital and missed the initial crossing of the Rhine. Later, my buddies told me I missed quite a show when they crossed the river. We had artillery and they continually shelled the Rhine all one night.

I rejoined my outfit when I was released. It was a heavy weapons unit. My weapon was a water-cooled .30 caliber machine gun. We were sent into battle several times. Behind us were our 80mm mortar crews. The .50 caliber machine gunners were behind them. In front of us were the air-cooled .30 caliber machine gunners and the 60mm mortar men.

I carried the tripod—that's what we mounted the machine gun on—because I was the number one gunner on our crew. I can still feel its legs hanging over my shoulders. When the action started, I'd flip the tripod over my head and the number two gunner would rush up with the barrel and we'd attach it. The number three gunner would bring up belts of ammunition and feed it into the gun while the number four man would bring up the water can to keep the gun cool. We each had to carry something and it was all heavy and very unhandy. All guns, front and rear, were to support the front line infantrymen. They were out in front of the light machine guns and the 60mm mortars. They got the brunt of the fighting. We fired over them into the enemy.

In Belgium and Holland

I saw quite a few American and German soldiers killed—a lot more than I wanted to.

We were in Belgium. It was winter time and very cold. I wore two pair of pants, three shirts and all the socks I could get on, trying to keep my feet warm. Once in awhile we'd get a bath. We then went into Holland. There was a big building where miners showered so we used their facilities. We hadn't had clean clothes or a shower for a long time.

We ate lots of C rations. If we stopped long enough, the mess trucks would bring up a big box of Ten-0-One rations with big containers of beans, hash, and stuff like that. Usually we'd just get three little boxes of C rations—and that was all—every day. I got a lot of heartburn but had to eat them to survive.

I was in the 79th Division. The Alsace-Lorraine Cross was on our shoulder patch. That represented an area in France. Our company commander was Captain English. Our officers led us into combat. Of course the guy who was really in charge of me was a sergeant 1st class. They commanded the squads.

I was involved in a few close combats that were a little too close for comfort. I had to shoot German soldiers and I came close to getting shot a few times myself.

We could hear the Germans talking

One evening we arrived at a little farm. It was way out by itself in the country. We were told to dig in. We dug a hole and mounted our machine gun. When night came, we took two-hour shifts as guards. We could hear Germans talking out in the dark and I thought, 'Boy, they are too close!' They were an armored company with tanks. They'd start them up and drive around. They were really noisy and it was one of my most scary experiences.

Germans unleash buzz bombs

When we were in Belgium, we were right in the path of the German's B-2 Bombers; buzz bombs. When they took off, we could actually see the ramps they were launched from, heading for England. They were jets and made a terrific noise that terrorized anyone targeted by them. Fortunately, we weren't the target.

In combat until the end

We were in combat until the war ended. For a while they sent us to Czechoslovakia to see what they were going to do with us. There wasn't any food there. Dockworkers were on strike so no supplies were coming in. We found a bakery that made these big loaves of black bread. They were about as hard as a table but we did have butter so we lived on it and the bread for three or four days until food started coming in.

Caring for displaced persons

We wound up in the Ruhr Valley, and then were sent to take care of people in displaced person camps (DPC). The camps we went to were Russian, Polish and Czechoslovakian. The Russians didn't want their displaced persons returned to them. They told us to shoot them if they gave us any problems. They would just as soon shoot their own soldiers or civilians just for saying something that irritated them. We got along with them because we had good cigarettes. Theirs were about five inches long and half cotton with very little tobacco. They loved our cigarettes. But, we wanted nothing to do with them after the war. They were so unpredictable. We were in kind of a no man's land with the Russians on one side and us on the other. They were always shooting off their guns and we didn't know which way they were shooting. They were crazy people.

Germans got out of uniform as fast as they could

The day the European war ended, we were up on hill in a big old house and had our machine gun set up. Down below was a valley full of trees. We could see German soldiers running into the forest and then run out again swinging their coats. They were getting out of their uniforms as fast as they could. They didn't want any more to do with it. We didn't fire on them because we knew it was over. I knew that. We didn't have to shoot them.

The house we were staying in had a double garage. Inside we found a 1941 Packard convertible. The Colonel found out about it and you know what happened then. He took hold of that bug!

We thought we were going to Japan

Japan looked like our next stop. A big invasion was being planned and a massive buildup of troops, similar to the D-Day Invasion, was needed. Nobody was thrilled with that idea since we'd served our time in combat. We heard that the Japanese would use every man, woman, and child to defend their nation, even if they were all killed. We heard that the Japanese swore to kill every allied *prisoner of war they held in Japan the minute we set foot on their soil. That alone would amount to the slaughter of thousands of helpless prisoners. But, we were soldiers. We took our shots, went through more training and were about ready to ship out when the atomic bombs were dropped and Japan surrendered. We were very glad to hear about that! But my tour of duty wasn't over. Not yet. Some of us were in for a big surprise!*

The Nuremberg Trials

The buck sergeants and staff sergeants were separated from our unit and we got the news, "You guys are going to be on the Nuremberg trials."

We wondered what that was all about. It didn't take long to find out because, very soon we found ourselves in Nuremberg, Germany where we were outfitted in white gloves, white helmets, white belts and white leggings. We found out that we would be standing guard at the trial of the generals, field marshals, admirals, and other top-level officials who had led Nazi Germany into war.

At the trial, only our colonel and lieutenant carried pistols. The rest of us were armed with billy clubs.

It was a historical time for us. The trial captured the world's attention and was extensively covered by the news media. Back home, in Satanta, Kansas, some of my relatives and friends went to the movies and saw a film clip of the trial. There I was, on film, standing tall over the top Nazis in the world, and it caused quite a stir.

In the Palace of Justice

The trial started on November 20, 1945 in the Palace Of Justice. The United States spent one million dollars on the courtroom, which was a tremendous amount back then. The walls were paneled in walnut and were about eighteen feet high. Thirty-two men were assigned to guard duty. There would be six or seven of us at a time standing guard next to the defendant's box. In front of us were their lawyers. Believe it or not, they each had a lawyer. Stenographers recorded everything. There were eight judges present. A section was available for spectators. Every seat had a headset. You could dial and hear translations in four different languages: French, Russian, German and English.

Herman Goring feels Kent's club

The Nazis did terrible things to people. Evidence of their atrocities against mankind was on display. They included framed pictures of tattooed human skin and lampshades made of skin. We were given orders to be very strict with the prisoners. Usually we had no problem. But one day, Hermann Goring, the former German Air Force

Left: Sgt. Kent Ross
Center: Nazi Criminal Seyss Inquart

(Luftwaffe) commander, got excited about something. He stood up and started talking real loud in German. I had my billy club and I tapped him on the shoulder. He looked around and I nodded for him to sit down, and he did. I was the only guard to actually touch one of the German officers. Goring was next in command below Hitler. He was quite large before he was captured but lost a lot of weight and was small at the time of the trial. He still tried to wear his uniform, stripped of insignia, but the clothes just hung on him.

Ernie Frazier

Rudolph Hess

Rudolph Hess, the number three man in the hierarchy, acted like he was goofy but he really wasn't. He wouldn't put on his headphones. Goring kept whispering to him to do so but he just sat there and read books all the time. Hess was in prison ten years longer than anyone else and was the only prisoner in the prison until his death a few years ago. The Russians didn't want to release him.

Rosenberg and von Ribbentrop

Eleven of those on trial were hanged. I have a video showing each of them after their deaths. My two favorite prisoners were Rosenberg and von Ribbentrop. They were nice guys. I brought them up to the courtroom from their cells. When we took them back after court, we took their ties, belts and shoelaces so they couldn't hang themselves. We took them through a covered tunnel to the elevator. Usually, I had the keys to the elevator. I would go up with the first bunch, leave the key in the elevator, let the guys bring the elevator down, then do it again until they were all seated in the courtroom.

Goring cheats justice

We had guards at each cell that looked in on the prisoners every two minutes and still Goring committed suicide. To this day I don't think they know how he got this cyanide or whatever it was. He always carried a pipe but he never smoked it. My theory is that he had a cyanide capsule in the pipe's stem and nobody detected it. It had to be something like that. Not even his lawyers could smuggle anything in, as they couldn't get close to him.

Walter Funk

Walter Funk was one who kept his weight. He was a little, rotund guy. He had a pinkie ring with about a three carat canary diamond in it. He told me, "If I go free, I'm going to give you this ring." I *thought that'd be all right, but it might have been illegal. But, I didn't get it because I left before the trial ended. He was a funny little guy.*

Ernie Frazier

Von Schirach

Von Schirach was the head of the Hitler Youth. He was the youngest prisoner, nice looking and sharp. He could speak good English and could tell us more about the United States than we knew. A lot of them could.
The trial lasted ten months.

I'd do it all again

I'd say that if I had to go to war all over again, I'd probably do it. Of course, I didn't know any better when I was young, but the U.S. is still the best country there is.

Kent still stands straight and tall and it's not hard to imagine him as a young G. I. standing guard in Nuremberg. He and his wife, Marie, are retired and live in Dodge City, Kansas.

CHAPTER 11

JOHN SCHLICHTING

"I fought at Midway, Guadalcanal and Bougainville"

John Schlichting was not only a fighting marine; he looked like one. His story is the tale of the young Marines who had to overcome starvation, malaria, and dysentery while engaging the enemy in a miserable jungle war that left thousands of their comrades dead or maimed for life.

Raw recruits ship out

I'd been attending junior college and joined the Marines on the 23rd of December 1941. The war hardly got started until I was there. I was sent to San Diego and taken in by a couple of those Marine Corps Drill sergeants. It was quite an experience in boot camp. They were making Marines out of shoe salesmen and what have you. They didn't have much time to do it, so the methods used were rather stringent sometimes.

I was just short of my 19th birthday. Of course I thought I knew everything then, but I learned a few things after that.

Ernie Frazier

I signed up for four years. The recruiters espoused all the benefits of being a regular instead of being a reserve. So, they talked me into being a regular and a four-year enlistment. As it turned out, that was just about how long the war lasted. Boot camp consisted of two weeks on the parade ground and two weeks on the rifle range. But, we packed in quite a bit of schooling because we would start at 6:00 in the morning and run until 10:00 every night. The fifth week, we were aboard ship going overseas. I don't know that we were actually Marines when we were finished but they called us Marines instead of a number of other adjectives.

We were put on a troop ship loaded with Marines and sent us to Hawaii. We joined a special weapons group in Hawaii and, it so happens I was put in a machine gun company. As far as training, I had about a month with a machine gun company and our primary purpose there was to guard against ground attack. I guess I was as proficient with the machine gun as any 19-year-old coming out of school who suddenly found himself in the middle of a war.

We had some training on the anti-aircraft weapons, shooting at some sleeves and other targets when we were in Hawaii, so we knew how to fire them.

<u>Preparations at Midway</u>

We learned to handle the guns and they sent us to Midway in preparation for the Japanese invasion. We knew the Japanese were coming because we had broken their code by that point. They used several devices to tell where they were going to hit. We knew they were intent on picking Midway, so we went in about ten days in advance of the Japanese. That gave us time to build up our fortifications. That was where I got into my first battles.

There were mainly Marines there along with a few U.S. Navy people. Midway had been operating as a radio relay station for the Navy for a number of years and there were a few civilian contractors who had built the airfield. It had been the stopping place for the first overseas flights to Japan and China by TWA's flying boats. They could not fly all the way across, so they stopped at Midway to refuel.

There were two battalions of Marines there along with an existing air group. Before the battle started, we got in six or eight B17's and also some navy TBF's, which were a brand new thing. I would guess there were probably 40 dive-bombers and torpedo bombers of the old vintage and probably about that same amount of fighter planes, which were called old Bruster Buffaloes, and a few Grumman F3F fighters.

At that point we had three carriers left and they were in position off the coast.

Japanese demolish our planes

The Japanese hit us on June 4, 1942. They had five carriers and by the time the first raid was over, they had pretty well demolished our air force. As I recall—the figures may not be exactly accurate—but I was thinking out of 40 dive bombers and torpedo bombers, we had 14 left that came back after the first raid. I believe we only had five fighters that could still fly.

We had set up machine gun pits on the beach in anticipation of an invasion. However, they attacked from the sky first, so all of us helped out on the anti-aircraft guns. The Japanese fighter pilots and bomber pilots were more skilled than ours. As our planes were trying to land they just swarmed over our boys. It wasn't a very good sight at all. We were probably 50 yards away from the airfield where this was happening.

There are two islands to Midway, Sand Island and Eastern Island. Sand Island is about a mile long, and about a quarter of a mile wide. That is where the big airfield was.

Our supplies were on Sand Island. There we had shore batteries, some which had been installed three or four years before on Wake, Midway, Johnson, and Howell—all around a perimeter. At Wake, there were still a lot of civilian employees working on the airfield when the war started.

Our machine guns were .30 caliber, .50 caliber and 37 millimeter. The anti-aircraft guns were 3 inch. The shore batteries were what we called 551's. About every ship around had one on the fantail. We also had a couple of 11-inch guns that had come from the Panama Canal. I remember helping some of the gun crews to make up canisters of ammunition loaded with nuts and bolts and other junk to be fired from the big guns.

At Midway, our fighters were able to shoot down a few of the Japanese bombers. We also hit some of the dive-bombers and fighter planes that were swooping in on us to strafe the island. I'm not certain but I think we shot down 27 planes. It's been a few years.

The battle for Midway never reached the island. It was an air and sea battle. Their fighter planes were all over the island and that's what we were firing at. Their troop carriers and battle ships never got to us. Our Navy stopped them, maybe 70 miles off shore. We got lucky and got one of their biggest carriers—I think it was named the Akake—when she had all her planes on deck, loaded and ready to go in for their second bombing run on us. A couple of our dive-bombers got to her.

Captain Henderson becomes a kamikaze pilot

Shortly after that, Captain Henderson, who had led a dive-bomber group out, was returning to base as the lone survivor of the mission. The zeroes were all over him and at about 10,000 feet he sent his plane into a dive, turning himself into an American kamikaze, and hit the biggest Jap carrier right at mid-ships. It was believed that he'd been hit so bad that he knew he wouldn't make it back so he carried his bomb all the way in. It was a 500-pounder and luckily it went right into the ship's magazine. You could see the smoke for 50 miles. That was kind of the turning point in the battle.

Wounded pilot lands with two dead crewmen aboard

That morning we only lost 15 or 20 men on the ground. However, of our torpedo bombers that went into battle that day, not a single one made it back. We had six new Grumman torpedo planes and only one of them made it. The pilot came right in beside my gun pit and could only get one wheel down. He had his head sticking out the side of the canopy trying to see to land and finally landed about 50 yards from me. We ran over and pulled him out. The reason he was sticking his head out was because he'd been shot through the throat and was coughing blood all over the windshield and couldn't see anything. I don't know if he survived or not but he had a gunner and a radioman in behind him and they were both dead.

Midway was truly an air war. No capital ships fired on each other. The battle was between air and naval forces. That may have been the first air battle on the sea. The Japanese got the Yorktown but we got more of their ships.

We got reports of what was happening at sea but we were too far away to witness it first hand. Of course we saw the flights going in and out but that was all.

I'd only been in the Marine Corps about four months and was a private first class. I made corporal before we went to Guadalcanal. Then I made sergeant and finally platoon sergeant.

We came back from Midway to Hawaii on the 4th of July and immediately began loading our ship. We didn't take long to get loaded and set out for an unknown destination. As I recall, it took 17 days to convoy down to Guadalcanal. We picked up a lot of ships and it was quite a convoy.

Guadalcanal

Our ships shelled the beaches before we began landing. Of course we didn't know if the Japanese were still there or not. We were circling around in a Higgins boat waiting for orders to land. Those boats could run right up onto the beach. When they did, a ramp would drop and you'd better get off mighty fast because you're just a sitting duck coming down the ramp.

The Japanese were building an airfield on Guadalcanal and had about finished it. They had 3,000 to 4,000 troops working on it. We landed about two miles east of them. At that point, we encountered none of the enemy. However, as we approached the airfield we met some resistance. They must have figured they couldn't hold it and fell back. Within two days, the airfield was ours.

Ernie Frazier

Japanese sink four U. S. cruisers in first hour

That afternoon—we came in on August 7th—Japanese planes flying out of Rabaul were coming in, attacking our transports with torpedo bombers. Our stuff was only about half unloaded. That night, the Japanese navy came in and sank four of our cruisers in the first hour of their attack. They also scattered or sunk our remaining troop transports. Of course the last thing to come off a ship would be food and supplies since they were the last things needed. So we wound up real short of food. Also, some of our artillery pieces got ashore but they couldn't get enough ammunition unloaded for them. That left us in a bad way.

At that point, the Japanese had complete control of the ocean and could bring in troops anytime they wanted. Their tin cans and cruisers would run around shooting up everything that moved. It wasn't a good situation for us, at all.

On the ground we set up mostly water-cooled machine guns to defend the airstrip. In a lengthy battle, an air-cooled barrel can melt down pretty fast. There were three men on a machine gun team.

Short of food and ammunition. Malaria and dysentery strike

We didn't have food or enough ammunition and the pressure was on 24 hours a day. There just wasn't any relief! We were really scrapping just trying to keep our hind ends together. Another thing: All the quinine came from Borneo and that had been blocked off for several years. So all of us started getting malaria and diarrhea and dysentery.

Some go mad

Some humans just don't have the mental make-up to put up with it all. There's a process whereby you have to block it out and just tolerate the misery. Some guys can't do it. One morning one of the sergeants in the gun pit next to me woke me up screaming and hollering something terrible. Unnatural screams. I looked over and saw him rolling around on the ground. I thought the Japs had infiltrated the area and knifed him. Actually he was beating himself on the rocks. All his fingernails were torn off and his face was all scratched up so I grabbed him and tried to hold him but I couldn't do it. A couple of other guys showed up and we got him down until one of the pharmacist's mates showed up and gave him a shot to quiet him down. We had a hospital and they took him over there. No one ever wanted to go to the hospital. It was made up of two long tents. They took everybody in one end. Later, they carried them out the other end. That's where the cemetery was.

I remember one night we got an announcement from naval division headquarters, which would have been Vandergrift, coming down from Admiral Halsey saying that they had fired Gormley, the admiral in charge of the South Pacific area. Bull Halsey was now in charge. He promised that the Japanese navy would never shell us again. Man, we were glad to hear that. It was cause for celebration. But, I would say that within thirty minutes of his promise, here came the shells once again! Big ones—battleship shells. After they pass overhead, they sound like a freight train has just cleared your head. They were big suckers. That went on for about thirty minutes, and then stopped as though ordered to cease firing.

Everything started flying out in the bay. We were about 200 yards from the beach and we scampered over to see what was going on. Between then and the next morning—I don't know how many ships blew up—but I know that seven or eight Men-O-War were burning at once. You couldn't tell whose ships they were.

I went back to the gun pit for a while, and then went back out about 9 o'clock in the morning. There were three ships dead in the water and a Japanese battleship in the bay that was just going around in a circle. He was all shot up and couldn't maneuver and wasn't firing on anybody. Our people tied a torpedo on a PBY and sent it out to see if it could hit the battleship. We got a hit and the battleship exploded, but a strange thing happened. It straightened out and went between Salvo and Guadalcanal and Cape Esperanee and then moved on out of sight. The report was that it sunk a little later because of internal explosions. From that time on, things changed in our favor.

We were still guarding the airfield. It was operating and we had planes flying out. I was lucky because I wasn't right in the middle of some of the worst battles and was a little ways back of the Tenaru battle. It was a little river about a mile east of the airport. The 14th Imperial Marines landed—their commanding officer was Tojo's nephew—and they were going to take back the airfield. We think there were probably 1,200 of them.

Oh, did you ever hear of a native of Guadalcanal, a Melanesian named Vooso? He'd been captured by the Japanese and tortured, but escaped. Now he was working for the Australians and held the rank of sergeant major in their army. One night, on guard duty, he saw the Japanese land and hightailed it to the airport to tell us what was going on. We immediately rushed a lot of people to the area to set up our 30's, 50's, and 37's on the riverbank.

Japs attact in waves

At about two or three in the morning the Japs came charging in, wave after wave. We opened up with everything we had and they just kept coming, running at our positions over and over again. Pretty soon the bodies were piling on top of one another. They wouldn't stop.

And our gunners just kept mowing them down.

They launched some small boats and tried to flank us. We sent out a couple of amphibian tractors and chopped them to pieces.

Photos of Japanese soldiers retrieved from one of their pockets.

When the battle wound down, we sent out a battalion to round up the stragglers.

We killed 1,100. They killed 16

That proved to be our best performance on Guadalcanal. Out of the estimated 1,200 Japanese that attacked, we killed about 1,100 and only took 26 prisoners. They only killed 16 of our men; would you believe that? We did have quite a few that were wounded.

Before we ever got to Guadalcanal, Australians, Mormons, and Catholic priests and nuns visited the area. A lot of the natives had reddish hair, which they colored themselves. They were very honest people but would ask us for anything we had. I remember one of them kept pestering me for a large safety pin I had and I gave it to him. The next thing I knew, he was walking around with it pierced through his nose.

Prior to the battle, DC 3's, C 54's and submarines were bringing in supplies and evacuating our wounded. But not every flight made it. I lost a good buddy on one. He'd gotten his leg shot up pretty bad so they loaded him on a DC 3. It barely cleared the runway on take-off, then lost power and crashed. It killed him.

I got off Guadalcanal in January 1942. I'd been there since August. Up until October we'd just been defending our little piece of dirt, trying to hang on until we could mount our offense. Fighting went on most of the time with the worst of it over by November when Dugout Doug let some of the Army come in. They did a lot of mopping up and began relieving the Marines.

Weevils supply good protein

We didn't have food when we first got there because our supply ships were under attack. I went from 180 pounds—hard as nails—clear down to 135 when I finally left the island. On the other side of the airport, the Japanese had a supply dump loaded with barley, rice, and fish heads. After they took off, we started eating their food. You give a guy a sock full of rice and two fish heads and he can live for a week. The fish heads provided some of the protein that we needed. We didn't care much for the food, even though

we ate it. The bad thing about it was that the rice was full of rat turds. We used to pick them out, but soon got tired of that and just started shoving them aside with our spoons. The barley was full of weevils and we did the same thing with them. Actually, the weevils were probably another pretty good source of protein.

You've got to stay alive. It got so I'd eat anything. I've even eaten stuff I would never admit to today. We were really in bad shape before our supplies came in and you'd eat any damn thing. Of course, everybody was sick by that time, everybody had malaria and there was lots of dysentery. Finally, we started getting shipments of a yellow synthetic--I think it was called Atabrine—which was a quinine substitute. It helped take out some of the fever and chills. And, like I said, nobody went to the hospital unless he was in terrible shape.

When you first go into combat and kill somebody, you might get sick to your stomach and it really affects you. But, you have to harden your mind and system to what you're doing because you see your friends getting killed and if you go crazy over that, you wind up getting yourself killed. You have to just block it all out and focus on your job and what you have to do.

Body parts

When a shell hits a gun pit and there are pieces of guys lying all over and you have to go over and pick up two legs, two arms and a head and put them in a bag, you don't know who you've picked up unless you knew who was in the pit. It's terrible but you just have to live with it. Of course, we had a burial detail going all the time. You see all of this going on and you just can't believe what your mind is capable of doing. It really is beyond comprehension.

Traumatized

Let me tell you a little story. My best buddy—you know everyone ties up with a best uddy—well, I knew this guy better than his mother. I knew every girl he ever dated, every drink he ever took and everything else about his life. One-day mail came and they dropped his at my CP. I called on the phone and told him I had mail for his platoon. He came over and suddenly we were under attack. He started up out of the pit. I pushed him aside and said, "I'll go first." So I went out with him behind. After the firing was over, I saw he wasn't with me so I went back. I found him. A shell had torn the back of his head off.

He was still spurting blood—if a guy is bleeding he's still alive—if he's not bleeding, don't bother. Anyway I picked him up and put him in the back of a jeep. He died soon so I took him down the road to bury him. I wrapped him in an old dirty blanket and dug kind of a shallow hole and put him in it. Then, I went back to work.

Three or four months later, I started to tell someone about the experience. You know, I couldn't recall my buddy's name. I tried to think of where he was from. I couldn't recall that, either. I knew him better than his mother knew him, but I couldn't remember anything about him...my best buddy. My mind had just blocked it all out. About thirty years later, a guy pulled up in my driveway from California. It was old Bill Briggs. He'd been there with us. So he came in and we had a great time, sitting having a drink at my bar and telling all of our old stories. He asked, "Do you remember Lynsch?" It struck me then, thirty years later; John C. Lynsch.

Probably the one thing that sticks out in my mind as far as near-death experiences go and the closest I got to getting sent home, was one day when the Japanese were coming over to bomb us. The announcement came down that they were on their way and sure enough, they came flying out of the clouds in one of their big V formations—about 25 planes. Our fighters got on them pretty fast and were giving them a bad time, shooting down one or two, I don't remember exactly.

A 1,000 pound bomb hits!

There would only be one Jap plane in the formation that had a bombsight and he would signal the others when to drop their bombs. Well, they must have got scared because they started unloading early and I could see this damn row of bombs coming right straight at us. I said, "Willy, get down low! That son-of-a-bitch is going to get us!" And it damn near did! They dropped a 1,000 pounder. It hit real close and blew our gun-pit in on us. The concussion threw dirt and junk all over us and the force of it wrapped me backwards around my gun.

Blood started running out of my nose and ears. I tried to make it over to the next gun-pit to see if those guys were all right but every time I stood up, the damn ground would come up and hit me right in the face!

I tried to stand up two or three times before I finally got smart and crawled over there. The guys there were OK, but I still couldn't keep on my feet so I crawled back. It was crazy. Finally, things got settled down so I told Willie to call battalion and tell them that no one got killed. Then I started getting terribly sleepy and couldn't keep my eyes open and I began to think, "Well maybe this is it. This may be the way it happens." I told Willie that I was going to crawl back in a little ammunition storage area and sleep. That was in the middle of the afternoon. When I woke up, it was daybreak. I'd slept all that time. I crawled out and asked the guy on watch, "How come you guys let me sleep?" He told me, "Well, we looked back in there and you were still breathing so we left you alone."

I walked around and found out that I'd gotten my equilibrium back. I was covered in blood and dirt so I went down to the river to wash up. After that I was all right except that I pissed blood for a couple of weeks. But there was no way that I was going to the hospital.

People asked if I got a Purple Heart for that. Well, I didn't. I guess it's because I never brought it up and didn't go to the hospital. If you could sit up and pull the trigger, you were OK. I never gave it much thought.

New Zealand

I still had some dizziness from the concussion and got malaria—malignant malaria—and it still crops up once in a while. Another thing you get in the jungle are rock sores and my body was covered with them. On top of that I had dysentery and everything that goes with it so, after Guadalcanal, a lot of us spent some time in a hospital in New Zealand. It was a good place to recuperate.

While I was there, an interesting thing happened. A kid from New Zealand would come in dressed in his school uniform, sort of a typical English outfit with short pants and long socks. I was cold and was trying to pull my blankets up but I was so weak I couldn't do it and I was using a few choice words. The kid saw my plight and said, "Yank, can I help you?" I said, "Yeah, pull the damn blankets up." He did—he was a nice kid about fourteen years old--and he sat down on the edge of the bed to visit with me. I never thought much about it but the next day after school he came by again and we talked some more. And he kept coming every day.

I finally got mobile and started moving around and he told me, "Mum says I can bring you to tea." I figured I had nothing to lose so I went home with him. He had a very nice mother, no father, but an old maid aunt that lived with them along with his two little sisters—one was seven and one was nine. They just sort of adopted me. I was their Marine and they were going to take care of me and see that I got everything I needed. Well, I kept in contact with them forever after and in 1980 my wife and I went to New Zealand to see them. This past December I took my son back and saw them again. They've been my extended family all these years and I wanted to perpetuate our family's connection.

The boy is now 72 and the girls are 66 and 64. Their name is Robbins. That's a good English name.

Bougainville and Rabaul

Bougainville was our next campaign. Rabaul was the big Japanese base in the Solomon Islands. It had an air base and a naval base, and Bougainville was next to it. We took Bougainville and by-passed Rabaul. We had enough air power by then that we neutralized their air power and whenever a ship tried to get to Rabaul, we would sink it. There were probably 20,000 Japanese on Rabaul and we stopped all supplies to them. We didn't care what happened to them. They just began starving.

We had a little problem getting onto Bougainville. We had to go in on landing craft. The island was very well fortified and we took a lot of casualties. On thing we did that was pretty slick when you think *about it, was at a place called Torquina Point—I'm not sure about the spelling—which had a little harbor that we came into. The Japanese had a couple of 75's set up just about six feet above the water line and they were riddling our Higgins boats as we came in. We landed on the point a little further down. We were supposed to be in the second wave but wound up being the first wave to arrive on the point. We tried to get to the 75's but were having plenty of trouble doing it.*

All of a sudden, here comes a big old tank hauler. It drops down the front end and out comes a bulldozer with a seabee driving it. We wondered, "What the hell is he doing? He doesn't know where he is." And all of us are pointing over at the 75 so he'd see what he was into. Well, he thought he was supposed to push it over, so he shoves the throttle wide open, went hell-bent and hit that gun emplacement square on. Japanese started running out in every direction. The seabee looked around and jumped off the dozer and came running back to us as hard as he could. He was madder than hell! Bullets had been bouncing off his Caterpillar—he didn't even have a shield up and hadn't realized that he was attacking a manned gun. We had a lot of fun with that!

I'd say Bougainville was more fun than Guadalcanal. The fighting wasn't as tough and we had all the supplies we needed. There's a rib of mountains down the center of the island and we drove right in and took that rib. Most of the Japanese were in behind it, on the other side. We set up there and let them have the rest. They fired some artillery at us, but we didn't care. We had them isolated and they were going to set there and starve. We were finally getting smart, you know. We landed there in August 1943 and stayed there three or four months. Then they decided to send me home. They took our whole outfit and put them in the 6th Marines and shipped them to Okinawa. I kind of wanted to go since they were all my buddies, but I decided I'd be stupid to do that and decided to rotate back to the states.

I was back here about three months and they decided to send me to Camp Lejuene to Chesty Puller's Troop Leader School and the Weapons School to teach me how to shoot machine guns. You know, all that crap. We were tooling up to attack Japan so, when I finished my training, they sent me out to California for more schooling. They were putting together replacement battalions to ship out to Japan and my Colonel asked me if I wanted to go, but said I didn't have to if I didn't want to. Then he started naming my buddies and all the other guys that were going so I said, "Yeah."

Japan next?

We sailed to Guam, which we'd occupied and hooked up with the 3rd Division. We were to make ready for an assault on Honshu, Japan. I never worked harder in all my life. It took about two months to get the outfit in shape. We were exhausted and everybody was strung out and we were all at each other's throats. We were finally ready to go with 116 combat loaded ships in Guam Harbor. But, we just sat there, waiting for orders to sail. Then we started hearing about a big bomb that was going to be dropped. We knew nothing about it but heard that a guy in another company knew a lot about it. So we went over and met this little, scrawny kid, and he sat there and started telling us all about what an atomic bomb was.

It ends

Well, the bomb was dropped and we never got to Honshu. I was very happy about that because assaulting the Japanese homeland would have meant tremendous casualties on our part. We would have had to fight every man, woman, and child since the whole nation was going to be forced to fight to the death.

Florence Burns

After the war, I came home and stopped by an apartment to see a friend of mine. While there, I saw this good-looking, dark haired girl in the hall and asked him who that was. "Oh, that's a new girl going to college up here." So when I left that evening, I said, loud and clear, "I'll be back about six tomorrow evening." Well, when I got back, she was there again. I went over and said, "My name is John." Her name was Florence Burns. Two years later I got her to marry me. I always accused her of engineering our meeting but she would never admit it.

She was my sweetheart for 49 years. She died of a heart attack in 1996. I've been alone since then.

I had a brother, George that was with the 1st Armored Division that fought in North Africa. He was taken prisoner when Rommel overran our forces at Kasserine Pass. Rommel destroyed about 400 of our tanks and just beat the hell out of our people. The Germans marched about 10,000 allied prisoners across the desert to Tunis. My brother said they got some ersatz coffee that was made from charred grain and a piece of black bread for breakfast. In the middle of the afternoon they got a cup of soup and another piece of black bread. At Tunis, they were put on a cattle boat and shipped to northern Italy. They were marched to the French border and shipped in cattle cars to Stalag 3-B outside of Berlin. He was an inch or two taller than me, weighed about 230 pounds and looked like Charles Atlas, the body builder, when he was captured. When he got home, he weighed 150 pounds.

I've got a friend that has done a lot of research on P. O. W. camps. The Germans put the prisons under the control of older officers, usually retirement age colonels. Some took the Red Cross packages that were earmarked for the prisoners and sold them. They'd get pretty good money because the German civilians were starving. My brother said that the officer running their camp wasn't too bad but they were short of food anyway. The commandant could rent out the prisoners to work on farms and he got to keep the money. Mostly the prisoners went to truck farms so my brother tried to get on those details because they could usually steal some food from the farm.

He told me that they woke up one morning and saw that all of their guards had abandoned them. The Germans had heard the Russian artillery was getting closer and closer so they took off. The prisoners knew where the German food warehouse was so they went over and broke into it. It was empty. So they went to the German's homes and kicked in the doors to get food. But, the civilians didn't have any, either. So George and the others just started walking west. After three days, they found the American army.

I had a sister, Sue Kohlman, that was a navy nurse. She stayed in the navy and retired as a full Commander. Both she and George are now dead. She did several tours on hospital ships and was on one at the Okinawa campaign and had an interesting story to tell.

I'd heard the story before but had no idea that my sister was the nurse involved. If it looked like a wounded trooper had a chance to survive, they'd take him in a Higgins boat to the hospital ship. One guy was hit real badly in the guts. She said that they brought him into the surgery room and opened him up. They found a 40-mm shell, unexploded, still in his belly. It took about a second and a half to clear the surgery room! But a doctor said, "I'm going back in and take that shell out of that boy. Will anybody help me?" My sister's a little crazy anyway so she said, "I'll go."

They cut the kid open and took a forceps and took the shell out. She laid a towel in a stainless steel pan and the doctor placed the shell in it. She asked, "Now what am I supposed to do with this thing?"

They were about two decks down and he said, "All you can do is throw it over the side." So she went upstairs carrying the shell and guys started jumping out of the way. It didn't explode and she threw it overboard. The doctor got a medal for his part. She got a letter of commendation. That's the way the military did things.

She told us the story some years later when she was home on leave. Her little niece asked her, "Well what did you do after that, Aunt Sue?" Sue replied, "Actually, I just changed my pants and went back to work!"

CHAPTER 12

FLOYD KIRBY

"I saw his body heave and slump down. He'd never see his new baby boy."

Floyd joined the National Guard in December 1940. He took a short discharge and re-enlisted in the Army Air Corps for three years. He wound up flying 50 missions out of Cherenola, Italy and was in the service until 1945.

Black pilots flying P-51's kept the enemy off the B-24's

Where we encountered the most fighter planes was over Polesti, Bucharest and Vienna. JU-88 and ME-109 fighter planes would rise to meet us. We were flying B-24's and I was the nose gunner. Our P-51's and P-38's tried to keep the enemy off of us. We had one group of black pilots that flew P-51s. Remember, the service was still segregated then. But, boy, we were glad to see them! They flew closer coverage for us than anyone and I mean they were good—exceptionally good!

We had to do 50 missions before we could rotate home. Pilots flying out of England across the channel only had to do 25. However, that was justified because they encountered fighter planes and flak almost immediately upon take off. When we crossed the Alps it was considered a two-mission flight.

It wasn't unusual for us to have three or four of our planes blown out of the air on a mission. Usually the two waist gunners could bail out. They always wore their parachutes. I didn't. But I wore my harness and had a snap on chute in the back. If I had to bail out I'd get up in the turret and go out the nose wheel of the ship. If you were hit hard it would be real difficult to make it and the ship would have to stay up a while before you could get out. Also, the ball, tail and nose gunners would take longer to get out because they didn't have their chutes on, either.

The ball gunner's position was terrible as far as I was concerned. It was located right behind the bomb bay and the gunner hung down under the plane in this little bubble. I flew it one time. Never again! I felt like I was suspended from a couple of pieces of string. I'm pretty tall so I was real cramped in there. Dysentery was common and once I volunteered to replace a sick ball gunner from another plane. That way I could log more time and rotate home sooner. However, it didn't take me long to change my mind. I saw one boy who'd flown a lot of missions over the Pacific and rotated home. He got restless and volunteered for a tour in Europe. He volunteered for everything. Well, his plane got hit and they went down. I decided to quit volunteering, figuring I didn't need to tempt fate.

Encountering heavy flack

We kidded each other a lot to keep our spirits up. One time we flew into heavy flak. It tore into my turret. I must've dug in as deep as I could to keep from getting hit. It would have decapitated me if it struck my head or neck. I was firing at anything that moved. Of course enemy aircraft wasn't attacking when flak was in the air. They were too smart for that. Our bombardier took a hit to the head but it wasn't fatal. We told him that his hard head saved him. A hit anywhere else would've killed him!

Shot up and forced to land

We made another mission into southern France where the anti-aircraft batteries got a lot more accurate. They trained their flak directly on us instead of just firing up a barrage and hoping we'd fly into it. They'd have four to six batteries tracking us from below. We'd see puffs of smoke coming out and we'd say, "Lord behold, we

Ernie Frazier

just hope that's a four battery unit, not six, because the next two will land right in our lap!" We got shot up real bad. Our plane was full of holes and we had to make a forced landing on a small island.

Floyd's recollection of the following incident brought back a flood of sad memories for him.

On one of our raids over Polesti we were flying at high level, thank heaven, because on one low level attack, errors had been made and a lot of our planes were knocked out by bombs dropped by our own planes overhead. I flew two high altitude bombardments over Polesti and they weren't milk runs. On one of them, our fighter pilot escorts were about five minutes late getting to us and boy, I mean we had two airplanes off our right wing that were shot completely out.

Counting the parachutes coming out

One loss kind of got to me because the boy that was flying in the nose—I'd gotten to know him pretty well—told me that he'd just received word from home that he had a new baby boy. I can still see him. I looked out of my window and saw his body heave up to get out of his chair, then he just slumped forward. We counted the parachutes coming out. There must have been at least six; possibly seven. My buddy didn't make it.

We were flying the lead on that mission. Our planes were stacked in formation and we were flying a little lower than the others. In my cramped area there was no way I could get my guns properly timed and sighted on the enemy planes. This ME-109 came in, knocked down my buddy's ship, then came back for more. We found out later that the boys on our right wing—I don't know why they were flying there anyway as it was their first mission—just froze at their guns. It looked like the nose gunner had a point blank shot at the ME-109 and we thought he could knock him right out of the air. But, the enemy plane got in again and knocked down another one of our B-24's.

The best dogfight you ever saw

Then our two P-51's came roaring in and we sat right there and watched the best dogfight you ever saw in your life. You see P-51's in air shows but you just can't believe how good they really were in combat. They came in on this ME-109—and I mean he was doing everything in the world to evade them—and they just drove him straight into the ground.

I always felt the infantry boys had it three times harder than us. They called us the white-collar boys. As soon as we completed a mission, we went home to a cot and sheets to sleep on, but it wasn't all pie and turkey.

A new major—he was really something else, kind of like a 90 day wonder—got assigned to administer our outfit. He saw us lounging around when we were off duty and decided to shape us up—make soldiers out of us. Our pilots conned him into flying on one of our raids. I think it was over Vienna. Our colonel, who was a super person and looked after us boys like a mother hen, led us in and it was a rough, tough target. My plane was flying on his left wing.

A B-24 folded like an accordion

Over the target, the Colonel's plane got a direct hit in the bomb bay, and, honest to goodness, that B-24 folded up just like an accordion and went straight down. No parachutes opened. No one survived. The new major was flying on our ship. When we landed he said, "I don't care what you guys do from now on. There's no way you can get enough for what you're doing up here. You'll never get me back up in one of those things again."

<u>Excerpts from S/Sgt Floyd Kirby's flight log</u>
(Every flight was a flirtation with death that only the very fortunate survived)
Not a complete log

Ernie Frazier

*April 29: Our big day—First combat mission. Bombed **Drmis**, Yugoslavia with eight 500# demos at 21,000 ft.—14:30.*

May 2: Second combat mission—bombed Spezia, Italy harbor with eight 500# demos at 19,750 ft. We were shot at with flak. It was quite an experience—6:55.

May 5: Third combat mission—bombed Pogodriga, Yugoslavia. No flak or enemy opposition. Dropped nine 500# demos at 21,000 ft.

May 10. "4th" & "5th" missions bombed Winer Neustaet Air Drom. Dropped 30 cluster fragmentation at 20,000 ft.—a very rough mission. Our group lost three 2-H'S. One on our right wing took direct hit with flak. No enemy aircraft opposition, thank God—6:40

May 13: "6th" mission bombed Cesena, Italy marshalling rail yard. Dropped nine 500# demos at 17,600 ft. Direct hits on target. Little flak but we were already past target before they opened fire—6:25.

May 14: "7th" mission bombed Pivuo Cabsco, northern Italy. Dropped ten 500# demos at 20,000 ft. on marshalling Rail Yard. Plenty of flak but we hit just at the side of it. No enemy aircraft opposition—5:10.

May 18: Bombed Belgrade, Yugoslavia. Dropped ten 500# bombs at 19,600 ft. Little flak, very inaccurate. No enemy aircraft opposition—6:05.

May 19: "9th" mission was supposed to bomb the railroad tunnel near Genoa, Italy but when we got within 30 minutes of the target, the weather was so bad we couldn't bomb so had to turn back. No flak. No enemy aircraft opposition. We were carrying two 2,000 lb. & two 1,000 G. P—6:15.

May 19: The "Wing" said, that since we didn't drop our bombs, the mission didn't count. So have to still sweat out #8.

May 22: "9th" mission bombed Piombino, northern Italy. Dropped forty 1,000 lb. demos at 19,600 ft. Encountered flak, but were in lead element so had passed the target before it got very bad. No E. A. O. (enemy aircraft opposition.) Bombed harbor.

May 23: "10th" mission bombed road junction south of Rome. Dropped 10-500 lb demos at 17,000 feet. No flak. No enemy aircraft—4:00.

May 25th: Bombed Carnoules, southern France. Dropped nine 500# bombs at 19,000 ft. on marshalling yards. Light flak. Enemy fighters but didn't attack our element—7:00.

May 27: Bombed Salon D. Provence, southern France. Dropped nine 500# at 20,000 ft. on the Air Drome. Intense flak but inaccurate. No enemy aircraft encountered—8:00.

May 30: Bombed Wels, Austria. Dropped nine 500# at 20,500 ft. Direct hit on aircraft factory. Got excellent mark from TAC Wing. Light flak. Few enemy fighters, but we weren't attacked—7:30.

Total combat hours for May: 80:45.

June 3: No combat mission. Flew to Naples—1:50.

June 4: "15th" mission bombed railroad bridge at Recco, Italy. No flak. No fighters. Dropped six 1,000 GP—9:55.

June 5: "16th" mission bombed Viadock at Merida, Italy. No Flak. No fighters. Dropped six 1,000 GP at 17,500 ft.—4:30.

June 7: "17th" mission bombed railroad bridge south of Canne, France. Direct hits on target. Lots of flak, very accurate. No enemy aircraft. Bombed at 22,000 ft. Dropped five 1,000 GP—7:00.

June 10: "18th" mission bombed oil storage tanks at Port Marghera, northern Italy. Direct hit on target, which started large fires. Dropped nine 500# demos at 21,000 ft. Heavy flak, but inaccurate. No enemy aircraft opposition—5:20.

June 11: "19th" & "20th" missions bombed oil storage tanks at Giurgui, Rumania. Good hits on target. Fires were started. Dropped eighteen 250# demos. Heavy flak. We were attacked by enemy aircraft but weren't hit. They knocked down two of our ships right off our right wing. We figured five got out of one ship and two out of the other. Bombed at 20,00 ft.—7:40.

June 13: "21st" & "22nd" missions were to bomb Munich, Germany but it was covered with a smoke screen. We bombed an alternate target, the marshalling yards at Innsbruck, Germany at 24,300 ft. with nine 500# bombs. Flew my first and last mission as a lower ball gunner. I had to take a boy's place that was sick. I was double scared today as we met around 65 to 70 fighter planes: ME 109s, ME 210s, ME H10s, & JU 88s. Of all times for my guns to go out, they did today. Also, plenty of flak and very accurate. We got 30 some hits on our ship. No one hurt—7:35.

June 14: Bombing and gunnery practice—4:25.

June 16: Started on bombing mission but weather was bad. Still, we flew—4:10.

June 19: Gunner practice—3:00.

June 22: "24th" mission bombed Pola, northern Italy at 19,000 ft. Flak moderate. No fighters. Dropped eighteen 250# bombs on submarine base—7:00.

June 24: Bombing & gunnery practice—4:00.

June 25: Bombing & gunnery practice—2:20.

June 30: "25th" mission target was Belhamer, Germany. Got within 40 minutes of target.

Weather was so bad we turned back. Ran into flak on our way up. Counted as a mission because we dropped bombs in the ocean—nine 500# clusters of incendiary. Too dangerous to land with them—6:10.

Total hours flown in June: 79.25. Combat: 63.50.

July 6: "26th" mission bombed aviation refueling station at Aviano, Italy. Very good pattern. No flack. No aircraft. Dropped nine 500# bombs from 26,000 ft.—6:00

July 7. Target Blechammer, Germany. Super chargers went out so we turned back. No mission—3:35.

July 11: "27th" mission bombed submarine base at Toulon, France at 21,500 ft. Dropped nine 500# bombs. Flak moderate but very accurate. Got two flak holes in my turret. Was too close for comfort but I didn't get hit. Very lucky. No fighters—8:00.

July 12: "28th" mission bombed Nimes, France marshalling rail yards at 21,000 feet. Dropped nine 500# bombs. Flak intense and very accurate. We had our closest call yet without going down. We got 25+ holes in our ship. Three big ones in our #1, #3, & #4 engines. Just too close for comfort—8:40.

July 16: "29th" & "30th" mission bombed Winne Neuorf, 10 miles south of Vienna, Austria—an aircraft engine shop. Dropped five 1,000# bombs. Flak was light. No enemy aircraft—6:50.

July 18: "31st" and "32nd" mission bombed Fredrishafem, Germany oil refinery at 24,600 feet. Dropped nine 500# bombs. Flak was intense and accurate. We got 14 flak holes. Flack flew in the wing fuselage by waist gunner. We got hit in the nose and the broken glass came right up under my fanny—7:30.

July 19: "33rd" & "34th" mission bombed Schleiszhein, Germany airport, north of Munich. Dropped five 1,000# GP at 22,000 feet. Flak intense and accurate. Got 10 holes and they were nice size. No enemy aircraft. When we came back to land the nose wheel wouldn't come down. Had to go around the field for an hour before we got the wheel down—9:15.

July 21: "35th" & "36th" mission bombed Brux, Germany air plane factory at 23,000 feet. Flak intense and heavy but inaccurate. We got only three holes. Dropped forty 100# GP. No enemy aircraft—9:00.

July 22: "37th" mission bombed Polesti, Rumania oil storage tanks at 23,000 feet. Flak intense but inaccurate. No enemy airplanes. Dropped five 1,000# GP—8:10.

July 30: "38th" mission bombed Bucharest, Rumania airplane factory at 24,000 feet.

Flak intense, incorrect and heavy. Enemy aircraft but our escorts (P-38s) took care of them. Dropped nine 500# DRH—7:00.

Total hours combat July: 74:00.

August 1: "39th" mission bombed railroad river bridge at Avon, southern France. Altitude, 21,000 ft. Light flak, inaccurate. Landed at Corscia, Italy—2:00.

(Report missing missions 40-41)

Aug 23: "42nd" & "43rd" mission bombed Merkerdroff, Austria Air Drome with 30 cluster OP Frag at 19,500 Ft. Met up with enemy aircraft opposition but again our luck was with us and hit the group behind us, knocking down 6 or 8. The six we saw exploded in the air. The other had an engine on fire or something else wrong but they went into the clouds and that was the last we saw of them. Some of them might have got home but I doubt it. No flak over the target, however, flak on the way home. It was too small but accurate.

August 26: "44th" mission bombed airfield at Bucharest, Rumania with nine 500# bombs at 25,000 feet. A very easy mission for a change. No flak. No enemy aircraft—8:15.

August 27: "45th" mission bombed railroad bridge at Borovica northern Italy at 18,000 feet. Another easy mission. No flak. No Enemy aircraft—6:10.

Ernie Frazier

August 28: "46th" mission bombed railroad bridge at Szlnoz, Hungary at 15.000 feet. Five 1,000$ GP. Once again, an easy mission. Hope they keep up for four more missions—7:20.

August 29: "47th" mission bombed railroad bridge at Szeged, Yugoslavia.

Total combat hours overseas: 207.40

<u>Planes in our squadron lost on combat missions</u>

No. 54 was the first one to go down over Giurgui, Rumania.

No. 51 was the second one knocked down over Giurgui. Both ships knocked down by enemy fighters—ME 109s.

No. 62 (Vivacious Lady No. 1) was third on the list. It pulled out of formation when hit by flak and had one engine knocked out. It started back to the field but never made it. We figure an ME 109 must have got it.

No. 55 was the next to go. It lost number two engine and had to turn around for home. Just as they left formation, we were hit by fighters and they were knocked down. The pilot had flown as our co-pilot for several missions. It was his last mission and his crew's first.

No. 63 was the fifth one to go down. It lost two engines. It was their first mission and naturally had a green pilot. The crew bailed out and all their parachutes opened.

Evelyn adds a few words

We decided not to get married until after the war so I spent my time working as a secretary for the superintendent of schools here in Dodge City. Like a lot of the women, I was involved with the USO and other wartime activities. Floyd finally rotated home. However, he missed the action and thought about signing up for another tour. I didn't go along with that idea at all! So, he got out.

We married in 1944. Uncle Sam treated us real good and sent us to Miami, Florida for our honeymoon. They called it R & R.

Floyd and Evelyn operated Kirby's Western Wear in Dodge City for many years. A tall, lean, cowboy—now past 80—Floyd defies his age, has won many roping awards and still ropes steers weekly for fun.

CHAPTER 13

MERL BEEMER

"We followed the battles, picking up the corpses and body parts."

I met Merl and his wife, Dorothy, at their cottage in Ft. Dodge, KS, an old cavalry fort that now serves the needs of area veterans. At the fort, I could almost see and hear the ghosts of blue-clad troopers from a time long ago, thrilling to the sounds of drums and bugles as the phantoms from an era gone by wheeled and turned on the parade field. My mind returned to the hard reality of modern warfare when Merl began telling me about what he experienced in WWII. The horrors of war swept over me as he described the grisly tasks he carried out with honor; and one has to ask, "Could I handle such duty with dignity and honor? Can a man who never carried a gun be as much a hero as one who did?"

Celebrities in the desert

Sammy Kaye, the Hollywood entertainer, was on the same train that took me an a lot of other U. S. Army recruits to Camp Young, a training camp at Indio, California, in November, 1942. He wasn't the only famous person we saw. General George Patton was there with his troops and tanks. Heat prostration was a big problem for the tankers. It was probably 120 degrees inside of a tank during the afternoon. The temperature in the desert fluctuated wildly and as soon as the sun dropped behind the mountains, we would scramble for our coats.

To the medical corps

After about two months of basic training, I went on furlough and was married before going on to Camp Bowie, Texas to enter the medical corps. The training was interesting and we learned to give shots by practicing on grapefruits. Our time there was brief, about two months and then we shipped out to England.

My outfit was the 64th Medical Battalion. We took on five clearing companies (troops that would go out and bring back our wounded for treatment) and, by coincidence; one of the troopers was my wife's brother, Harry. He was a pharmacist and we went all through the war together—through all five major European battles. Our training continued as D-Day was on the horizon. But we didn't know it.

Meeting a blizzard of firepower at Normandy Beach

Then, one day, we were shipped out on a sea covered with ships—a truly spectacular sight—and headed toward Normandy Beach.

As we approached, the Germans opened up with artillery, mortars, rifles and machine guns. About 100 of us were crammed onto an LST landing craft. It surged forward and we began plowing through the water toward the beach. As a medic, I carried only a pack, no rifle. We huddled down and bucked the waves, shocked by the intensity of the battle all around, knowing that we'd soon have to jump in the water, unarmed, and face a blizzard of enemy firepower. All around us, G.I.s were being cut down.

I saw dozens, if not hundreds, go down and we had precious little time or opportunity to help most of them. Bodies were floating around our boat and blood was everywhere.

Somehow we landed, got unloaded, and began to help everyone we could. Our boat was never hit. How we survived the next two or three days on the beach, I'll never know. But, we survived. Our foothold was secured after three days or so and we moved inland, following the infantry.

We were caught up in a whirlwind of activity that kept us so busy we had little time for fear.

Ernie Frazier

The worst scenes of the war were at the hedgerows

Then we got to an area known as the hedgerows. The hedgerows became a notorious battleground because the Germans had mined the area. When they'd open fire on our troops, the men would dive into the hedgerows for shelter—right into the minefield. It was there that I saw many of the worst scenes of the war—the entrails and other body parts of our men that were blown clear up into the tree branches and were just hanging there.

A medic who cared for the dead

While I was a medical corpsman, my assignment was far different than you might imagine. Our unit was assigned the task of picking up, identifying, tagging, bagging and transporting the bodies of our troops that fell in battle.

I was a private. In addition to my other duties, I became the battalion stenographer and recorded whatever happened. A lot of it I kept in my head, but I did have a little booklet I picked up in Germany—a 1936 calendar that I logged information into. Battles were pretty well going on non-stop. Our artillery was firing over us at the enemy and they were firing back. So, we were in artillery fire a lot of the time that was flying both ways over our heads. Also, our planes were overhead and the Germans were trying to shoot them down. It's funny, but I don't remember ever really being scared. You learn that you can't operate under fear and you learn to control it. You have a job to do and you do it.

Loading dead Americans onto trucks at St. Lo

I remember the battle of St. Lo in France. The headquarters company actually served as a graves registration unit. We'd load dead American soldiers onto 2 ½ ton trucks. Then, we had to get up on the trucks, take the men's dog tags and register the bodies. We saw every form of injury imaginable. We'd see their wedding rings. That could really get to you if you let it.

Merl's lookout mission

After we made it clear across France, we wound up in Luxembourg—too close to the front lines. We were forced to retreat—something we had never done. We were retreating back over the same road that the 82nd Airborne was coming up on and we had to give way. I was on the last shuttle going back and the Germans were at the bottom of the next hill. For some reason our lieutenant said, "Beemer, go up on top of that hill and be a lookout." I didn't like the idea but I had to go. The ground was covered with snow so I squatted down so

Tech Cpl. Merl Beemer (rear) & PFC Worley.

I wouldn't stand out like a sore thumb. Down in the valley I could hear the sounds of small arms fire as the battle was on. Before long, trucks were sent to pick us up.

Fleeing the area

I rolled down the hill like a snowball and we fled the area, leaving all our equipment behind. That's the closest I ever came to becoming a P. O. W. In recent years I've thought about the incident. I wondered if I wasn't sent to be a sacrifice. I couldn't think of anything else. I guess I might have stalled a few Germans long enough for our men to start escaping from the area.

Registering bodies at Bastogne and the Ardennes

Everyone's heard about Bastogne and the battle of the Ardennes. We were there, registering bodies in the bitter cold. The snow was about a foot deep and the ditches were full of American and German bodies. We lost an awful lot of people there. The bodies were packed and frozen so we got a big maintainer with a blade (like they used to plow potatoes with) tipped the blade down and tumbled the bodies out just like potatoes.

We got to do a little deer hunting when we were camped up on the Danube River. I'd picked up a Norwegian rifle and a couple of shells. By the time it was dark, every one had a deer but me. Finally I shot at what I thought was a deer's head sticking up and I hit him. When I got to him, I saw I'd taken his whole front quarters out. We cleaned four deer that night and left the remains to float down the Danube.

The horrors of Ohrdruf Concentration Camp

Another horrible experience was going through a concentration camp. General Eisenhower wanted our troops to see the atrocities. I think he thought there might be more battles to be fought and he wanted our troops to be fighting mad. We entered the camp at Ohrdruf, Germany just after the Germans had pulled out. They'd taken all the P. O. W. S. and German camp workers that they could load in their trucks. Then, they just machine-gunned the rest. When we drove in, there were bodies all over the camp. The latrine was just a big 40' X 40' pit with a boardwalk and railing all around. It was full of human excrement and bodies were floating in it.

Some of the people had been worked to death and were stacked like cordwood in boxcars, head-to-foot, head-to-foot, all the way up either side. Others had been stacked on the ground with a railroad tie between each layer of bodies. After the stack got as high as they wanted, they doused it with gasoline and burned it all.

Like two ships passing in the night

After the war, I got home and found out something interesting. My brother and I were at the same intersection in Germany once and didn't even know it.

Now Merl leads the singing on Sunday mornings at the Ft. Dodge Soldier's Home Chapel and Dorothy plays the organ. Dorothy told me that she worked in a bank during the years that Merl was away, waiting for him to come home.

CHAPTER 14

VERNON V. SCHRAEDER

"The copilot was screaming so loud that our men in the back couldn't hear anything."

Vern completed flight cadet training in May 1940, and was sent to Thunderbird Field in Arizona to learn to fly Stearman PT 17's. He completed single engine training, thought he did well, and was dismayed when the Army Air Corps sent him home—back to Kansas and Ft. Hays State College where he enrolled for CPT training as a post graduate student and got his private pilot's license. Then came December 7, 1941, followed by a visit from an Air Corps recruiter. He enlisted in January, 1942, was sent home, and then was called up in August for bombardier-navigator training.

He earned his commission at Big Spring, Texas. In Windover Field, Utah, his gunnery training—primitive by today's standards—included sitting on the ground with a 50 caliber machine gun and firing on a flag mounted on an unmanned jeep traveling through some rocks. In Walla, Walla, Washington, they formed a crew and practiced flying B-17's. They ultimately were sent to Gander Lake, Newfoundland and flew from there to Ireland.

To Snedderton Heath Airport, England

We landed at the airport near Lake Loch Loman. There was a Red Cross mobile van there and an old gal was singing " On Yon Bonnie Bank" for us. Soon we were assigned to the 96th Bomb

Ernie Frazier

Group, 413th Squadron at Snedderton Heath Airport about 14 miles southwest of Norwich, England. Here we got the good news that the casualty rate per mission flown was only 4%. The bad news was that we'd have to fly 25 missions. 4 X 25 = 100% casualty rate! Unfortunately for us, their predictions were extremely accurate! Fortunately, we sustained no casualties on our first 24 missions even though we were riddled with flak and enemy fire on a lot of them.

The B-17 was known as the Flying Fortress. Our pilot was 1st Lt. Robert Dickert from New York. 2nd Lt. Robert C. Scott, the copilot, was from Harlan County, Kentucky where the legendary feuding Hatfield and McCoys lived. 2nd Lt. Ken Stone, the navigator, was from Bristol, Connecticut. Our tail gunner, Staff Sgt. Charles W. Gafford from Wichita, KS manned flexible twin .50 caliber machine guns. The ball turret gunner, Staff Sgt. Bob Meyers, from Bellingham, Washington, hung in a little bubble-like turret from the bottom of the plane. The two waist gunners, Staff Sgt. Herman Rennow of Altoona, Alabama and Staff Sgt. Wilbur Haugen from Minnesota fired hand held .50's. I was a second lieutenant and the bombardier. Charles A. Rayburn, of Chicago, was our radio operator-gunner. Our engineer, Tech Sgt. James P. White of Lexington, Kentucky stood behind the pilot and manned the top turret.

Bombing a "heavy water" plant

One mission sent us to Rejuken, Norway to bomb a "heavy water" plant that was controlled by the Germans. We didn't even know what one was. Normally we bombed from 30,000 feet. This time we were ordered to drop to 12,000. We were sent in to destroy it during the noon hour, as we didn't want to kill civilians. There was no opposition because the Germans didn't want to admit they controlled a plant there. Later we found that "heavy water" is used in the development of atomic bombs.

Overloaded planes crash on take-off

Flying was dangerous but just getting off the ground was as bad or worse at times. We carried a 2,000 lb. bomb on one side. On the other was a 1,000 gal. fuel tank, which alone exceeded the weight that the plane was designed to carry. Our pilot, Dickert, would brace himself, brake hard and rev the engines until the plane shook. When he snapped off the brakes, the plane would jump and we'd get off. Some weren't so lucky. On one mission the plane just ahead of us crashed on the runway and was on fire when we flew over it. There were 10 guys aboard. All died.

Just getting the planes up to 30,000 feet with our loads would take as long as three hours circling over England. The 8th Air Force could put up a total of 1,000 planes. On a mission we'd have 300 to 400 being stacked in formation.

Next door in England was a group who was noted for being the disaster group. On one mission they sent up 16 planes. Only 6 returned.

German fighters shoot down B-17s

We bombed Bordeaux Airport in France from 13,000 feet. We sighted in on the target and didn't just drop bombs because everyone else was. I sighted right in on the door of the hangar. I could see guys running down on the ground. I don't know if my bombs went right in or not because we were beyond the target when they exploded, but I had my bombsight right on that door. When we circled Bordeaux to head out over the North Sea, German fighters swarmed in and shot down B-17 after B-17. We were one of the lead planes and the guys behind us were falling like flies. Our plane barely escaped.

German buzz bombs were launched from cleared out areas in the forests. We'd come in single file and bomb those facilities. This is what we called a milk run!

Paris, Braunschweig, Gelsenkirchen, and Frankfurt

Paris was occupied and heavily fortified by the Germans. We bombed the Cam Ball Bearing Factory and did "pylon eights" around the Eiffel Tower. The Germans shelled us unmercifully and a lot of our planes never came home. An antiaircraft gun could be set to explode flak shells up to about 30,000 feet. So, if we were bombing at a lesser altitude, you were flying through flak. We also flew missions over Braunschweig and Gelsenkirchen and other targets in the Ruhr Valley. Those targets, along with Frankfurt, were heavily fortified. We encountered tremendous flak and lost lots of planes. And men.

Firing at 50 below zero

Our equipment was primitive compared to today's weapons. Our machine guns were probably designed 50 years earlier to fire under normal conditions. At 30,000 feet, the temperature is at least 50 below zero. After about three shots, the thing popped out bullets about like a cork gun shooting. We somehow stumbled along and won the war. Our commander for a long time was Brigadier General Travis who had an air base named after him. Our division commander was the famous General Curtis E. Le May. He pinned the Distinguished Flying Cross on my uniform.

In another battle I looked down at one of our B-17's. It took a direct hit and broke clear in two. The front half was spiraling and I could see the guys in it clawing, trying to get out of their seats so they could jump. I don't know if they made it or not because we passed by them in a minute or so. A German pilot who'd parachuted from his plane drifted down from above. He was so close I could see the expression on his face. You could tell he thought he was going to get hit by our plane.

A 20mm shell hit Charlie

The odds makers proved to be correct on our last mission. It was over Braunschweig—25 missions equals 100% casualties. We caught heavy flak and fighter planes swarmed all over us. We were hit hard and had to peel out of formation and abort our mission. We had a new co-pilot flying on board. All of us were scared as hell but he was scared to death. I don't know whether it was flak or firepower that blew off our number two engine, but it was gone. Charlie, our radioman slumped over and died when a 20mm shell tore in and killed him.

Two bail out. New man goes berserk.

At that point our new man was screaming. He'd pretty well gone berserk. The men in the back of our plane lost communications either because the radio went dead when Charlie got hit or the screaming was so loud they couldn't hear.

They knew we were under heavy fire and dropping fast. The two waist gunners, ball gunner, and tail gunner all bailed out. There wasn't much left of our plane when we got down to 3,000 feet or so. About then, two P-47's were flying back to refuel and fell in alongside us. Thank God. It's all that saved us. The Germans got one look at the fighters, decided they'd had enough, and flew away.

Lt. Vern Schraeder (2nd from left) and crew examine damaged plane.

Dropping fast over the Zider Zee and the White Cliffs of Dover

I went to the bomb bay to unload our live bombs. The doors were stuck open—nothing was working—so I stood on the catwalk and pinned and toggled those bombs out into the Zider Zee. I remember seeing the White Cliffs Of Dover and wondering if we had enough altitude to clear them.

Thank God for those fighter pilots

Our men who parachuted out were all captured and imprisoned by the Germans, except for Wilbur T. Haugen. He hid out and evaded *capture for seven months until rescued. We still talk on the phone. He sent me a copy of a letter that he wrote years ago about his experiences. I hope you can use it in this book.*

Author's note: Wilbur T. Haugen's letter appears in this book.

Bob Meyer, captured, endured the "Black Death March."

Bob Meyer, our ball turret gunner, was sent to a German camp only forty miles from the Russian front. I read a lengthy letter he wrote about his experiences. He was shifted around from one area to another, then on February 6, 1945 the prisoners—some 300—were herded out to participate in what became known as the Black Death March. The march lasted until May 2 and covered about 650 miles. They slept in ditches and barns with two men sharing a blanket or two and survived mostly on potatoes. When they stole some chickens the farmer reported it to their guards. They had to open their jackets and sacks and chickens fell out all over the ground. The Germans mounted machine guns on tripods and ordered them to line up. It looked like they were going to be cut down. A British soldier yelled at the prisoners and told them not to run. Evidently the Germans, honoring the Geneva Convention, would only fire when prisoners were escaping. Everyone stood their ground and finally, after a long time, the Germans put up the guns and they continued to march. The prisoners never had their clothes off for 86 days, couldn't get water for bathing, and were covered with lice. One town they marched through had just been bombed by the Allies. The townspeople were armed with big rocks and clubs and Bob felt they would have killed the prisoners if the German guards hadn't fixed bayonets and more or less held them at bay.

He said he saw an awful lot of men die from dysentery and trying to escape. One died of appendicitis. Rescue came in the form of a group of English soldiers on May 2 who attacked the German guards and ran them off into the woods. When he was finally rescued, Bob said he weighed about 70 pounds and was nursing broken ribs. The Germans smashed his chest with rifle butts when he fell exhausted to the ground.

Vern went home after the war. He became a farmer and was involved in local politics. He is proud of his military service even though it meant he had to bomb Germany, the home of his forefathers. A widower, he lives alone.

CHAPTER 15

WILBUR T. HAUGEN

"We were deep into Germany when we encountered their fighter planes"

Wilbur Hugen (kneeling 2nd from left), Vern Schraeder, (top right)

Vern Schraeder obtained the diary of his former fellow airman, Wilbur Haugen, for inclusion in this book. It's the story of the long months that Wilbur spent hiding from the Germans after being shot down over enemy territory. I met him at one of my book signings in his hometown of Albuquerque, NM. We got to talk for just a few minutes, but it only took that long for me to feel as though I'd known him for years. Vern had warned me that Wilbur might be worn down from a long battle with cancer. But, the man I met stood proud and tall and I could envision the young airman who'd parachuted into the teeth of the enemy—and survived!

Wilbur's diary

Pegasus was the name we had given our B-17 when we arrived at our base in England in October 1944. As mythical as was the winged horse in Greek mythology, so it seemed a myth that we would survive the twenty-five bombing missions for which we would be assigned.

We were thrilled to realize that we had flown twenty-four missions up to February 10, 1944. Whereas we had many close calls, we suffered most with the loss of two crews from our own barracks. One of their planes had been blown to "smithereens" by a direct flak hit, and the other by being chewed up by the propellers of another B-17 from their own formation.

The last mission

The day of February 10, 1944, our last mission, started out in a normal routine. We had flown deep into Germany when enemy fighters were encountered. One of the planes was rammed by an ME-1-09 that split the fortress at the waist doors. The second collided in mid-air with a bomber while negotiating their bomb run. The enemy fire injured our navigator, knocked out the top turret gun, hit an engine and riddled the side of the airplane to the extent that the oxygen supply was destroyed.

Since I was a waist (right side) gunner, I didn't know exactly what had happened. When I collected my thoughts, I noticed that our radio operator, just ahead of my position, was lying on the floor. Believing that he might be out of oxygen, I went to him to administer an emergency supply of oxygen. While kneeling to adjust his facemask, I noticed blood on the floor. I realized then that Rayburn, the radio operator, was dead.

Due to the loss of oxygen, the pilot had dropped our plane out of the formation and was now heading for home. I returned to my position to find that a fighter was now firing on the tail of our plane. These shots struck the plane elevators and reached to the wings. It was at this time that orders were received from the pilot to bail out. Without any questions I proceeded to exit from the nearby door.

Parachuting under enemy fire

The few lectures we had in parachute jumping were not to pull the rip-cord immediately but to delay the opening of the chute as long as possible in order to expend as little time in the air as possible. I opened my chute as quickly as I was able. I was obviously very high and drifted over a considerable amount of countryside.

When I was able to determine the shape of buildings, I struck the ground. I barely missed a barn and luckily landed in a nice, soft, plowed field. My chute rested in a nearby tree. Without any knowledge as to where I might be, with friend or enemy, I waited for a farmer who was approaching. I detected in his question to me the word Tommy (British). I said, "No, I am an American." I could tell he didn't understand so I said, "United States." No response. "Minnesota." No response. "Minneapolis." When I said "Chicago," he understood. He grabbed me around the shoulders and shook my hand.

By that time some boys had taken the parachute and hidden it. The farmer escorted me to his house where I met his family and many smiles. Soon there must have been 50 people in and around the house. Included in this group was a young man who could speak English. His name was Wilhelm Smudde. He asked many questions and translated to the interest of the people. I distributed the gum and candy that I had in my pocket and asked the fellow to show me our location on a map that I had available (silk handkerchief). He drew a mark on the map but put it in his own pocket and said, "We will help you." I knew now that these people were Dutch.

A fugitive

Almost immediately a young girl came running into the room and said that the German soldiers were coming. Smudde told me to got to the woods a short distance north of the barn and stay there until he came after me. This I did and found a shallow hole and some tree branches to hide myself in. Whereas I had hoped he would come to me before nightfall, it was now late afternoon and very quickly the day turned to night. Finally, in despair, I realized I would have to spend the night out.

During the night it started to snow and turn cold. I attempted to stay warm by digging a hole in the sand covering myself with it. I tried to sleep to no avail. I walked and jogged and tried to forget my plight. If I had known where I was, and had the aid of the map, I could have left the area. Finally, at about 5:00 a. m., I went back to the farmer's house and awakened him. He recognized my problem and invited me to go into his barn. There, in the warmth of the barn, I immediately fell asleep on the hay. At about 8:00 a. m., Wilhelm Smudde came and awakened me. He had an overcoat, a hat and bicycles. He invited me to follow him on the bike and we drove approximately two miles to the edge of the village of Oldenzaal. There we entered a small home that had recently been evacuated. The furniture had been stacked and was covered. Since I was still wearing flight boots, he had cautioned me not to step on the patches of snow and give away our entrance to the house.

Wilbur eats a month's supply of meat at one meal

I was instructed to stay in a bedroom of this house until his return. I knew that he was going to attempt to find shoes and other clothes to replace my flight outfit. I had given him French Francs, which were supplied to each flier by the Army to be used in such emergencies.

In mid afternoon, Wilhelm returned with a new pair of shoes and a pair of trousers. We then drove our bicycles into the city where I was taken to an apartment of a young family. Upon my arrival, I was treated to a vegetable casserole and a grilled pork chop. I ate the chop and a portion of the casserole, as I was very hungry. Later I was to learn that the pork chop was the family's monthly ration of meat.

Ernie Frazier

Henrik Pieffer

The people were extremely friendly. The young children had a great time playing with my flying suit that I had now exchanged for a suit of clothes, a shirt and a tie. In the early evening and after another meal of poached eggs and toast, a young fellow by the name of Rudy Fleer came and escorted me to the family of Henrik Pieffer, a local baker. Pieffer and his young wife were also delightful people. They, too, entertained me by serving a very rich pastry with coffee. Rudy Fleer had to interpret our conversation, as the Pieffers did not speak English. Later in the evening I noticed that Rudy had gone to the telephone and had a conversation with someone. He noted my curiosity and said that he had called the home of the local parish priest and made arrangements for my staying at the priest's house. The Pieffers were nervous about an American being in their bakery shop on a Saturday and the possibility of my discovery by a customer.

Rudy was scheduled to come after me at 7:00 a. m. Saturday morning. It was not until almost 8:00 a. m. before he arrived. It was a comparatively short walk to the parish house, but, as we approached the main entrance, we noticed a policeman standing at the door. Fleer instructed me to stop as he made conversation with the policeman. The policeman informed him that German soldiers had just left the parish house after a search of the premises and could very possibly return. Fleer then returned me to the bakery where I was secluded in a bedroom.

I stayed at the Pieffers for three days. Each evening we visited in their living room and during this time an identification paper (persoonsbevis) was prepared for me. We had a set of pictures made up at our home base in England for just this type of emergency. I remember that my identification card was made up with the name of a person who had been born and reared in Surabejo, Dutch East Indies. I left the Pieffer residence on February 16 very early (approximately 3:00 a. m.)

Dodging Germans on the trains

A young man (name unknown) and Pieffer escorted me to the railroad station. En route the police stopped us as we were violating curfew. They obviously believed the explanation that it was necessary to meet the early morning passenger train. Upon arrival at the depot, the young man purchased two passengers passes, one for himself and one for me. I was instructed to follow him through the depot where we boarded the waiting train. We then traveled to Hengelo where we changed trains. Then, on to Arnhe, Nijmegen, and finally, Roermond, arriving there in late afternoon.

In Arnhem we again had to change trains and there was several hours delay between trains. In lieu of waiting around the depot and risk that someone would question us, my guide took me to meet a friend of his who happened to be a local newspaperman. I remember that as we walked together to the newspaper office we passed a German officer dressed in an immaculate uniform. Upon arrival at the office, I was introduced to the guide's friend who was obviously very nervous. Since many people were at desks throughout the large room, an apartment key was given to the guide and we were asked to leave the office and go to his apartment.

His apartment was very gaily decorated and I noted that several American magazines—Life, Saturday Evening Post, and Esquire—were lying on his library table. Later, we visited with the owner and he said that in the next week a German Army medical officer who'd just returned from the Odessa Front would be visiting with him. He went on to say that the German had been a local Dutch boy who had gone to Germany for his education. Later he had been drafted into the German Army. He was of the opinion that the German and an American would have a very nice visit.

The train trips were otherwise uneventful. I always had the feeling that the other passengers in our compartment recognized me as an American. I am sure that in a number of cases they were looking over their books that they were pretending to read. German soldiers were always observed on train platforms.

Ernie Frazier

The Lovens

Upon our arrival in Roermond, I was escorted to a bakery located in the main business district of the city. We were met at the door by a very dignified lady named Jane Loven. Mill Loven was the head of the household that included two sisters, a brother and their aged mother. I was taken to their upstairs apartment where I was introduced to the family. Jane could speak English very fluently. She could also speak six other languages. While I stayed at the Lovens, a living room and a bedroom were made available. On the third day of my stay, two other Americans arrived who were the same type of dependent as me. They were Ray Slomowicz of Buffalo, New York, and Ted Simmons of Cleveland, Ohio.

We stayed with the Lovens until approximately two weeks after Easter of that year. Time passed very slowly. Even though we had some books and playing cards and a spring operated record player, we felt very confined. During the very early morning and in the late afternoon, marching German troops passed on the street in front of the bakery. The one notable thing about their marching was their singing. Not only was it spirited, it was in four-part harmony.

Periodically, the Lovens would invite us to their living room for conversation and treats.

On one occasion they were particularly disturbed with the Americans. Apparently an American bomber had dropped bombs on a Dutch village. They grilled us very severely as to why this was done. We were not permitted to go outside during this time and they didn't want us to be seen at the windows for fear of us being seen by outsiders.

Approximately one week before Easter, the old mother (late 80's) became deathly sick. The Lovens desired that we not be in the house as other members of the family and neighbors would be visiting the family. We three Americans were taken to a neighbor. This family was much less affluent than the Lovens. We were housed in a very small bedroom. The lady of this house had moved to Holland shortly after World War I. She was anti-Nazi but very sympathetic to the German people who were now subjected to heavy firebomb attacks by Allied aircraft. She didn't seem very friendly to us. In this same house there also lived a Jewish couple. The Jewish lady spoke excellent English and was very friendly to us. She explained the feelings of the German wife and attempted to apologize for her.

The Baer family

We stayed at that house several days and then were returned to the Loven residence for another night. During that night Grandma Loven died. We were taken to her room where the family was gathered to await her death. Early the next day we were taken to a farm some distance from Oldenzaal. The name of the family was Baer. This farm stay was very pleasant. The home was typical of the Dutch farms we had read about when we were children. It was a very pleasant house with a dairy barn attached to the kitchen and other farm buildings to form a large court where ducks, chickens and rabbits wandered about. We were permitted to be in this enclosed area during the day and we helped with the chopping of beets, etc., for cattle feed. We enjoyed sitting with the family during the evenings. We attempted to play games, but, since they didn't speak English, there were many laughs.

Shortly after Easter we returned to the Loven apartment and were told that lines of communication had been established with the Belgian underground that would permit us to return home at an early date.

We left the Lovens on April 14th late in the afternoon. We Americans walked to a nearby residence where a fourth American (John Lyons, Portland, Oregon) joined us. We were loaded into an automobile, presumably to be driven over the border to a rendezvous in Belgium. In lieu of crossing the border, however, we were driven to a remote farm. It was quite dark when we arrived so we were not able to recognize other persons who were also gathering there. We did understand that there were four Frenchmen and a number of other people who were carrying rather heavy cargo. Later we were to learn that they were trading in black market goods. This farmer had apparently made a business of guiding this illicit trade. These people, 12 or 15, then formed a caravan and we proceeded to walk through forest and field. We were instructed to be very quiet and do no talking. By this we understood that we were going to move into Belgium by bypassing the border patrol.

We must have walked a number of miles during the night up to the point that we actually crossed the border. Here we heard birds chirping, saw signal lights, and finally approached a building where the contraband was unloaded. The four Frenchmen and we four Americans were instructed to walk to a nearby burned out building that could be seen in the moonlight. The person who guided us said that he had to return to Holland but someone would soon meet us to guide us into Belgium.

Was the guide shot?

We waited at the rendezvous point throughout the night but there was no indication of anyone meeting us. As a matter of fact, shortly after our guide left us, we heard a gunshot from the vicinity where the caravan ended. This sound made us suspect that we wouldn't be having any more guidance.

As dawn approached, the four Frenchmen left, walking south. A short time later we four Americans made a decision. Since we couldn't be at this location when it became light, we took a vote as to what we should do. I voted to go to the building where the cargo had been left and find out what had happened. The other three voted that we follow the Frenchmen. We followed the Frenchmen.

Since I had a compass, we determined to follow a southerly course as well as we could. We attempted to avoid main roads and stay on wagon tracks and fence lines if we could. We did cross several highways, however, and in at least one instance, when we stopped by a farm to ask directions, we were waved away by the farmer. After much walking we crossed a pasture, stopped at a stock tank and a well pump for a drink. We could see the smoke of a village ahead and were deciding what to do when a farmer with a one hose cart passed by at the end of the pasture. We ran and told him who we were—as if he didn't recognize us. He laughed and said that his brother was in the White Army (Underground) and he would help us. We followed him for some distance. Then he asked us to wait at the edge of the woods. He'd been clearing some land of brush, which he bundled and stacked in large piles. Not knowing how long we might have to wait, we decided to build a shelter of the bundles. We worked vigorously for several hours and were becoming quite comfortable when we saw our rescuers approaching. They were four big men. On was dressed as a mailman and one could speak English. They gave us a most welcome reception.

They escorted us to a residence in a nearby village, Maaseik. Again we were treated very warmly, given food and a bed over a period of two days as I remember. On the morning of the third day, the brother of the farmer came to us and said that we were going to board a train and move toward Liege. The train ride was without incident but there was much apprehension on our part. There were few people in our coach and, fortunately, no Germans were seen. We felt very conspicuous.

Drunken guides

We stopped at a village a short distance north of Liege, Belgium. I believe the name of the village was Ans. At this point, all passengers disembarked. As we stood at the exit of the train, we could see the four gentlemen who had guided us previously standing along the depot wall. Our guides were in good spirits. They greeted us as long lost buddies with laughter and much talk. They were drunk. Despite the fact that we were in a large crowd of people, the four Belgians pushed a path through the crowd and forced entrance onto the last remaining space at the front end of a streetcar. As we rode toward the city, we could see the other passengers looking at us and smiling. It was then that our guides must have discovered their loose tongues and decided we should make a quick exit. The streetcar stopped in a rather remote area and we eight men dashed down the road and hid ourselves behind some buildings along the road. After a time of waiting, we walked approximately a mile to our planned destination.

Ernie Frazier

Marie

We were escorted to a small cafe run by 'Marie' and her husband. This cafe was located in Ans, a coal-mining district at the north side of Liege. Marie prepared a large plate of French fries for each of us with a fried egg. I don't believe any food has tasted better. That evening we were interviewed in a room at Marie's by a leader (Paul) of the underground force in Liege. Paul had brought a barber friend with him so we got haircuts that were badly needed.

That night we were taken across the street from Marie's to the small home of a miner. The house was very small so the four of us were placed in a small bedroom. We stayed in this room for about ten days. While we received but one meal a day, our main discomfort was knowing that the food we were getting was being sacrificed for us by the miner and his wife. We could see through the crack in the door that the man and wife were picking at only a few crumbs for their meal.

We voiced our concern to Paul on several occasions. Finally, we told him that unless we were moved we would leave on our own. He didn't want this to happen; not only for our own safety, but also for the safety of those we might know. In the late afternoon one day (early May, 1944) Paul took Ray Slomowicz and Ted Simmons to a new location and the next day returned for John Lyons and me. Paul led us to a restaurant where we were introduced to a young girl who was to guide us through the City of Liege to Chenee, an eastern suburb. We boarded a streetcar and traveled to the main city plaza where we were to change streetcars. Soldiers were visible all along the route. There were several on the streetcar, also.

Close encounters

At the Plaza where we changed streetcars, I noticed a very well dressed German officer on a sidewalk across the Plaza. We three were the only persons waiting for the streetcar. I then noticed that the officer started walking directly toward us. I thought for sure that he was going to stop directly in front of me but luckily he walked right by me without a hint of recognition.

We boarded a nearly loaded streetcar requiring that we be crowded onto the entrance platform. I was standing by a young woman who had a large bouquet of flowers in her arms. Since we were quite closely packed, these flowers would occasionally brush across my face. When the girl discovered this was happening, she laughed and started talking. When my response could only be my nicest smile, our guide rescued us by getting us off at the first stop. Unfortunately, this required that we walk a considerable distance before we met our next host.

Madame J. Ziane

Our rendezvous for Madame J. Ziane and her daughter was along a river parkway leading into Chenee. We stayed in their home until July 15, 1944. Her home was a three-floor apartment. She had three children. Her husband was a prisoner of war in Germany. Madame Ziane is probably one of the bravest women I have known. She was very active in the Underground and often ran messages for the Central Organization. On one occasion there were approximately 16 Americans in her apartment for a few hours as some major movement of airmen was taking place. Food was adequate but on one occasion she walked ten miles into the country to where a relative lived and returned with twenty pounds of flour on her back.

We always had access to a radio at Madame Ziane's despite the fact that radios were forbidden. We listened to BBC and a German news station, including William Joyce (Lord Haw Haw). In late May, bombing attacks near our residence became heavy. We saw several American airplanes struck by anti-aircraft fire that showered debris over the yard. Again we were very much confined as we were allowed into the backyard for a few minutes, only after dark.

We followed the news of the Normandy invasion on June 6, 1944 very carefully. Things were beginning to "look-up." Apparently as the news improved, people were taking more chances and escapees from German labor camps were returning to their homes in Belgium. As a result, police were making more searches of homes, some in the neighborhood where we lived. The children were sent to the relatives of Madame Ziane for security. Finally, on July 25, 1944, the breakout took place at St. Lo. It was determined that John Lyons and I should be moved from the vicinity.

John and a man from the Underground left the household together, then Madame Ziane and I followed. We walked a distance to a point where we were to meet a bus. John and his partner were sitting on a retaining wall overlooking a river and Madame Ziane and I were about fifty feet from them. Just as the bus drove up to the stop, a tire on the bus blew out requiring that the passengers be unloaded. Many people were milling around just as a Gestapo car drove up to a point directly in front of John and his partner. When we saw this happen, I told Madame Ziane to go home and that I would leave alone.

The Gestapo picks up John Lyon and his Underground partner

She said no, that she wanted to see us through. We crossed a small footbridge and from the opposite side of the river witnessed John and his partner entering the Gestapo's car. Knowing that there wasn't anything we could do, we continued to walk the footpath. We had walked some distance when who should be running toward us but the man who had just been with John. He asked to see my registration card. I showed him what I had and he asked, "But where is the work paper?" That was an attachment to the registration card signifying that you were doing essential work in Belgium; otherwise you were shipped to Germany as a slave laborer. Obviously the Belgian had sufficient proof of his exemption, including discharge papers from German hospitals as a result of war injuries. John also had not revealed his identity that would implicate the Belgian.

Ducking the Gestapo

It was determined that we should now return to the main road so we re-crossed the river. No sooner were we back on the main road than the same Gestapo car passed us again. We almost panicked. Madame Ziane really took an extra effort to describe the beautiful flowers in a resident's yard so that we could keep our backs to the road. The crisis passed and we boarded a bus. On this bus—standing room only—were some friendly German soldiers. They were attempting some conversation. To avoid a confrontation, we got off the bus and continued walking.

A warning from a motorcyclist

We walked for a distance when a motorcycle with a sidecar swung around on the street and stopped us. The Belgian man with us said that the motorcyclist was an underground compatriot and he had just seen the Germans set a roadblock just ahead of us. We then walked into a nearby restaurant that was obviously friendly to make new plans. I had just gotten seated when the proprietor came to me and asked if I would mind going upstairs to talk to his young son. He was learning English and wanted to talk to an American. So I went upstairs and met the boy. We had just begun to talk when a fellow came running in to the room and said that the Germans had just come into the restaurant. We fled out the back way to a house a short distance away. I waited there until late afternoon when George, a leader in the Underground, came to finally take me to my destination.

George

I had met George before. He was a very handsome fellow who had worked for the Ford Motor Company in Detroit. He drove me into the country on the back seat of his motorcycle. I stayed overnight at a farmhouse. The next morning an old fellow (name unknown) came to the farmhouse to escort me to his home. He lived in the little village of Forte. We walked across the countryside to avoid any major roads. Forte is an isolated little village with a church and a number of substantial stone houses and a chateau—a large farm with a protective wall around it.

A Jewish family, refugees from Brussels, lived in one of the houses of the village. The man had been in the textile industry and had visited the United States many times. Two other Americans were living in the home of the old gentleman who had escorted me to Forte. The business of this household was the slaughter and sale of farm animals. The house was equipped with large, walk-in refrigerators.

Ernie Frazier

As a matter of fact, the second day there, a young bull and a sheep were butchered. Floyd Kisner, one of the Americans, was experienced in slaughtering and helped the old gentleman.

On the second day of my stay in this household, the sister of the old gentleman took me to her home, which was several miles distance across the valley near Floron. Several days after my arrival in her home, another American, Emile Adabie, whose home is in New Orleans, joined me. A highway passed near the house where we lived and we began to see evidence of the retreat of the German army—including soldiers walking—and equipment being towed by other vehicles. They surely appeared to be beaten. We heard on the radio of the rapid advance of the Allies and the people were beginning to prepare for a celebration.

About September 1, 1944, Abadie and I were brought back to the house in Forte. Approximately 25 airmen gathered there awaiting the arrival of the American First Army.

Gunfire at the Chateau

We were all sitting in the loft of the house one day when a great amount of shooting and explosion took place at a Chateau located nearby. We all jumped to the ground and scattered in all directions. The residents in the houses also fled. I didn't run very far, but hid myself in brush and trees to await the end of the disturbance. Toward evening I decided to go back to the village to see if I could find anyone around as I was all-alone. As I got close to the house where we had been staying, I was stopped by several Belgian men who had arms and asked who I was. I, of course, informed him that I was an American that had gotten separated from the main group when the disturbance occurred at the Chateau. One of them spoke excellent English and he told me that the Chateau had been used as a gathering place for Belgian fighters who wanted to get revenge on the Germans. Several German dispatch carriers riding past the Chateau had been killed by the partisans, which accounted for the retaliation by the Germans. He asked me if I wanted to go to the Chateau. I said no that I would just as soon stay away from there.

Partisans are shot

The fellow took me about three miles from the village to the house of a farmer and his family. They were very poor but seemed pleased to give me a place to stay. I slept in their haymow at night and stayed in the woods during the day. On my third day there, a large cloud of smoke could be seen rising over Forte. The farmer informed me that German Soldiers had returned to the Chateau and set fire to all the buildings. Those partisans who attempted to escape were shot.

The following day I was returned to Forte. The people were really beginning to celebrate. We were greeted by the people. By the time I reached Forte, all the airmen had returned and everyone was awaiting the arrival of the American First Army.

Late that afternoon a forward patrol consisting of two jeeps drove through the village. We lined both sides of the road as the jeeps passed between us. We finally got their attention by saying, "Brooklyn."

The ladies of the village had cut many flowers and showered the jeeps with them. We were loaded onto the jeeps and taken to their bivouac area. The commander of this unit loaded us on trucks and moved us back to a tank company where lodging was found for us in available houses. I believe this date was September 8, 1944, almost seven months from the date of my jump into enemy territory.

The following day we were loaded onto supply trucks that were returning to Paris. En route, German soldiers were also picked up and returned to prisoner of war stockades.

The final day of our trip to Paris was Sunday, September 12, 1944. Each village we passed through was bedecked with flags and flowers and the people were dressed in their finest. I am sure that we were as happy as they. Our final stop was the Hotel Maurice in Paris. We were still suspect as far as the American Army was concerned and were not allowed to leave the hotel. The Hotel Maurice had full occupancy so, for that night, we were escorted to a small hotel nearby. The following day we were flown to London via a C-47 where final debriefing took place. In London, I was to learn that our plane had returned safely. Four of us gunners had bailed out. Three of them were captured and imprisoned until V. E. Day.

Ernie Frazier

October 8, 1944, was the approximate date that I returned home to be re-united with my family.

Afterward

On May 5, 1983 I had the privilege to visit with Madame Ziane and her husband at their home. On November 19, 1985 I received word of her death.

The Gestapo had captured John Lyons

John Lyons was captured by the Gestapo as feared on July 25, 1944. Later I learned that he had been imprisoned in a Stalag Luft and had returned to his home in Portland, Oregon after the war.

I received a letter dated October 22, 1983 from the Loven family. They wrote that they were ordered by the Germans to leave their home on September 11, 1944 as it was too near the river Maas. Their home, built in 1773, was the oldest and nicest house in town. It was bombed on November 11, 1944. In January, 1947, they were awarded the Medal of Freedom along with a letter from General Eisenhower. In addition, they were awarded The Silver Laurel Leaves from Canada, and received letters from General Charles de Gaulle and Sir Winston Churchill. The Lovens not only aided American pilots but helped many French soldiers fleeing German prison camps.

She finished by saying it was quite an anxious time, but a nice time, and said it was "nice sport" and asked that I write to her with some details of my life.

Those brave residents of Holland, Belgium, and The Netherlands risked torture, hanging, or being shot to death if they were caught assisting the Allies. This book honors them as well as our fighting men.

The people and families listed below are some of the unsung heroes who risked everything to help Wilbur and scores of other military and civilian personnel in their desperate flight from the Germans:

(1) Wim Smudde, Steenstraat 22A, 7571 BK, Oldenzaal, Holland

(2) G. Tydhof (Family), Hulsbekenkamp 12, 7576 VA, Oldenzaal, Holland

(3) H. J. Tydhof (Family), Schipeleidelaam 65, 7576 PB, Oldenzaal, Holland

(4) G. Ancone, Timmer, Meubelfabrink, Oldenzaal, Holland (moved to Australia)

(5) Rudolph Fleer, Padangstr. 48, 7535 AA, Enschede, Holland

(6) Loven (Family), Zwartbroekplein 10bv, 6041 HX, Roermond (Limburg), Holland

Renee Ziane, 39 Rue Large, 4600 Chenee, Belgium

CHAPTER 16

GENE EASTIN

'Tell my wife that I love her.' "That's all he said."

    The winter of 1945 in France was brutal. The Rhine River lay ahead. The 3rd Division, 30th Infantry, had methodically pressed forward over snowy fields and through frozen streams, pausing only to dispatch mortar crews and riflemen with grenades and bazookas to silence the deadly pillboxes and machine gun nests blocking their way. However, the Germans weren't the only major enemy they encountered in their push toward the Rhine. The weather was equally as deadly. Streams of curses split the air every time a soldier broke through the ice and found himself floundering in freezing water. Without any means of thawing out, the troops would continue their agonizing march in frozen clothes and sopping wet boots. Everyone tried to thaw out at night. They slept in foxholes, rolled up in sleeping bags or blankets. Some soldiers didn't realize the importance of getting out of their wet boots. Their feet were never dry and frostbite took a terrible toll. Fear, pain, and exhaustion were their constant companions.

    They were fighting their way to the Comar Pocket to reclaim the real estate lost to the Germans in the Battle Of The Bulge, an area renowned for hosting some of the greatest tank battles of the war. Audie Murphy, the most decorated hero of WWII, fought in the small towns of Holtzihr and Riedwihr. His story, deservedly, has been told many times and this episode is not about him. It's about Pvt. Gene Eastin who embarked on January 1st, 1945 on a refurbished Queen Mary—the famous luxury liner—for Glasgow, Scotland. After only seventeen weeks of basic training, he found himself packed below decks with thousands of other young soldiers, replacements for exhausted allied troops.

On January 23, only 22 days after leaving the states, he lay in a ditch pinned down by a steady stream of .50 caliber machine gun fire, rocked with concussions from the 88's barrages, beside a dead man he hardly knew. He braced himself and waited for orders. A few weeks earlier, at age 19, he'd been cutting wheat on his family farm, full of the hopes and dreams of youth. On a frozen, foreign field, his dreams would become nightmares.

G. I.'s ripped to shreds

The assistant platoon leader, a kid from Missouri, was in the ditch with me. I've always regretted the fact that I couldn't remember his name and didn't know how to contact his family. He's the one that yelled to the platoon leader to deliver his message of love. "Tell my wife that I love her." That's all he said. Within seconds, flying shrapnel from an exploding shell tore into his body and he died beside me.

Many of our troops, less fortunate than my squad, were caught in the open field. Trapped, they were only able to run a few yards before German machine guns ripped them to shreds. Then the 88's (howitzers) opened up. Scores of our men didn't have a chance.

Our platoon sergeant yelled for us to stay in the gully. That probably saved our lives. Part of a squad behind us had tried to run over a little ridge to escape. They'd been riddled to pieces by the machine guns.

Our orders were to take this little French village. We'd sent out advance scouts to see if there were any German tanks in the area. No reports of enemy tanks reached us. Now, there was a lull in the firing. We held our position and kept our heads down. Then, from the distance, we picked up sounds we never wanted to hear; the clanking of steel treads on frozen turf.

Ernie Frazier

The SS tank

We could only wait and it didn't take long. We pretty well resigned ourselves to dying when a German tank, manned by Hitler's elite SS troops, lumbered into position with its massive gun barrel slowly traversing on its turret. It stopped and aimed down the length of the ditch.

It was the biggest gun barrel I'd ever looked down. But, luck was with us. The tank commander must have been raised by decent people. He could have blasted us right there but he gave us a chance to surrender. Maybe he sensed that the end of the war was approaching. We threw down our arms and came up out of the ditch. I remember that I was amazed, shocked, at the huge number of American soldiers I saw dead and dying on the battlefield. We thought most of them had escaped while we were pinned down.

One German wanted to shoot us

They took us to a little village and lined us up. The Germans had a heated discussion. I asked a G. I.—he was Pennsylvania Dutch—what they were talking about. He said that one of the Germans wanted to shoot us right on the spot! I shrunk back and tried to disappear in the rear ranks.

The Germans wasted little time. One of our soldiers, a G. I. from Texas, was suffering from shell shock. The Germans took him away to an unknown fate, and then marched us out under an overcast sky that prevented our planes from attacking. We marched for miles and finally crossed a long bridge into Stuttgart where we were to undergo interrogation. It was exhausting and we fell down and slept wherever we could.

In boxcars

A '40 & 8' boxcar holds forty men or 8 horses. After a couple of days, we were loaded, about a hundred prisoners to each car, and shipped to Berlin and on to Nuremberg. It was terribly crowded and we had to take turns sitting down. There were instances when they'd pull the train onto a siding a day at a time. It took about a week to get there.

Burying prisoners

A week later we were shipped to Hammelburg, one of the worst camps. I had to work on a detail to bury prisoners who had starved to death. We ate watery soup, allocated tiny portions of Red Cross rations among dozens of men, and had no way to sterilize our utensils. Diarrhea hit us all. We only had one bucket for a toilet and couldn't even get to it. We had no way to clean ourselves. It was terrible.

Those of us with farming experience were sent to work on small German farms that worked Polish slave laborers, both men and women. I worked a team of oxen hitched to a farm wagon. We hauled manure out to the fields and did general farm work.

The German townspeople we encountered were friendly. Most of them had relatives in the states. Soon we heard small arms fire and knew the Allies were coming. The people asked us what to do when the Americans arrived. We advised them to hang white sheets out of their windows. That didn't last long. The SS troopers told them to either defend their village or they would burn it down.

Liberated!

About 100 of us, joined by British prisoners, were marched to Nuseburg at night. The British were great improvisers and cooks. They'd get a little box, then cut a tin can into a fan that became a miniature bellows. They'd put in a handful of wood chips and cook up a complete meal over the tiny fire. We obtained food by crawling out a window at night and raiding nearby farms for chickens and potatoes. Nuseburg was terribly overcrowded. Soon Patton's 4th Army arrived and began liberating us.

When asked about the current condition of our country, Gene felt that over 50% of our people believe in God and he hopes future generations will continue that belief. He said he always carried a New Testament and other prisoners were constantly asking to read it.

The prisoners even conducted church services in the camps. He has few regrets about the sacrifices he made to keep our nation free.

After all, it's still the best country there is.

Gene was a farmer after his military service and became active in the Republican Party. After retiring from farming, he accepted an administrative position with U. S. Congressman, Keith Sebelius who is now deceased. He later worked for U. S. Representative, Pat Roberts, who is now a U. S. Senator, R-KS. Gene's contributions to the party were recognized when he was selected as one of the 46 potential electors from Kansas in the Electoral College. As such, he and five other Kansans cast direct votes for the president and vice president as the state went Republican in the 2000 election. Few Americans are ever awarded that privilege.

CHAPTER 17

WILLARD DAVIS

"When we sat down to eat, there would be a dead man or two beside you."

Tech Cpl. Willard Davis & Marjorie

When it was pitch black, the unit slipped into the swamp. They were on patrol and ordered to keep silent. Ears were finely tuned to the night sounds all around. Terror gripped the men--some of whom were barely 18 years old. Occasionally a soldier's scream would break the silence as an alligator rose to rip into his thigh, or, more frequently, a giant rattlesnake, disturbed in his nest, would sink his fangs into a leg covered only by canvas leggings. Several died from the wounds. Others had complete mental breakdowns and were sent away. It was May, 1942. They were at Camp Rucker, Alabama training for the real war ahead. Willard's wife, Marjorie, participated in our interview.

Ernie Frazier

Tough training

Willard : *As far as I was concerned, the training was about as bad as the war, at least psychologically. In combat you're busy fighting off or attacking the enemy and trying to stay alive. Even though men were dying all around, you have no time to think.*

A new bride

Marjorie: We were married about six months before Pearl Harbor. He was called up in May but, as a family man, was allowed to come home to settle up business before they called him back—for keeps that time. I felt the weight of the world was on my shoulders. I'd never had a job away from home but found a job in Pratt at Duckwalls. After six weeks, another soldier's wife and I rode a bus three days and nights to Alabama to see our husbands who were due to get their first pass. At the camp, we located Willard's company and asked some soldiers if they knew him. They did and one went into a building to locate him. A career officer appeared right then and told us he knew we liked the boys but the army wanted to keep undesirable women out of the camp. He took us to a sergeant to deal with us. We had no base passes but explained that we were married to two soldiers there. He was very kind, got some passes made out, and told us where to find our husbands.

Her pay was $10.00 a week. Rent was $7.00

I got a job in a dime store outside the base and rented a room with a bath for $7.00 a week. The hours were from 7:30 a. m. to 7:30 p. m. except on Saturdays when I worked until midnight. The pay was $10 a week. After rent, I had $3 left—that was all—for lipstick and food. The town processed peanut butter and it was very cheap. I ate a lot of it and little else. Later, I followed Willard to another camp in the desert outside of Phoenix, then to San Luis Obispo, California for more training. He shipped out from Lincoln, California and I went back and worked in an Army store in Pratt until he returned home.

First combat: the Philippines

<u>Willard:</u> The 81st Infantry sailed for the Philippines in June of '43 on a troopship packed with 3,800 men. I'd been trained in communications—how to get up a telephone pole or a tree with spikes mounted on your boots and string wire. On board the ship we were trained to fire the huge guns in the event the sailors got wiped out. We saw our first combat in the Philippines. I was up in a tree stringing wire in advance of our tanks. The Japanese opened fire on me, sending a round past my head, splitting the wire. I jerked my spikes out of the tree and plunged down as fast as possible. I survived that battle. Later, on Ulithi, we got into heavier fighting. I was pinned down for about four hours without a radio strong enough to contact my unit. A huge rock separated me from a Japanese soldier. Neither of us would raise our head and neither knew when the other would attack him. Finally another trooper realized my predicament and called in some firepower, driving off the main Japanese force. They captured the soldier on the other side of the rock.

Japs, snakes, and land crabs

On the Philippines, the Japanese, as well as tropical snakes up to twenty feet long, terrified us. Some had heads as broad as a football and about sundown you'd see one rise up, at what appeared to be about ten feet in the air, and look around the swamp.

The Japanese would attack at night. Angar Island was only about five miles long and a mile wide. Land crabs covered the beach. Their shells clattering against the rocks made a distinctive noise and we got used to it. When the Japanese began to infiltrate our positions, it was a dead give-away when they crossed the beach. Their boots hitting the rocks changed the tune and we knew those weren't crabs coming in! The Japanese were desperate for food and were trying to cross our lines to steal our rations.

Ernie Frazier

No atheists in foxholes

It's terrible when you're pinned down behind a log with a steady stream of bullets splintering the wood and you hear your buddy screaming. You can't do a thing to help him until artillery is called in to clear the area. Only then could I run over to my buddy. All I found, and I carried it back to our position, was one arm. I don't care what they say, war is hell! Lots of guys maintained they were atheists early in their training. It's funny that no one in a foxhole ever declares that he's an atheist.

Lonely at home

Marjorie: I was at home, working and lonely, and, I have to admit, sometimes resentful of the couples I'd see strolling to the movies while my husband was on the islands of the South Pacific. There was an air base nearby and I had many an opportunity to go out with a lot of airmen. I never did but some of the girls I knew ran around with them. A lot of them couldn't face their husbands when they returned home. I had relatives that visited or wrote often and it was a great help to me. My sister-in-law, Marguerite Frazier, wrote to Willard and to me each week that he was in the army and we've never forgotten it.

Colonel shot between the eyes

Willard: I was a tech sergeant while we were fighting in the Philippines. I was sent out to put up a wire to our outpost. When I got up a tree, I saw the Japanese coming in so I dropped back down and lay flat on the ground. We needed communications established in the worst way. The battalion commander, a colonel, showed up with our company commander, a captain, along with the first sergeant. They provided cover fire so I could get back up the tree. As soon as I got the line in, it was shot in two so I had to fix it again. Then the colonel and the first sergeant headed up to our outpost. Suddenly, the sergeant came running back and announced that the colonel had just been shot square between the eyes.

Eating with the dead

I was getting paid about $21 a month at the time. I'd keep five for a little Bull Durham smoking tobacco and a little ice cream if the civilians could supply it. The rest went home. Insects weren't too bad. The worse thing was when you sat down to eat. There'd be a dead man or two lying next to you.

There were a lot of heroes around us all the time but one of our men really sticks out in my memory. One night he crawled through the enemy lines and into the rear of a Japanese mess hall. He could understand some Japanese. He overheard conversations and brought some important information back to us. That took a lot of guts; a lot of guts. It was things like that that won the war.

I think the closest I ever got to getting killed was when we were laying wire to an outpost through a minefield, which is just a little hard on your nerves. Mortar fire started coming in. I jumped in a jeep. The driver was spinning around in a circle to escape the mortars. In the rear of the jeep were five gallons of gasoline. Shrapnel hit the can and cut it to pieces. We tore over a small hill and escaped.

The Christmas tree wilted while she waited

Marjorie: When the war was over we were overjoyed. My folks came into town and joined a big celebration. Then I found out that Willard was going to Japan with the occupation forces, a terrible blow that just tore me up.

One December day I got a telegram notifying me that he was back from Japan, in Seattle! I decorated a Christmas tree just knowing he'd be home for the holidays. Well, the tree wilted and dried and I waited. He finally got home the last day of December, 1945 and we had a wonderful Christmas then. He'd been in the army for 3 years, 8 months, and 7 days.

We have never taken it for granted that we survived those times and are still together. We have really slowed our pace and are happy to be retired and have the health that we do.

Ernie Frazier

Willard operated a barbershop in Larned, Kansas and Marjorie worked in a local bank until they retired. Their son, Randy, a dentist, pursued a career in the army. Prior to his recent retirement, he attained the rank of Colonel and became commander of Dentac at Forts Riley and Leavenworth.

Their daughter, Iris, teaches school in the Kansas City area.

CHAPTER 18

MARVIN CLARK

"We landed the first 90-mm anti-aircraft gun on Normandy."

Marvin spent most of his life trying to forget his wartime experiences. He told me he seldom ever talks about his time in battle. However, his memory is strong and he had a remarkable story to tell.

They needed bodies for replacements

I was 20 when I was drafted into the Army on November 13th, 1942. My basic training was at Camp Haan ,California, in the Mohave desert followed by a move to Camp Pickett, Virginia, for amphibious training.

My wife, Ella, was able to live off-post near the various camps while I was stationed in the States.

After about a year, we were sent up to Ft. Dix, New Jersey and boarded ships for England. I really don't think they toughened us up a lot. They just needed bodies for replacements as fast as possible so the training wasn't all that great.

We spent eight months in England training on our guns and killing a lot of time before the invasion. We trained on 90-mm anti-aircraft guns and supporting .50 caliber machine guns. A lot of our time was on what we called "dry runs". We simulated our attacks on an area of abandoned houses that the British set aside for us. We'd blow them to pieces. We actually loaded onto our landing craft several times getting ready to sail to Normandy; then they'd call it off and we'd have to unload and wait for another day.

Ernie Frazier

We didn't actually know what we were practicing and loading for but our old colonel told us the last time we loaded that we would be the first to ever make an amphibious landing with our type of guns. "If we make it," he said.

We knew that we would be attacking somewhere, but we had no idea as to when or where or what it would be like.

We still didn't know the last time we loaded up that we were on our way. In fact, we were well under way before we were told that this was it.

Scared to death at Normandy Beach

I remember when we were approaching the beach that I was scared to death. There's no question about it. You don't know what to expect. We were just a bunch of kids and we didn't really take anything serious until we were facing the German guns.

Going in was really awesome. We could look in either direction and see nothing but ships from one horizon to the other. The Germans started bombarding and machine-gunning our ships and our men in the water. Our ship didn't get a direct hit but every time we tried to come in, they'd open up and drive us back. We'd pull back and circle around until we felt the coast was clear, then try it again. We wound up making three runs at the beach before we could get unloaded.

Medics spread out one guy's intestines

For a while, they brought wounded troops onto our ship for treatment. I sat there most of the night watching the medics work on one that had got hit in the stomach with shrapnel. They had his intestines spread all over a table and were trying to sort everything out. One of the medics stopped for a smoke and I asked him, "There's not much chance for an old boy like that, is there?" He said, "Well, as long as his heart isn't blowed out, we've got a chance to save him."

He said they gave him over $7,000 worth of penicillin right there. I often wondered if he made it.

Another guy, he was a big, redheaded soldier, was hauled in. He'd been hit right through the large part of one leg; shot clear through with a .50 caliber machine gun bullet. When the medics got to him, he said, "I'm all right. Take care of these other boys first." A .50 caliber leaves quite a hole. I figured he was pretty gutsy to just lie there and wait while the others were attended to.

Landing with nine ton guns

Our outfit did become the first to make an amphibious landing with 90-mm guns. We brought them in on LST's, our landing craft. In fact, we brought in a battery of four on one ship and there was also a battery of field artillery on our ship. The 90-mm guns weigh about nine tons so it was quite an accomplishment. An LST is a big boat. We went in and they unloaded the smaller field artillery first.

An LST couldn't run right up on the shore. The reason all of our guns didn't sink was because they were so tall and we pulled them in with what we called a prime mover. They were like huge front wheel drive trucks with tall, dual wheels.

A real-life nightmare

It was a sickening sight—a real-life nightmare going on all around us. A lot of our troops had tried to wade ashore quite a while before we got there. Hundreds were drug under by their equipment and drowned. Hundreds more were floundering in the water and we could see the Germans cutting them to pieces. The water was already full of dead Americans when we got there. Soon the beaches were, too.

Crews were already starting to pick up the bodies. I've thought about it an awful lot over the years. The bodies were put in mattress covers and stacked up until it looked like a snow bank for as far as you could see. There was no way that they could find all of the bodies. The water was just full of them. They used our ship as a hospital ship while we were waiting to land. I don't know how many wounded we took on but there was a bunch of them that had been shot up. We learned about war instantly. It just all happened right now.

Ernie Frazier

My outfit was the 413th Anti-Aircraft Battalion. When we first went in, we were independent. Later, in France, we were attached to the First Army and the Third Army after it landed. So, we were attached to whatever outfit needed us.

After we landed, we set up our gun right on top of the ground so we could get into action as quick as possible. We had a big, heavy metal box that sat on the ground under the gun, surrounding the axle.

A shell hits the gun emplacement

A German plane came over and fired a 40-mm shell. Talk about miracles! That shell hit right in the middle of the steel box and exploded. Not a one of us got a scratch! The box contained the blast, sending the force straight up.

I was a fuse setter. The barrel on those guns was over 20 feet long. The shells were about 3.5" around and 40" long. I believe the projectile on it weighed 23 pounds. It had a fuse in the end that had to be set. Let's say I set the fuse for 30 seconds and we fired the shell. If it hit something before 30 seconds were up, it would explode. If it didn't, it would still explode in 30 seconds.

All I did was use a clock to match pointers with. It gave me a reading as to how fast a plane was coming in on us and at what angle. When I got my fuse ready I'd holler "Cut!" and a guy would turn a crank and that would set it.

It took a nine-man crew to man the gun as I recall. One guy was an azimuth and elevation man. I was getting my readings from those guys because they had the plane in view. A couple of men on our crew were killed during some of our battles and we lost several from our battery.

I take my hat off to our front-line infantrymen anytime. Our guns were positioned quite a ways behind the lines.

Knocking out 16 tanks

Ever so often they'd take our unit and break it down. We'd leave our radar equipment behind, take our guns and go up to operate as tank or personnel destroyers or whatever else that was needed. We'd be firing point blank—we could bring the gun barrel right down to ground level-- so we didn't need much equipment, just our guns and ammunition. I recall that we were credited with knocking out 16 tanks.

We carried rifles so if the tankers didn't surrender, we could take care of them. One time one of my buddies—his name was Adams—and I were off several yards away from our gun, filling up sand bags. We didn't have any weapons but an old German soldier came out of the woods and surrendered to us. He was armed and could have picked us off anytime but he came to us because we were unarmed and he had been waiting for a chance to give up.

Unimaginable fire power at Remagen bridge

The bridge at Remagen was where some of our greatest battles were fought. Several other anti-aircraft units were in place there as well as us. The firing was so intense that we couldn't see anything but tracer bullets flying from every direction. You couldn't imagine it. It was the worst mess of fire I ever saw. That bridge had to be taken or else the Allied advance would halt right there.

We were quite a ways behind the main force when they took the bridge. Then we were called up to protect the bridge so we had to drive as hard as we could all night to get there. It was daybreak when we pulled in to set up our battery and the Germans began shelling us. Our mess truck was hit just as we turned off the main road. It killed the driver. His name was Wolf. The shell just blew the whole front end off the truck.

As soon as we got clearance, we crossed over and set up on the other side. It finally caved in and the engineers had to build pontoon bridges across the river.

The Germans were sending in airplanes to attack us. They wanted to knock out that bridge real bad. We were positioned within a half-mile from the bridge, firing at the Germans as they swooped in.

Ernie Frazier

The Battle of The Bulge

We got right in the middle of the Battle of The Bulge. The Germans broke through our lines and were shelling us. We could see a line of their shells dotting the ground, coming toward us in a perfect line. It was going to hit us but for some reason they raised their sights just enough that the shell that was meant for us hit our sandbags instead and blew them apart. It makes you wonder, "Why did it happen that way? Is somebody up there taking care of us?"

Our little battery was named the Fighting 413th. We fired smoke shells for the bomb release lines and got a lot of commendations.

Germans killed most of our green replacement troops

We went up to destroy the buzz bombs that the Germans had developed and were using on us. The Germans broke through our lines and cut us off. Our First Division was on leave and two battalions of infantry replacements came in to take their place. They were new kids that had never seen any action. The Germans attacked and destroyed almost every one of them. Our officers got some tanks from another outfit and they came in and opened up a road for us to escape. They were shelling us pretty hard and our colonel (Lieutenant Colonel Donald "Sandy" McGrain) got hurt. A piece of shrapnel cut his jawbone and one cut the hamstring in his leg. He'd heard our call for permission to leave and wanted to come down and see for himself just how rough it was. We lost a lot of our big guns and heavy equipment. Later, we pushed forward and recaptured some of our stuff.

We didn't lose any people in our anti-aircraft batteries but the infantry, as I said, lost a tremendous amount.

Shrapnel hit one of our lieutenants, Lt. Flood, but it didn't kill him.

We pulled back into Belgium and sat there about a month until we could get our equipment back. We'd even lost our personal items—blankets and clothing—and had to get re-supplied.

A lot of mistakes were made. One time an unidentified plane showed up on our radar and didn't respond to our messages to identify himself. So, we opened fire and hit the plane. The pilot bailed out and we ran over to him. It was an Englishman in a British plane. He just failed to respond when he should have.

I was a corporal, a T-5, which was the rank my gun position called for.

It's hard to remember a lot of the stuff I saw. I haven't even talked much with my family about the war.

Earning five Bronze Stars

I do remember the miserable conditions when it was sopping wet and freezing cold. I'd roll my blanket out and lay down on the ground. The mud would squish up all around and ooze into everything. We didn't freeze but fighting in the mud was just terrible. I think that's why I've got so much arthritis today. Both of my knees have been replaced and my joints in one shoulder are wearing out. But, I'm in damn good shape compared to a lot of them.

We lived mostly on c-rations and k-rations. Occasionally we'd outrun our food supply so if we were where we could, we'd hunt deer. We shot quite a few and would even make up deer sausage to eat.

Just before we were called into battle at the Remagen bridge, we had raided some chicken houses and were boiling up eggs in our helmets. The battle ruined our egg dinner.

Our unit was awarded Bronze Stars for each major battle. There were six given and our unit got five.

Gary earned 14 Oak Leaf Clusters in Vietnam

Our oldest son, Gary, is the guy that really deserves the credit in our family. He was in Vietnam and won 14 Oak Leaf Clusters. You get one for 25 combat flying hours. He was even awarded the Bronze Star for valor after he got home. He died a few years ago in an electrical accident. Then, eight months later, his wife died. But, he was the hero in our family.

I was fortunate. In the three years I was in, I never had to face the enemy head on like our infantrymen did. Our firing was all at long range, behind the front lines. For example, when we got into the

Ernie Frazier

big bomb raid at St. Lo, there were 15,000 planes in that raid. Our guns could shoot about 20 miles firing straight ahead. If we lobbed the shells in with high trajectory fire, they'd go a lot further. We were pulled back to about 12 miles behind the front lines because the town was going to get pulverized. Our planes dropped some of their bombs short of the target and killed quite a few of the guys that were up closer. Even that far back, the concussion from the tremendous bombing that went on would shake us just like we were in a strong wind. After the bombardment, we went into the town. You wouldn't even know a town had been there. There was nothing but piles of rock and rubble—no buildings at all.

I tried to forget it all

The next raid was at Aachen. We were sent up to the bomb line and fired smoke bombs to guide our bombers onto the target area. We lost none of our men in that raid and won a commendation from General Jimmie Doolittle. We fired shells that day until we melted the paint off our guns and warped the tubes so bad that we had to replace some of them. I got out in September 1945 and tried to forget it all.

CHAPTER 19

EDGAR FRANK COMBS

"Firebombing Tokyo was a scary thing."

Edgar Combs shares a characteristic that is common to many of the warriors in this book. He doesn't look or act the part of a military man. During the many years I've known him, I never heard him speak of his wartime experiences until his sister told me that I should hear his story. I did and found it remarkable.

Wrong answers for the psychologists

    I enlisted at age 17 in the Army Air Corps with the goal of being a pilot. Unfortunately, I didn't come up with the right answers for the psychologists and the other interviewers so I decided I'd become a radio operator. My hearing couldn't differentiate between loud sounds so I flunked that test too. That's when they gave me the choice of either being a ground crewman or a gunner on an airplane. I took gunnery school.
    Basic training was in Wichita Falls, Texas. Since I was just a big, skinny, tough farm kid, I sailed right through the obstacle courses and even a 20-mile hike didn't bother me. Gunnery school was more fun since we got to do a lot of target practice. Before long I was assigned to a crew to be a tail gunner on a B-24. I heard they called them flying coffins. We trained & flew on them for a while until my assignment got changed. The B-29s were coming out, men were needed to man them, and I wound up taking a lot of training for that. My status changed from tail gunner to being a replacement for

Ernie Frazier

disabled airmen and I was assigned as the left blister gunner on a flight crew in Peyote, Texas. That's where I was involved in my first action.

On one training flight we went out with a full load of bombs and gasoline and flew to a bombing site. We were to drop the bombs, fire our guns, then fly 1,000 miles to see if we could complete what was a simulated combat mission.

<u>Shooting up our own plane!</u>

We dropped the bombs and began to circle down, lower and lower and began firing at the targets. I was a blister gunner on the left side of the plane. We had five turrets mounted with .50 caliber machine guns and the tail gunner had a 20-millimeter cannon. Our training mandated that we gunners change turrets from time to time and familiarize ourselves with the way the turrets fired. It was a dangerous maneuver if the gun barrels were hot and we had specific steps to follow when we switched turrets. Well, I changed with another gunner and we forgot one of the steps. One gun barrel was red hot and as we swung the turret around, it fired automatically, three times. Those three bursts blew out two of our engines! Things looked bad but they got worse.

Our fuel tanks still had a lot of fuel plus we had two huge fuel tanks stored in the upper bomb bay. We'd already dropped the bombs that'd been in the lower bomb bay. With two engines gone, we weren't going to complete our 1,000 mile trip. We had to abort our mission and try to get home in one piece. We circled back over the bombing target and dropped the fuel tanks. The bottom tank fell free.

The upper tank stuck and pulled a connection hose loose. That sprayed fuel back into the airplane. Our radio operator was pretty sharp. He shut down all of equipment as quick as he could and said, "Don't anybody smoke or use anything that makes any sparks!"

Our pilot radioed the base and asked for instruction. They asked him how serious the situation was and would the ship explode before we could land. He said, "I think I can make it." They replied, "That's a very dangerous situation."

We were in bad shape. On top of everything else, the bomb bay doors stuck open because the bomb bay fuel tank jammed the doors. We got our parachutes on while they debated whether to have us bail out and let the plane go, or to try and bring it in. We were ready to jump if we had to. The pilot said, "Well, I can bring it in."

He landed it as smooth as silk and we didn't get a scratch anywhere. We got a black mark as a crew, but our commanders let us stay together and put us through more training. One piece of advice we heard was, "Now, when you move your turrets, don't turn the control lever loose. Hold onto it until you get there."

B-24's blow up in training

Another training mission took us down around Charleston, South Carolina. We didn't shoot it out this time but one of our engines conked out anyway. Our pilot called for instructions and was advised to land at a B-24 base there. While we were waiting for a ferry plane, we watched the B-24 crews train. They called them flying coffins and we found out why. In just one morning, one of them blew up and another one crashed. The very next day another one blew up. I decided there must have been a providential reason why I was no longer assigned to those aircrafts. Eight died in one of the wrecks and several were killed in the others. Casualties were expected in training so the survivors weren't grounded. They just got more training and tried again.

Ernie Frazier

Bombing Japan

Nebraska was the staging area for B-29s and we flew from there to New Mexico, California, Honolulu, Midway and on to the Mariana Islands. We would be flying out from a base on Tinian Island to bomb Japan.

Our planes were so heavily loaded that it looked like they'd crash in the ocean before they could gain enough altitude to survive. It was scary. Only one plane could take off at a time and the flight leader was the one guy who was supposed to know where we were going. If it was cloudy, a pilot could lose track of the leader and had to get on the radio to get instructions, in code, as to what corrections to make to join up with the formation. By the time we'd get to Japan, we'd be flying in tight formation so we could muster tremendous firepower if we came under attack.

Foul-ups

Strange things happened. We had one flight commander who'd come under enemy fire before. We were going in on one bombing target and he lost his nerve and pulled away without dropping bombs. Our pilot was unhappy because the commander was supposed to lead us into the target whether we got shot at or not. On that mission, our pilot followed him out and we didn't drop our bombs until we got over the ocean. Of course, that didn't do a lick of good and our pilot was enraged. We'd risked all the men's lives and went through all the time and expense of flying to Japan, only to abort our mission out of fear.

The next time we flew out, the same commander did the same thing and avoided the target. Our pilot just peeled off the formation and came back over the target and we dropped our bombs where we were supposed to. He thought he was doing the right thing but back at the base the top brass told him, "You don't do that. You don't break formation unless you are hit or something is wrong with your plane." Our pilot answered, "Okay, but give me somebody who will go to the target."

They did just that. However, our new commander was a man who would ride his throttle. An engineer usually sets the throttle on the B-

29. He had instruments to show him the most efficient way to use his fuel, and fuel was precious. This commander didn't trust his engineer so he took the throttle away and set it where he wanted it. That usually meant using more fuel than he should. His plane ran out of fuel over the Pacific and they went down. Only one man survived.

Fire bombing Tokyo was a scary thing. Usually there were about 27 B-29s that made up a flight. We used our own weaponry and had no fighter escorts near by. They'd be up ahead of us or back behind because if we saw a plane to shoot at they didn't want to be too close. Right over the Japanese islands, the Kamikaze pilots would attack.

We were on a bombing run right over a huge thermal cloud. We were at about 10,000 feet and the cloud was boiling up toward us like a massive oil fire. It caused a tremendous turmoil in the clouds all around and we could see the fires burning down in the target area. I was flying tail gunner instead of blister gunner because they needed less weight for additional fuel. In flight, the only way to get out of a tail gunner's station was to pop the tiny square door and throw yourself out backward. I was sitting there with my hand close to the trigger for the window and my other hand on the gun. The plane was rocking us around. My head swung to the right and I saw a Japanese fighter plane right on our tail. I didn't even have time to fire when he fired a rocket; it barely went under our wing, missing the plane—then peeled off and escaped so I didn't get a shot at him. That was the closest I ever got to the enemy. I could see the pilot, he was that close. They didn't have pressurized cabins like us and he had on a helmet and goggles and stuff like that.

Flying air-sea rescue missions

We escaped that but I saw some tragic stuff. On some flights, our plane would be assigned to air-sea rescue duty and we wouldn't carry bombs, only rescue equipment. On one flight, we received a message to watch for a fighter pilot. He and his plane had both been hit and he was going to bail out. Sure enough, we spotted him parachute out and drift down. One of our Navy submarines was in the water and they were supposed to pick the pilot up out of the water while we circled above. A twin engine Jap plane—we called it a

Betty—showed up. It had six guns mounted and a turret gun. Our radioman tried to drop a smoke bomb where the pilot went down but the pressure in our plane blew the thing back inside. The sub wouldn't approach the pilot with the Betty coming in ready to attack. We swung around and fired on the Betty. As soon as he saw us, he fled the scene. We dropped another smoke bomb and the sub surfaced and began searching. We never did know what happened to the pilot.

The worst thing

Abandoning a friend in combat was the worst thing I had to do in the war. We were on a bombing run when one of our planes got hit, probably with flak, knocking out and blowing up one of its engines. When going into a target, you have to go in at full bore and pick up all the speed you can. The pilot in the injured plane couldn't keep up and began to drop back. We could see fighter planes rising up to pick him off so I opened up with my machine guns to try to drive them off.

"Who's firing?" Our pilot asked. I answered, "This is Combs, left gun." He said, "Well, quit that. You're not doing them any good. We may need the ammunition later."

So, I quit firing. I can still see that plane as it dropped back and the fighters just swarmed all over it, circling like buzzards. They knocked the plane down and we saw some chutes open, but not all of them, so I don't know whom or if any actually survived.

It's terrible to just go off and leave your friends and not be able to do anything for them.

Twenty-one missions over Japan

We flew 21 missions bombing Japan. Usually we were bombing shipyards and other heavy industries. Yokahama was a big industrial area so we would bomb that a lot. We dropped a variety of bombs, sometimes they were 1,000 pounders and other times we let them have it with cluster bombs or firebombs that would spread apart and cover a wide area.

I don't think a bullet ever hit us since we pretty well kept enemy fighter planes away from us. But, flak was another matter. One of our turret gunners almost got it when a piece of flak hit the turret a few inches from the little bubble he was sitting in, just barely missing his head. Our plane had a huge tail and it wound up with a lot of holes in it. Flak would come up no matter where we were. The Japanese had some pretty sophisticated equipment on the ground—maybe they got it from the Germans—and they could put a searchlight on our plane and synchronize it with their flak guns. We were really scared of those lights. I was flying tail gunner one night and was alone back in the tail. All of a sudden our plane flipped up on one wing and started to slide down. I was getting pretty nervous. Nobody said anything, so I asked, "Is anybody up there?" I didn't get an answer so I prepared to pop open the window and parachute out.

About that time the plane kind of leveled out, slid over a bit and revved the engines back up again. The pilot called out, "Is something the matter with you back there, Combs" I said, "Yes sir, I didn't think anybody was here but me." He said, "Well, we wanted to get out of that spotlight. We didn't want it zeroed in on us so we dropped down and got out of there as fast as we could."

It was close to the time for the atomic bomb attack and our whole island was under tight security. Saipan was only ten miles from where we were and we knew that something was up. No one told us anything about the bombing until the bombs were dropped on Hiroshima and Nagasaki. Shortly thereafter, our government wanted to get the word out to Japan that we were going into an all out effort to win the war so they ordered up all the aircraft and ships they could find from the Navy, Air Force, and Marines.

Devastation at Hiroshima

Our planes all got up about the same time and we were soon flying in a whole armada of airplanes. The air was just full of planes and the Navy had their war ships in the water. We were just showing them what we had and what they would have to put up with. The people of Japan got messages from our military commanders telling them how futile further resistance would be. In the meantime time we flew over Hiroshima to see what it was like. It was something awful. We saw total devastation.

Ernie Frazier

The war ended soon after that. I was discharged as a staff sergeant and wound up working on my Pappy's farm back in the states. I've had quite a few jobs over the years, as diverse as being a Protestant minister to riding shotgun on an armored truck. Then, in 1972, I found myself in a war zone again. I'd taken a civilian job with the Army Aviation Command in 1967, designing packaging and shipping containers for parts for our military forces in Vietnam.

To Vietnam as a civilian in 1972

In 1972 I volunteered to go to Vietnam to help coordinate and bring back retrograde aircraft to be repaired and refurbished for further service back in Nam. The cultural shock I was in for, seeing the difference in attitudes in a lot of our civilian and military personnel that came about between WWII and Vietnam, was heartbreaking.

Rampant crime

The saddest thing I saw was that drugs were everywhere. The troops had it available to them at any time and place. It was that prevalent and nobody seemed to care much about it. Also, the black market in military equipment was rampant. If there were a market for it in Nam, shipments of equipment we needed would disappear as soon as it was unloaded. It was pretty obvious that some of our people were willing to let our materials go to the black market as long as they got a cut out of the deal.

The French and Catholic influence was great. We had young Vietnamese women in our offices that could speak and write three languages: Vietnamese, English, and another one. They appeared to be of a pure race, had been educated by the Catholic Church, were very intelligent, and their families usually ran the stores and local businesses.

On the other hand, another group had migrated in and did a lot of the hard work. They were mostly Buddhists, didn't care much for the Americans, wore red robes or black pajamas and had many prostitutes in that group. The prostitutes operated both in the hotels and on the streets. They were everywhere and their little brothers would come up and proposition you for their sister, aunt, mother, or whoever. It was a kind of culture you didn't want to raise your family in.

Who cares?

I spent two brief tours in Nam, always on military bases, as it was dangerous to leave them. Besides the graft and black market and drugs, the big differences between Nam and WWII was that in WWII you had to stick with the rules or you got into big trouble. In Nam, I saw and heard the attitude of " Who cares?" by some of our people. The government didn't and that attitude was noticeable in them and Vietnamese civilians.

The Vietnamese officials working with us were terrified as the war wound down and they saw that we were preparing to abandon them to the Viet Cong. Their chances were very bad and they said that they would be killed after we left. Maybe they were, I don't know. We had people disappearing from our offices left and right. One morning I went to our office and none of the young women showed up for work. We sent people to find them but they'd disappeared. Some speculated they went to join the Viet Cong but I don't think so. I think they wanted to escape and went to Thailand or the Philippines or someplace like that.

Not wanting to fight the system any longer, I resigned my position about 6 months before the end of the war and headed home. Again.

Frank is tall and unassuming, a humble, gentle man who came from a strong Christian background. After his military service, he worked for some time as a minister but found he wasn't cut out for it. He was a stockholder and worked in his family's automotive supply business until it was sold. He and his wife, Emily, are retired and live in Rogers, Arkansas.

CHAPTER 20

ARNOLD (GABBY) HARTNETT

"I found out that paratroopers got an extra $50 a month and I signed up."

The recruiter "misunderstood."

I was only 18 in April of 1943 when I was drafted. I wanted to go into the Air Corps but got assigned to Camp McCall, North Carolina for basic training. Evidently the recruiter misunderstood me. I wonder. I wound up in an airborne infantry division, not the Air Corps, and was assigned to a glider regiment, which also trained regiments of paratroopers. We trained constantly in gliders and they were real interesting. You could get about 27 men in a glider. Less if we hauled a jeep or other equipment. They'd carry a lot of weight.

I found out that the paratroopers got an extra $50.00 a month and I could get that if I took jump training. So, after about 9 months I volunteered and was sent to Camp Forrest in Tennessee to go to jump school. But I was still assigned to a glider regiment.

The training was rough. I'd never thought about a man 27 or 28 being old, but a lot of them just couldn't keep up. We did a lot of running and calisthenics, jumped out of mock airplanes and slid down cables to learn how to land. Discipline was tough. When we'd get a break—if we didn't sit just right and were so tired we couldn't do anything else—we'd have to do a quick 25 push-ups. It was hot and humid—miserable.

Brutal training can be funny..sometimes

I think the training in our division might have been a little different than some. Our officers were put through the training right along with us. It was funny to see one of our colonels running around one day holding a handful of sand, saying, "I am a bad colonel. I spit in the sand." A sergeant made him do it.

Sergeant Jones was our First Sergeant and I'll always remember him. When we went overseas, he was transferred out. He'd have probably been killed if he went over there.

G. I. humor was pretty grim. We had to eat a lot of mush for breakfast and we hated it. One morning we were lined up outside the mess hall and heard gunshots. A soldier had committed suicide. Someone said, "Oh shoot, he heard we were having mush for breakfast again."

We were in a pretty congenial group and weren't trying to emphasize that we were tough paratroopers. In Tennessee there was a little old town we'd go into when we were off duty. It had an alley with bars on both sides that attracted the G. I.'s. Even though we were both in the 17th Division, the paratroopers and the glider people tangled occasionally. One time they closed the alley for a week or two because we tore the place up. The owners liked the G. I. money but not the expense of fixing it up.

Practically our whole division shipped out of Boston on one big troop ship. We weren't in a convoy. It was a fast ship and we zigzagged all the way to baffle any subs that were lurking around.

Riding in dangerous British gliders

We landed in England and did the same old stuff, more training except now we got to take rides in some British gliders that were really a lot bigger and heavier and more dangerous than ours. They could hold about 50 men.

Ernie Frazier

In to relieve the 101st trapped at Bastogne

The Battle of The Bulge was going on and the 101st Airborne division was surrounded at Bastogne, Belgium. We had a division made up of two glider regiments and one paratroop regiment, the 17th Airborne. Our regiment consisted of two battalions. We were sent in to relieve the 101st.

We quickly wound up in the thick of battle and ran up against some really stiff resistance. I was the gunner on a mortar team in a weapons platoon and carried a 40- mm mortar barrel. Other guys carried the base plate, tripod and ammunition. We lost so many people that they had to reorganize our regiment.

No overshoes; a fatal blunder

I was confused about what part of Belgium we were in. It was wintertime—cold with snow on the ground. The morning we were to attack we were ordered to turn in our overshoes. I think our officers felt we'd move better without them. That was a fatal blunder.

Things didn't go well. Our artillery laid down a barrage for us, but it was a little too close to us and not close enough to the Germans. 'Friendly fire' wounded several of our lead scouts. Our artillerymen quickly adjusted their range and began pounding the enemy. But, when we attacked, they were waiting and our outfit took a pretty bad beating that day.

In a German mine field

On thing that stands out in my mind, four of us were taken out to a German mine field, instructed as to the location of the mines, and told that some of our soldiers who were surrounded would probably try to escape and come through here. Our job would be to guide them through. Only one group appeared. They had an officer with them and none of them knew the password. They thought we were the enemy and we didn't know if they were or not. We finally figured it all out after quizzing each other on the New York Yankees and everyone else we could think of and I said to the officer, "Follow me and I'll lead you through." He replied, "I don't think there is a land mine here." I was kind of a smart aleck kid and I told him, "Okay, you just walk on through and I'll lead your men later." He decided then to follow me through.

I was fortunate that I didn't have to spend a lot of time in combat and never got into hand-to-hand fighting. The infantry companies would go ahead of our mortars and we'd fire over their heads to try to take out machine gun nests and things like that. The infantrymen were probably 100 to 200 yards ahead of us. Our machine gunners were right behind the infantry and the enemy like to wiped out our infantry that day. Our sergeants and a lot of our good friends we had been in barracks with—they pretty near got the whole group of them. I wasn't that close, but I could see them getting shot. It was a horrifying experience.

Artillery devastates the 106th Infantry Division

The 106th Infantry Division was on the line when we made the first drive and the Germans just pretty well wiped out the division. It was devastating. They were hitting us with 88 mm howitzers. You couldn't see the shells, but you could hear some of them coming. I saw lots of our troops mowed down right in front of me. I walked by our platoon sergeant's body. He'd been killed a little earlier.

Artillery coming in on you is kind of frightening. In fact, I'd probably say I was scared out of my wits, but you can't respond to being scared. We just had to move on.

I remember another incident when several of us jumped into a foxhole and landed on a dead German.

Frozen feet and a hole in the helmet

There was snow on the ground, it was really cold, and we had no overshoes. I don't know if I got frostbite the day of the battle or later when I was on patrol, but my feet began to freeze.

During the battle, I got hit. Either a mortar shell or some kind of an artillery shell hit my helmet and punched out a hole probably 1.5 inches in diameter. It knocked me out momentarily but I came around and it really didn't hurt me too much. I caught a little piece of metal in my head and it's probably still there to this day.

The battle had been fierce for a couple of days and I'd never want to go through that again. You asked about seeing bodies. Yes, I saw lots of them. Most were Germans. The first day of our attack, the Germans seemed to be stronger than us but they were involved in a desperate fight. Their supplies couldn't keep up with them.

We were at the outskirts of Bastogne. It was foggy and our planes couldn't get in to drop food to the 101st. When the weather cleared, the U. S. Air Force basically came and freed them; bombing, firing tracers, and dropping supplies and ammo so they could maintain themselves.

I can honestly say I'm not sure that I ever killed anyone. The Germans didn't bother too much about picking up their dead, this close to the end of the war. Fortunately, I never was on a burial detail.

Hospitalized with cousin Florene

Between the head wound and the frostbite, I got sent back a hospital full of GI's on the outskirts of Paris. My bed was out in the hall and a group of nurses went by. I thought, "By golly, I recognize that one gal." When they came back by again, I hollered at her. It was my cousin, Florene Volker. We had a good visit. Later I got shipped on over to England.

Fortunately for me, my feet weren't as bad as a lot of guys—some lost their feet. I had blisters come up on my toes but I didn't lose anything.

My division made an airborne landing over the Rhine River behind the German troops while I was still in the hospital. After I was released, I rejoined them and we began patrolling the Rhine. We were eating K-rations and C-rations. If you've ever had to live on them, you know you're soon craving some fresh food.

We wound up on a troop train that stopped at a food depot. The poor guard saw us jumping out of our boxcars and head for his food. He couldn't stop us and we picked up cases of whatever we could find. I remember one thing; we grabbed a gallon of peaches and ate them until we were sick. But, I did feel sorry for the guys trying to guard the depot.

We took some German prisoners. I guess some of our guys could have killed them, but we were humane and we didn't.

The war ended and we waited for the Russians to come in to take Berlin. Our job was to move German people out of their apartments and homes. My whole company wound up in one big apartment building and the families who lived there had to move across the street. Some things happened there that I wasn't too proud of. We had the authority to confiscate, say, a radio if we needed it. But, we were supposed to return it. One German lady who lived in our apartment building had a big nice clock with a pendulum that would swing and she'd come over sometimes to wind it. We had one ornery son-of-a-gun who threw his bayonet at the clock until it was destroyed. It upset the poor lady something awful and I was very proud that she knew I had nothing to do with that. I was glad to think I had enough character that she could see I wasn't involved in the incident.

Guarding Cat Houses!

We got sent back to France to await shipment back to the states, then over to Japan. The war there hadn't ended yet. About 25 of us got pulled out for special military police duty. It was a good deal. We had a home, a cook, and could go out and buy the best food. I thought we had it made. We guarded cathouses and things like that. We'd take the women down to get examined by the doctor once in awhile and we'd patrol the streets. I guess we had it too soft so we got broken up and had to go back to our company. I got transferred to a paratroop battalion and was sent home on a little Liberty ship. It was as rough as it could be—nothing like the giant ship that took us over. Guys were sick and were moaning and groaning all over the place. Someone stole the chaplain's communion wine and that didn't go over too great.

On the way home, the United States dropped the first atomic bomb. I was glad. I thought that atomic bomb was a great weapon.

Ernie Frazier

A ticker tape parade in New York

We landed in New York, came by the Statue of Liberty and down the Hudson River. They had a ticker tape parade for us. I got 30 days leave before I was to ship out to Japan. When that was up I reported back to Ft. Leavenworth. In 20 more days I would have enough points to be discharged so they sent me back home for another 20 day furlough. Then, I finally got out.

My discharge says, "Gold 33, WD 45, Rhineland, Ardennes and Central Europe." It says I was wounded in action in the Europe Scene, African, Middle Eastern, January 11, 1945. That was my frozen feet. I got the Purple Heart for my feet.

Gabby and his wife, Betty, live outside the little village of Ensign, Kansas. He worked in a grain elevator and operated a farm prior to their retirement. Like many WWII vets, he isn't bitter about what he had to endure during the war. He accepts it all as something that had to be done if we wanted to remain a free nation.

CHAPTER 21

DON SMITH

"Our planes towed us into battle, then turned us loose."

Don enlisted in the Enlisted Reserve Corp, (ERC), right out of high school, in the spring of 1943. Little did he know that he'd soon be riding into combat on an airplane without engines.

Flunking college

I didn't get called for a while so I went to Washburn University in Topeka, Kansas and flunked about everything. I knew I was going to get called up and I did in the fall. I reported to Ft. Leavenworth and was put in the Army Specialized Training Program. They sent us to Ft. Benning, Georgia where we took the Army's Specialized Training Forces program. I wound up one point short of qualifying to go on with the training so they kept me around picking up cigarette butts and other menial jobs. I wasn't too happy about that. Dad had been in WW I and I'd picked up some kind of ideas about the glamour of war. I particularly wanted to be in the 35th division because that was his outfit.

They finally sent me to Camp Wheeler, Georgia to the Infantry Replacement Training Center. That consisted of seventeen weeks of intensive basic training to qualify as a combat infantryman. I said we were trained to become cannon fodder.

Ernie Frazier

Jump school

Another guy and I got the idea it would be a great idea to go jump school at Ft. Benning. I wore glasses and passed the physical and my eye exam. He didn't wear glasses but he didn't pass the eye test and was disqualified. Another guy told me I was crazy to go to jump school. He said it was an invitation to get killed. I decided against it and finished my basic training. I got a leave for a couple of weeks and then reported to Ft. Meade, Maryland as an infantry replacement. You know, I can't imagine anything more expendable than an eighteen year-old infantryman. The government didn't place a very high value on human life, particularly on some kid who would do whatever he was told.

We sailed from the east coast in a massive convoy of troop ships with an armada escort stretching as far as the eye could see. We were having submarine and U-Boat scares and I guess they figured it was safest to travel in a convoy. In about two weeks we landed in Liverpool, England. They herded us like cattle into boxcars and shipped us to a replacement depot where they assigned a bunch of us to the 82nd Airborne Division. I'd never heard of the outfit but that was immaterial. It was right before the June 6, 1945 invasion of Normandy that the 82nd Airborne participated in.

To the 325th Glider Infantry

They assigned me to the 325th Glider Infantry. Fortunately, the 82nd had already embarked for Normandy and the invasion started without me. So, we stayed in England and did a lot of close order drill and physical training. About fifty percent of our division that landed—they went in at night and everything was screwed up—were casualties. Fortunately, with the resourcefulness of the American soldier and some good leadership, they did some great work in Normandy, in back of Omaha Beach, and captured St. Mary-Eglise. Several of the guys got the Silver Star and other decorations.

They came back to England and we were taken into the outfit. I remember shortly afterward we had a division review for General Eisenhower. I remember going by the reviewing stand. Usually the generals were on a platform but Ike was on the ground. When we went by and they gave us "eyes right", I thought Ike had tears in his eyes because of the terrible losses the division had sustained.

On about September 15th they notified us we were going to go to the airport the next day to fly out on an airborne invasion of Nijmegen, Holland.

The British 1st Airborne division was dropped at Arnhem and they suffered terrible losses. The Germans had captured the road up north and they were cut off and lost about everybody. Nobody could get in to relieve the British and it turned into a real slaughter.

Crash land first—Germans next

The gliders we were riding in slid silently through the air. Any engine noises came from tow planes that brought us from England. When we got over Holland, the Germans opened up with ack-ack guns. We braced ourselves. The gliders that survived would crash land. First, we'd worry about the landing, then, the waiting Germans. It was September 17, 1945.

Our planes turned us loose and we landed the best we could. It was a very inexact science and we had all kinds of casualties. I was lucky and didn't have any trouble. The division commander then was General Jim Gavin, 37 years old and the youngest division commander in the United States Army. I remember seeing him on the ground with an M-1 rifle and a little aide following him around.

Our time in Holland was spent capturing Nijmegen and the very big and important bridge that crossed the Rhine there. We had to capture that and the battle carried on for two or three weeks. It never stopped. Some of our men had submachine guns. I was armed with an M-1 rifle. I was only a private at the time. I hadn't even made PFC.

Bombarded

One night we stopped in a forest. It was kind of dumb, really, because of the tree bursts. We dug big slit trenches and foxholes and in the evening a British armored, self-propelled 105 pulled in close to us and began firing. Instantly, the Germans would pinpoint where the shells were coming from and return fire with their own artillery. We were under bombardment all night and it was a very harrowing experience. I survived it all and got well acquainted with some of the British tank guys. The Irish guard replaced the British when they left. They liked the Yanks and would sit down and visit with us.

We stayed in Holland through October. Then they took us off the line back to Reims, France and we stayed in the stable that was built there by Napoleon. One night we saw a good movie, Saratoga Trunk, starring Gary Cooper. When we got back to the stable, the 1st Sergeant told us that the Germans had broken through in Belgium and in the morning we had to be ready to head up there. We didn't have any winter gear, just regular spring equipment. We got it and our ammunition and were loaded into trucks in the morning.

Bastogne

We headed for Bastogne but we beat the 101st Airborne up there so they sent us on through to Werbonnet, north of the Bulge. It was snowing heavily and we could see we were getting into something bad because there were soldiers retreating back through our columns. We found out that the Germans had broken through our lines and were advancing toward Antwerp. Our mission was to see to it that they didn't get any further north. The 101st was trapped in Bastogne, which is right in the middle of the bulge with St. Vith on the south and the 82nd on the north. We were now under command of Field Marshal Sir Bernard Montgomery, the British commander.

It was pouring snow. The Germans were everywhere, then nowhere. At Malmedy, American soldiers threw down their arms in surrender only to be herded together and massacred by the Germans. Utter chaos and confusion reigned. We were up in the Ardennes Mountains and didn't know where the front was or anything else.

Patrols and firefights

Our outfit was mostly on patrols. We had isolated firefights where the enemy would fire on us and we'd return fire. We were to stay on the ground and fight like a regular infantry unit. The snow was deep and all we had on our feet was our regular G. I. boots. We were cold, had frostbite, no food, and were low on ammunition. Supply planes dropped off food by parachute, mostly K-rations in a box and maybe a can of ham or chicken and a couple of biscuits. Finally we got some winter gear and got C-rations sometimes, which were a little more sophisticated. G. I. rations always had cigarettes in them. We were the generation of smokers and we're now paying a hell of a price for it in the area of emphysema.

All this time I never got hit. But I was homesick, blue and cold. We went through the snow across the Siegfried line. One night we were on patrol and I was carrying the radio. We reached a firebreak cut in the forest and a German machine gun opened up on us. Lehrman Wilson, a good buddy about my age with a lot of similar interests, was hit and killed. We took a couple of prisoners. I don't know if our men killed them or not. They might have.

A squad leader at eighteen

I was the youngest guy in our outfit, not yet nineteen, but the company commander decided to promote me to corporal and make me a squad leader. I was confronted by the older troops who didn't like the idea, but I was pretty gutsy and didn't take much off of them and we got the thing settled.

Christmas

On Christmas day, 1944, it had been snowing and our rifles were frozen shut and our feet were frost bitten. We were in the march toward Germany when the skies opened up on a beautiful, sunshiny day and our planes were able to drop supplies to us.

From then on we did the grunt work and were in one continuous combat after another, driving the Germans in full retreat. Soon we had a great big German army trapped between the Russians and the Americans. The Germans opted, wisely, to surrender to the Americans.

Ernie Frazier

We met the Russian army up where the Elbe River runs out of Germany and empties out into the North Sea. We partied with them and established a good rapport. Our officers told us to be nice to them since they were our allies. That was the exact opposite of what occurred during the Cold War.

Ludvickslust Concentration Camp

About that time, Germany surrendered. We'd captured thousands of prisoners and I was kind of in charge of making sure they didn't go anywhere. A concentration camp was outside of Ludvickslust. The Germans had buried Jews and displaced persons who starved to death in mass graves there. Our division commander made the Germans dig up all those graves and re-bury the people in the main street of the town. I'll never forget that.

They sent us on to a little French resort on the Meuse River named Epinal where we awaited orders. We heard that we were going to Japan to participate in the invasion there and, to put it mildly, we weren't too happy about that. Then orders came down that the highly decorated 82nd Airborne, the All-American division, would be the division occupying Berlin.

That's when I got hit. But it wasn't by enemy firepower.

Mangled by a truck

We wound up in Kaiserlautern, Germany and I had the job of setting up a place to spend the night on our way to Berlin. One morning I was riding in the front seat of a jeep on the way to take a shower. The driver cut across in front of a big army truck and he struck us broadside. That pretty well ended my army career. I was taken to a French hospital with a broken back, leg and arm along with assorted other injuries. The pain was bad and I was pretty well out of my head. They finally sent me to the 96th General Hospital in Frankfurt and I was severed from my outfit. Someone stole my high school graduation watch and anything else I had of value. I was in a big body cast from the eighth day of August until about the first of November and it really tried my patience. The cast went down my left *leg to my knee and my right leg down to my toes with a bar between my legs and I could just barely sit up a little bit. Among other things, they put a plate in my right femur. Eventually they took us to Bremerhaven on the North Sea and shipped us home on a hospital boat. When we docked I asked if they'd take me up on the deck so I could see the Statue of Liberty. They carried me up on a litter. It was a great feeling to be coming back to the states.*

I spent the winter of 1945 in the Camp Carson General Hospital in Colorado. In April they advised me I would be getting a discharge.

I graduated from Washburn University in 1950, got married and ultimately was elected county attorney of Ford County, Kansas.

State representative, county attorney, and district court judge

In addition to his legal practice, Don was instrumental in founding a bank. He also served terms as a Kansas state representative, Ford county attorney, and district court judge.

I was sad to read that he died at his home in Dodge City, KS on January 19, 2002.

CHAPTER 22

ORVILLE BREHM

"I rode the death train at St. Valerie."

Sgt. Orville Brehm

Fate has a strange way of creating circumstances, usually with no plausible reason, that determine who will live and who will die in a given incident. Most soldiers who die on enemy soil are killed in battle. However, in war the enemy is only concerned with numbers of soldiers killed not how they died. Each body counts the same.

The 565th Quartermaster Railhead Company, composed mainly of men from Indiana, Ohio, Kentucky, Kansas, Texas and Missouri, was activated in April, 1944. Orville Brehm had been drafted into the Army in March and was trained in Camp Carson, Colorado, a rather scenic if rugged place; and Camp Rucker, Alabama, which sported swamps, stifling heat, snakes and alligators; and Fort Myers, Virginia, which wasn't too bad.

Soon they were on their way to Kaiserslautern, Germany where they would begin operating food warehouses and distribution facilities. Orville, by then a corporal in the 565th Quartermaster Corps, was placed in charge of a night crew. Their primary duties were to receive bulk quantities of canned food and G. I. rations and break them down into manageable units to be transported to troops in combat. General Patton's tank crews were beginning their push into Germany and one of the primary missions of the 565th was to keep them fed. As the combat units moved forward, the Quartermaster Corps followed behind. It appeared to be a safe duty assignment. But the hazards of wartime travel and sabotage awaited them.

Riding the 40 & 8 boxcars

On January 18, 1945, our unit was on the move. At Le Havre, France we'd been loaded aboard the infamous 40 & 8 boxcars. Many were without tops, and we were riding through the night pelted with rain that was rapidly turning to snow. We were living on cold C-rations and morale had hit an all time low. Our car was right behind the engine.

I don't know why—nobody knew why—but the train went off on a siding and the engine switched ends. Now, instead of riding in the front of the train, we were riding on the tail end.

Fate was coming into play

The train had picked up speed for some reason. All night we'd traveled at about 10 to 20 miles per hour. But when we got to St. Valerie, we were doing about 60 and not slowing down! The station was constructed of brick. We crashed right into it. The old French rail cars buckled up and piled on top of each other and spilled out all over the rail yard. Men by the dozens were trapped underneath the wreckage. Since we were in the rear of the train, none of our men were killed or injured.

Everyone jumped out and we began rescuing the injured and the dead.

Then, one of the great tragedies of the war—a crime by our own commanding officer—happened right on the spot.

Remains of St. Valerie Station

Devastation at St. Valerie Station

Arrow points to the first car of the 565th

Ordered to abandon our comrades

While our comrades were screaming to be rescued, our company commander ordered us onto trucks and out of the area. He said that someone else would take care of the carnage and we were forced to leave. It was a terrible experience and even caused one of our sergeants to argue over his ordering us to leave. But, it did no good and we were soon loaded on trucks and vacated the scene. None of us ever forgot having to abandon our men and could only pray that rescue would come soon. The engineer and fireman along with 145 other men were killed in the wreck. Some 400 more were badly injured.

It was impossible to determine the cause of the wreck but an interview with a 12-year-old French boy revealed sabotage as the probable cause.

As far as our C. O. was concerned, Lieutenant Thomas Shusky, who was promoted to captain, replaced him when we approached the front lines in Germany. He was one of the swellest guys I ever knew and he stayed on as our C. O. for the remainder of our time. We never knew what happened to our C. O. that ordered us to leave the wreck. The army didn't keep enlisted men informed of the fate of their officers.

Misery at Camp Lucky Strike

Our next stop was Camp Lucky Strike, a captured German airfield that was mostly a sea of mud. The camp was very new and we had to put up our own tents to live in. Since we were sunk in a swamp of mud, we went out and raided some straw stacks and tried to pack the floors with straw. Probably for the first time in our lives, most of us were cold with no way to get warm, and hungry with no way of getting enough to eat. We resorted to digging up frozen potatoes and made soup out of them. Sometimes we could borrow some bread from the French.

There were two stoves per 25-man tent. We were issued a small amount of wood. We used it and "borrowed" whatever else we could find and were able to keep the fires going for part of each day. There were no lights or electricity and we soon learned how to make candles out of most anything. Everyone quickly learned the value of soap, candy and cigarettes. It was so bad that we had to break ice in shell holes to get water to wash in. Believe it or not, it felt warm to the skin. We were that cold.

It seemed like forever but we were only at Camp Lucky Strike for 23 days. We were then loaded onto trucks and transported about 30 miles where we boarded boxcars bound for Rheim. We were freezing so we tore wood from inside the boxcars and used it to build fires on the floor for warmth and cooking.

At Rheim, Troyes, Chalons, Conthill and Neustadt

We weren't in Rheim very long until we were shipped to Troyes. We got in there at night and began breaking down rations the very next day. On February 16th we left Troyes for Chalons where we began breaking down rations for thousands of troops, including the 101st, 82nd, and 17th Airborne Divisions.

A month later we were transferred to the Seventh Army, which had arrived at the French border. On March 17, we came into a little town named Conthill. We slept in pup tents that night and in the morning started a ration dump along the railroad tracks leading to the front. The Seventh Army had begun their march to the Rhine.

Guarding prisoners

While we were in Germany, we were assigned the additional duty of receiving, working, and delivering prisoners of war to stockades at the rear. One night I was in charge of a work detail of German prisoners and called them into formation. I saw that one prisoner was missing. No one had any answers for me as to his whereabouts and I was getting worried. My job was to see that none escaped. Finally someone said that he was lying sick behind a building. I checked it out. Sure enough, he was one sick soldier. Fortunately, no prisoners ever escaped from my detail.

We left Conthill in trucks on March 25 and moved toward the front. Along the way we came across the signs of battle—tanks, *trucks, and other burned out relics of war. We arrived about 4:00 p. m. at a displaced person's camp on the edge of Neustadt, Germany. Our officers left to go to town to arrange quarters for us. While they were gone, some of the displaced people passed out liquor to the men. By the time our officers returned, a good number of the men were feeling no pain.*

Our billet, for the night, wound up being a big hotel. The next day we were moved into a telephone building. We were only a few miles from the Rhine and we set up another ration dump to supply troops that were preparing to cross the river.

France, Luxembourg, Belgium, Holland and Germany

It took a lot of traveling around to keep up with our advancing armies. On April 4th we left Neustadt for another three-day train ride through France, Luxembourg, Belgium, Holland and Germany. Outside of Cologne, we were transferred to trucks for transport into the city. However, the Germans were still shelling Cologne. Our truck drivers (they were black as the army wasn't integrated yet) claimed they couldn't find the way to town. We had no argument with that and went back to the train to sleep the balance of the night. In the morning they hauled us on into the city without any problems and we spent a few nights in one of the suburbs.

We left Cologne and went about 150 miles to Ehrang. It's close to Trier, the oldest city in Germany. We were there, breaking down rations when Germany officially surrendered.

Thirty-thousand miles at sea

The odyssey of the 565th didn't end there, even though the war in Europe did. In fact, their travels would take them over 30,000 miles on sea. Notes regarding their trip home were cited by Harry N. Smith in collaboration with two others known only as King and Dusing. A copy was given to Orville some 50 years ago and a condensed version of those notes follows.

May 21: Train ride to Marseilles
45 days later: Boarded Navy transport General Randall

July 22: Passed Rock Of Gibraltar.
July 29: Arrived Panama Canal. Only allowed to visit USO there. Hot, nothing to do.
August 16: Arrived Marshall Islands
August 20: Anchored in the Caroline Islands
August 23: Stopped of Leyte. First land we'd seen in the Philippines.
August 24: Anchored in the Bay Of Bantangas. A battalion of troops unloaded here.
August 26: Anchored in the Bay Of Manila
August 29: Disembarked, loaded onto trucks and taken to a mosquito infested rice paddy. Slept in tents covered with mosquito nets.
September 3: Boarded train to Agoo, near the Lingayen Gulf. Put up tents, played volleyball, explored, took in some cockfights. Most of our original cadre were rotated out on the point system and sent home.
October 18: Loaded on an LST for shipment to Japan. Slept on the deck.
October 27: Landed in Japan.
October 28: Landed at our station in Fukoko and began issuing supplies. Shortly thereafter, many men completed their service and were shipped home. Pattison went home and Thomaszewski become C. O. Then he went home and Brown was promoted. Finally, the company was deactivated and we were transferred to the 363 Quartermaster Company. Very soon, the rest of the men were sent home--except for Pop Lehman and Joe Orwitz. In another tragedy that struck randomly at the old 565th, both men were killed when hit by a truck, the very night before they were to leave for the states.

Orville is a retired real estate executive in his early eighties. He married Mary Johnson after the death of his first wife who died after a car wreck that almost killed him. He is still a globetrotter. He and Mary travel frequently to Guatemala to deliver humanitarian supplies to a church mission in Guatemala operated by their daughter and her husband.

In October 2000 they rode in a balloon at the annual balloon festival in Albuquerque.

CHAPTER 23

ALBERT ROTMAN

"Sometimes I flew in 'Flak Bait'. She's on display at the Smithsonian."

Two of my brothers wound up in the tank corps. I was 26 and had a farm deferment but that didn't last for long. My number came up; I joined the Air Corp, and was inducted at Ft. Leavenworth, Kansas. They gave us a mechanic's aptitude test that I must've aced because three days later three of us were sent to Tucson and five days after that I was working on aircraft. I didn't have to go through basic training.

Flight engineer, mechanic and top turret gunner

We trained on BT trainers—basic trainers—and pulled maintenance on BT13A's. They were two-seat trainers used for training cadets and weren't armed. I got there in November and in March they sent me to a mechanic school in Lincoln, Nebraska. I wound up with scarlet fever for 21 days. After I got out, they sent me back to Tucson. I volunteered for gunnery school and trained at Kingman, Arizona. From there we went to Shreveport, Louisiana to pick up a crew. Our training there was at Lake Charles Airbase just out of New Orleans.

We picked up a new B26 at Hunter field, in Savannah, Georgia, a twin engine, 2,000 horse power aircraft. I became the flight engineer, the mechanic on board and the top turret gunner. There were guns mounted on the fuselage—we called them package guns—which the pilot could fire electronically from his seat. We had a tail gunner and a gun in the nose that the bombardier could fire. There were eight guns on the inside that the radio operator could fire out the side doors. I was in the turret, behind the bomb bay on top of the aircraft. I could rotate 360 degrees and had two .50 caliber machine guns that I fired manually with my hands.

We were assigned to the European Theatre and flew out from Hunter field in Savannah, Georgia. Right off the bat we had engine trouble and had to spend a night at Fort Dix, New Jersey to work on the plane. From there we went to Bangor, Maine and then we spent a night in Goose Bay, Labrador. It was July and the weather was rough. Then we flew out of Goose Bay, Labrador to Greenland, and on to Iceland, which was a tricky place. It'll all be clear, then suddenly they'll close the airstrip down for a while, because of bad weather, and you have to wait your turn to land. We made it over to Prestwick, Scotland and the pilot and I took the aircraft over to North Ireland and did a little practice flying.

I was an enlisted man. My job called for the rank of staff sergeant but I got promoted to tech sergeant. I think that happened because when we were on a training mission, our company commander over-shot a landing field. Just beyond the White Cliffs of Dover, we crashed through a fence and wound up in a muddy cabbage patch.

We had seabees stationed there with a Caterpillar. As flight engineer and mechanic it was my responsibility to get the plane out of the mud. The seabees worked with me and we were making progress when the seabee lieutenant tried to take over and tell us to get it out. He was

Albert Rotmen (4th from the left) and crew with B-26.

with him. Of course, I was only a sergeant and had no control over him. Things heated up and pretty soon my company commander came over and said, "When my sergeant says move, you move, and when he says stop, you stop!" Those seabees were really happy that I, a sergeant, had control over their lieutenant. We eventually got the aircraft out of the mud. I was promoted to tech sergeant shortly after that.

In August, 1944 I flew my first mission. It originated in England and we flew across the English Channel. I wound up flying a total of 57 missions. The radio operator's diary tells a little about each one.

Our specialty was bombing bridges, road junctions and things like that. Our ground troops would pull back then we'd fly in to soften up the area for them. After we were done, they'd come back into the area again.

We had a guy named Pecos who wrote about the old 322nd Bomb Group of the 449th Squadron, or outfit, and the missions I was on. He told how the Luftwaffe was sometimes low on fuel and would wait until our heavy aircraft came over, the B-17's and B-24's, then come in pursuit. Down below, their anti-aircraft guns were letting us have it and our planes took a lot of flak.

I flew at times on 'Flak Bait', the plane that flew 202 missions and wound up in the Smithsonian. The aircraft I was normally assigned to had a rather unique name, 'Cock-in-hand' which happened to be the name of an English pub.

The Germans had their best gunners at Brest

Brest was a big problem for General Eisenhower. Our army and navy had it surrounded on land and sea but the Germans wouldn't surrender and it turned into the biggest siege in the war. On September 3rd eight B-26 groups, four A20 groups and 10 to 12 fighter groups, along with 500 heavy bombers from the 8th Air Force, were sent to bomb Brest. That's probably the most scared I ever got in combat. The Germans had some of their best gunners at Brest. We'd usually approach from about 11,000 to 12,000 feet. Their flak would go up a lot higher than that. In order to protect ourselves we took evasive action. We figured it took 20 seconds to get out of our altitude so we would change course every 20 seconds. We could sit up there and see the flak go right where we would have been if we'd stayed on a straight course. They always say, "Well, the flak was so heavy you could ride over it." That's the way it was at Brest.

Our group's target at Brest was the bridge in the center of town. We were loaded with four 1,000-pound bombs and made four or five trips over there. Once we dropped to 1,000 feet and had to make four passes before we finally dropped our bombs. We were receiving small arms fire.

Our plane is hit!

Steel, lead and fire were whizzing by so close that I could see it right out the window. We got down to 400 feet. Some of our plane's fuselages were hit with metal from exploding material that was bombed.

We took a hit to our engine harness on that trip. We were lucky, and made it through all right. Some of our planes didn't. I was looking through this stuff a while back and found out that we'd lost a lot more people and planes than I realized. We flew in a box formation with planes on each side and above and below us. Sometimes we'd have a group of 36 flying in formation and I couldn't see everything that was going on. Every so often a plane would drop out. Later we'd find out that they weren't coming back.

Metz was another mission that flak was heavy and we suffered some hits.

We had a lead pilot, Captain Fort from Texas, that I liked. He usually had a way of avoiding some of the flak. Our losses and damage weren't nearly as great as a lot of the planes. Later on, we got a new company commander who wanted to go straight in on a target. We knew the ack-ack guns were just waiting for us on the bomb runs.

I believe it was the 344th group who bombed a bridge and there was a whole trainload of German equipment coming to it. The bombs slowed it down and they radioed back for our fighter planes. Boy they got the whole train!

I remember that we bombed Baueaif-Tille Airfield many times. When we finally got control of it, we had to repair it before we could use the airstrip.

Ernie Frazier

Flak hit my canopy

You never knew when you were going to get it. The canopy over the dome where I was sitting got hit with flak and I've still got it around here somewhere. It looks like a chunk of an axle that came off a machine. The Germans were firing .88 mm anti-aircraft guns. The explosions caused a terrible air turbulence that jerked our planes around quite a bit.

We sent 36 planes to bomb the Siegfried line, a long stretch of concrete tank traps and other obstacles. It was almost impregnable, and we never even dented the fortifications.

Jumping John jumped from 90 feet

Some funny things happened. We had this one guy we called Jumping John. He jumped out of his plane three different times. His last jump was from 90 feet and he lived to tell about. I was on the ground and saw it happen. His plane was coming in for a landing, badly shot up. He misunderstood what the pilot said, and out he went. They say that chutes blossom at 87 feet. He was a pretty good-sized guy and was lucky to survive the drop.

Liberating Americans at Bastogne; a merry Christmas!

The happiest day of my life, and I think I could say that for everyone in our squadron, was when the sun came up on Christmas Day and we were ordered to bomb around Bastogne. Our forces fighting there were trapped, freezing, running out of ammunition, and on the brink of annihilation. It felt good to be able to aid them. We knew how desperate the situation was for our ground troops and we let the Germans have it with everything we had. We bombed road junctions, supply lines, trucks, tanks, troops, and artillery-- anything to halt their advance. Of course the Germans weren't asleep. They fought back—they had five to seven divisions surrounding our ground positions—and they fought back. We lost several aircraft that day.

One of our crew made it back even though they had one engine and a tire knocked out. Fortunately the engine was on the opposite side of the tire. That made it possible for Captain Fort to land the plane.

After the war, I looked over some of the books I have that tell of the casualties our men suffered. I know that I didn't pay the ultimate price. My brother, who passed on in his 80th year, was in the tank corps. He was wounded and wound up in a hospital; however, he didn't go back to the states when they released him. Instead, he returned to his outfit and was wounded again. In 1958 he had to have a lung removed and lived until 1998 with only one lung

Right after I was discharged, I became the commander of our local VFW in the small town of Downs, Kansas. We, along with the American Legion, conducted six military funerals that year for men from our area that fell in the war.

Decorated

I was awarded the Air Medal and two silver oak leaf clusters. Those indicate 55 combat missions.

Albert farmed for many years after the war. Now retired, he lives with his wife in Cozad, Nebraska.

CHAPTER 24

WENDELL SWANK

"Floating down, I thought, 'Mrs. Swank's little boy, you're a long ways from home'."

Wendell never dreamed he'd be in a war, shot down over enemy territory, parachute from an airplane and become a prisoner of war.

Never believe the recruiter

Before I enlisted, two years of college were required before you could get into flight school. They lowered that requirement and would admit you if you had a high school education and could pass the entrance exams. I qualified and was admitted to the Aviation Cadets as a civilian. My draft number was coming up, so I went to Kansas City and talked to a recruiting sergeant who taught me lesson number one: never believe the recruiting sergeant. He told me to enlist and go down to Jefferson Barracks with my paper work. They'd put me in the Army Air Corps and I'd go straight to flight school after basic training.

Well, I swallowed his story and enlisted. They sent me to the infantry and I began basic with the 30th Division at Ft. Jackson, South Carolina, on the first of March 1942.

It took me until July to get my transfer to the Air Corps. I was sent home for 60 days and found a summer job and met my future wife before being called to active duty.

My first classification was navigator. For reasons I never knew, that was soon changed to pilot. One hundred eight of us started primary training and 49 got our wings.

I remember our colonel told us, "Don't worry about washing out of pilot training. We'll either make pilots out of you or kill you!"

We graduated from flight school in Tucson in June 1943. We joined a B-24 crew as co-pilots; they had graduated just before us—and flew to El Paso for phase training. None of our class got any first pilot training. We went straight in as co-pilots.

We were there until November, and then went up to Nebraska to be outfitted to go overseas.

We got a new crew and flew to the 44th Bomb Group that was stationed in England.

Our fighter escorts ran low on fuel

On the 22nd of February, we were sent on a mission to bomb an aircraft factory at Gotha, Germany. There were 40 planes in a bomb group and 10 groups were on that run. We'd been assigned an old B-24D that didn't even have a ball turret. They'd give the new crews the old planes. It would fly and that was about all. It was around noon when we crossed the border into Germany and hit a 100 mph head wind. Our fighter escorts left us when they got low on fuel.

Six bullets barely missed

The Germans hit us when they saw we were unescorted. Their first plane came in about one 1:00 0'clock high and took out our number three engine, the one right outside the co-pilot's window. I saw oil come out of the engine and tried to feather it, but it was too late. About that time, I felt some stuff on my helmet. I didn't have a scratch. The pilot asked me, "Is Swanky all right?" I said, "Sure, why shouldn't I be?" He said, "Look at your window." I looked and there were about six bullet holes right beside my head.

Ernie Frazier

Only one engine left!

Right then our crew started yelling that planes were coming in underneath. About five attacked us. We were a sitting duck because we couldn't reach them without a ball turret. They got two more engines, meaning we only had one left. Our controls weren't operating too well, either.

Our pilot ordered the bombardier to unload our bombs. The bombardier yelled, "I can't! The electricity is all shot out!" We had a T-handle attached to a cable positioned between us. It could be used in an emergency to unload the bombs, so I grabbed it and gave it a jerk. All that happened was I came up with the T-handle and a foot of cable.

I don't know whether bullets or shrapnel were tearing us apart, but when I crawled over to the radio room the carpet there was riddled to shreds.

Bail out!

The pilot told us to bail out. I went back and held the wheel while he got his pack, then he held it while I got mine. The bomb bay door was open so I moved over there to jump out. Well, here came our engineer up through the bomb bay. He said, "Swank, push back and you go first!" I told him, "No, we haven't got any time to be heroes. Get out of here!" He didn't want to so I put my foot on his shoulder and kicked him out through the bomb bay. Incidentally, we had no parachute practice, only instruction. Our first pilot was behind me. He couldn't see the engineer down below so he began hitting me on the head to get me to jump. I jumped right after the engineer. We were up about 18,000 feet and it took me probably ten minutes to drift down. I wasn't panic stricken or anything. I remember looking around and seeing the blue sky and the puffy, white clouds. It was beautiful and a thought went through my head, "Mrs. Swank's little boy, Wendell, you're a long way from home!"

There were 10 men on our plane. The bombardier didn't survive. All we know is that he and the navigator were up in the nose. They were supposed to pull a cord and the door enclosing the nose wheel *would fly off, giving them a place to jump from. They couldn't get it off so they had to crawl back to the bomb bay and bail out. The navigator said he thought that the bombardier bailed out, but none of us ever saw him again.*

WESTERN UNION TELEGRAM

MARCH 6, 1944
THE SECRETARY OF WAR DESIRES ME TO EXPRESS HIS DEEP REGRET THAT YOUR BROTHER SECOND LIEUTENANT CLIFFORD W SWANK HAS BEEN REPORTED MISSING IN ACTION SINCE TWENTY TWO FEBRUARY ON MISSION TO GERMANY PERIOD IF FURTHER DETAILS OR OTHER INFORMATION ARE RECEIVED YOU WILL BE PROMPTLY NOTIFIED PERIOD.
UL10 THE ADJUTANT GENERAL.

Knocked out and captured

There was a high wind that blew me over backwards when I hit the ground and it knocked me out. I was lucky that I was out in the country. When I woke up, some German civilians were there. They'd already stripped off my parachute and my Mae West life jacket and had me on my feet. There was a man under one arm and a kid about twelve years old under my other arm. They walked me over to a little car, about like a Volkswagen, which they'd driven out to the field. They threw me in the back seat; I was still about half out. A big German man in a black coat drove the car over to a little village named Wessel. We went to a house and he took me in through the back door. Inside was a room with some bunks. He pointed out one and I went over and laid down on it. I was still woozy.

After a few minutes, they brought in a couple of other airmen I didn't know and then led in the waist gunner from my crew.

Heil Hitler!

The big German was standing by me so I sat up and tried to talk to him. A loud speaker, probably an air raid warning, was going off, and the German didn't say a thing to me. He just picked up a telephone and spoke to someone in German, which I didn't understand, hung up and said, "Heil Hitler!" I knew right then we weren't with friends.

They bought in another man from my crew and three more airmen. A couple of civilian policemen and the big German in the overcoat came in, took us out and marched us about a mile to town, to a building in the town square that looked like a courthouse.

They took us upstairs to a large room. A German army officer was there and I think he paid the civilians for bringing us in. They waited until about a dozen more prisoners showed up, then took us down and put us on a train bound for Dusseldorf.

We arrived after dark, got off the train and marched 12 or 15 blocks through the bombed out city. Our planes had blown holes through the ceilings and roofs and we could see the sky above.

They took us through an arched gate into the first building and into an office. Behind it was a row of cells. I figured it was a guardhouse from an air force base.

Just then, a German sergeant brought our navigator in through another door. So, there were four of us together from my outfit. The navigator and I were the only officers; I was a second lieutenant and they put us in a cell by ourselves. The cell doors were solid with a little peephole in the middle. It was February 22nd and really cold. They threw in one blanket for us to share. Our cell had a wooden bench with a sloping headboard. The floor was cement. The room measured about 10' X 12'.

My leg was still hurting from my jump and I was hobbling around, trying to get warm. Pinkie, my navigator who was a Jewish boy from New York City, looked around and said, "Swank, I'll be good to you. You can take the bed and I'll sleep on the floor." That was a joke. One was just as hard as the other.

I was really tired, so I slept that night even though the accommodations were pretty lousy.

You're Jewish, aren't you?

In the morning, the German sergeant came in. He was about 40 years old, had a big gray beard, and could speak perfect English. He *let us out and told us that we could go down to the end of the hall to use the latrine. We talked for a little bit and he looked at Pinkie and said, "You're Jewish, aren't you?"*

"No, no," Pinkie said, "I'm not Jewish."

The sergeant told him, "Well, you can go on down to the latrine."

When Pinkie got out of earshot, the sergeant said, "He can't tell me he's not a Jew. But it doesn't matter to me. He's got on an American uniform and I don't really care where he came from. I just made that statement."

As I went down the hall, I heard some people talking and I recognized the voice of my first pilot. I yelled to him through the door and he told me they'd come in that night and everyone of our crew was there except for the bombardier. We stayed there until about 11:00 that night; we got called out to go to an air raid shelter. The British were staging an air raid. We went down into the shelter; it was real crowded with women, children and everyone that could get in along with the guard watching us.

We stayed about a half hour, then they took us out and marched us down to the train station and we got a ride to Frankfurt. It was called Frankfurt On The Main, distinguishing it from Frankfurt On The Oder, which was east of Berlin. The civilians didn't like us, but the German soldiers protected us. We then got on a streetcar and were hauled over to Stalag Luft which was an interrogation center.

WESTERN UNION TELEGRAM

MAY 28, 1944
FOLLOWING UNOFFICIAL SHORT WAVE BROADCAST FROM GERMANY HAS BEEN INTERCEPTED QUOTE AM A PRISONER OF WAR IN GERMANY. AM WELL AND WAS NOT HURT WHEN SHOT DOWN. PLEASE NOTIFY (LAVERE?) AT ONCE. I CAN WRITE THREE LETTERS AND FOUR POST CARDS PER MONTH. MAY RECEIVE ALL SENT. CONTACT RED CROSS REGARDING PACKAGES. TELL EVERYBODY HELLO AND WRITE OFTEN AND I WILL DO THE BEST POSSIBLE. LOVE AND KISSES. WENDELL. SIGHED SECOND LIEUTENANT CLIFFORD W SWANK. UNQUOTE THIS BROADCAST SUPPLENTS PREVIOUS OFFICIAL REPORT RECEIVED FROM INTERNATIONAL RED CROSS STOP.
LERCH ACTING PROVOST MARSHAL GENERAL.

Ernie Frazier

Solitary

We got split up and I went to solitary confinement in a small cell. It had frosted windows and a heater that I could sit on without burning and they pitched me a couple of blankets. I spent the night. In the morning they brought me some ersatz coffee, (I don't know what it was made from), and some black bread and jam. I stayed there all day. The guard would take me to the latrine. At noon, they fed me a bowl of soup. Supper was more black bread and jam.

That night, I was getting ready for bed when the guards came down and told me to get my clothes; they were taking me to another cell.

Interrogation

They shut the door on me. No sooner would I lie down to go to sleep until they would come knocking on the door and come in and start asking me stuff like, "What is your name? What is your name? What's your serial number?" They didn't torture me; they just kept this up over and over to harass me.

At about 10:00 the next morning they took me over to another building and into an office. A German major was there. He spoke good English, asked me to sit down and offered me a cigarette and made small talk for a while. Then he got my name, rank, and serial number again, which is all I was required to give under the Geneva Convention. But then he wanted information about my group and squadron. I said, "Well, you know Major, I can't give that out. I've given you my name, rank, and serial number and that's all I'm going to give."

He loosened up a little, visited with me some more, and then started asking the same questions again. I'd tell him the same thing.

So he asked me, "Did the people that captured you treat you all right?"

I said, "Yeah, they treated me all right. I didn't expect the country club welcome."

He told me, "We know they didn't beat you, but sometimes our soldiers steal from the prisoners. Did they take anything from you?"

I replied," They took my watch."

He said, "Oh, that was a G. I. watch. We can keep that."

"Well," I said, "that may be right, but the band was given to me by my fiancée. She sent it to me for Christmas this year. So that band is mine."

He picked up the phone and called someone. Within five minutes, a knock came on the door. A German lady walked in, called me by name, and then walked over and handed me my watchband.

I thanked her and went over to sit down and look it over. The major walked up and again asked me, "Now what was you squadron and group?"

I just leaned back and laughed and said, "Major, you know I'm not going to tell you that."

"Well, you go over and sit in that cell for three weeks and you'll be glad to tell me."

He called the guard who took me back to my cell. Just as it was getting dark that night, the guard came for me again and told me to get my clothes. We went over to a big, long barracks and he shoved me inside.

It had a long hall with rooms on either side. They were full of American prisoners. I looked in the rooms and came across a sergeant that was a good friend of mine. Believe it or not, his name was Jimmy Doolittle. Of course he wasn't the general.

I asked him, "Jimmy, what are you doing in here?"

He jumped up, gave me a hug and told me I was the first guy he'd met in there that he knew since he was shot down over Austria 10 days earlier. He asked if I wanted a cigarette, somehow he'd held onto a pack, and I said, "Sure." So we had a smoke.

The next morning we were taken to another camp. Red Cross people were there with parcels containing towels, razors, soap, cigarettes, sweaters and underwear—that sort of thing. We could send a card home. I sent one. My daughter has it right now. She's making copies of my wartime memorabilia.

Showers were available so we took one. Then we were to assemble in front of a building where we would be fed. A guy was there who looked at me and said, "Why you s. o. b.!"

I said, "I don't think I know you."

"Yes you do," he said. "You're the guy that won all my money in a blackjack game a couple of weeks ago!"

His name was Bob Jacobe from Kansas City. Well we hung around together from then on until we got back home.

Two nights later we were taken to the freight yard at Frankfurt. There were four boxcars and they loaded eight guards and 20 prisoners into each of them. The cars had straw at one end and a stove in the middle.

They brought us in some cheese and stuff to eat and the train pulled out that night. We rode for four nights and three days, and then unloaded at Barth, Germany. They took us to our prison camp; it was about a mile away. We took a shower and were led into our barracks. We spent the next 14 months there.

We'd get Red Cross parcels that were supposed to be enough food for one man for a week. We'd get about ½ of what we should've gotten. The Germans fed us some potatoes, barley, cabbage, and sometimes, a dead horse. We'd wind up with about two meals a day from all of that. As officers, we didn't have to work so all we did was keep clean.

Six weeks on turnip and cabbage soup

We didn't get any Red Cross supplies during February 1945 or the first two weeks in March. Also, the German food supply slowed down. We went for six weeks on a daily bowl of soup made from turnips and cabbage. There was no meat or salt. We had 18 men at our table and each day we'd get one pan of soup. Someone had to ration it out so nobody would get more than anyone else and they drafted me to do that. That went on for six weeks and was the only time in captivity when we really got hungry. We dreamed a lot about chocolate bars and other good stuff.

During air raids the Germans made us go in the barracks. Jim McCord, a first lieutenant from Fort Scott, Kansas was with me one day and he said, "Swank, we can go outside and sit down and watch the raid and no one can see us." So, we sneaked out and were watching the B-17's and 24's coming over, heading toward Berlin.

The Boothill Coffee Club Volume I

All at once we heard a loud ka-whang, whack! A bullet had hit the steps right between us.

Later McCord said, "I ran back into the barracks as fast as I could and Swank pushed me all the way!"

That's the only time I got shot at while I was a prisoner.

After VE Day, we were liberated and I got 65 days leave. VJ day was declared while I was home and the war ended.

I'd gotten married while I was on leave and we went down to Florida so I could be discharged.

I spent the next 40 years in the automotive and tractor parts business before I retired.

Ernie Frazier

CHAPTER 25

ORVILLE BERGER

"I was there on D-Day."

I met Orville at a Korean War Memorial service where he told me he was in WWII and participated in the Normandy invasion on D-Day.

Tough training

I was sworn into the Army on April 3, 1942 at age 27. My outfit, the 358th Infantry, was reactivated with the 90th Infantry Division on March 25, 1942. Basic training at Camp Barkley, Texas, included 25 mile hikes and night exercises in the mesquite. My training at there lasted about a year. That included three months when I was sent to radio school at Ft. Benning, Georgia.

Then we engaged in two weeks of maneuvers against the 77th Division in Louisiana. After returning for a short time to Camp Barkeley, we went to the Camp Granite for maneuvers in the Harquahala Mountains. After that, I got home for Thanksgiving, and then we went on a troop train to Ft. Dix, New Jersey. We took a little training there and then I was sent to Camp Kilmer to attend International Morse Code School.

Sailing to Europe

In March, the 90th Division was alerted to ship out for a secret destination in Europe.

We sailed at night from New York Harbor on the M. S. John Erickson and arrived on Sunday, the 8th of April at Liverpool Harbor, England.

My training was as a radio operator so that's what I did. All messages were encoded as secret, top secret or top-top secret. I remember the wooden barracks in England. They had no lights, the ventilation system was poor and there was a lot of smoking among the men, which stunk up the place.

The Second and Third Battalions and the special units went to Camp Stuart Common near Bewdley. The First Battalion went to Camp Coton Hall for more rugged physical conditioning. On May 12 we were resettled as a regiment at Llanmartin, near Newport, Wales.

We were 'sealed' in the camp. Everything was secret. Commanders attended strategic planning sessions in a headquarters building that was boarded up. We continued the rugged training schedule.

Something big was coming up

On June 4th we went to the dockside at Newport, Wales and were loaded onto two ships, the Bienville and the Excelsior. We joined several other ships and sailed quietly to a rendezvous point off Cardiff, Wales. We knew something big was coming up.

Then we heard that the D-Day invasion was on. Paratroopers had been dropped behind enemy lines the night before. Plans for our outfit were unveiled. Our chaplains conducted services that attracted a larger than usual attendance.

The common troops hadn't gotten any prior word about the invasion and all we heard was that we were going to unload cargo at Utah Beach. The LST we were on was operated by the Limey Merchant Marines. (They had some rum for us, and it was the rottenest stuff I ever tasted.) The hull held 17 vehicles, with a ¾ ton in one corner. We stayed in the harbor for a day and a night, and then got orders to unload. The fog was so heavy we couldn't see anything. When we finally landed, we saw balloons tied to 300-foot cables and wondered what they were. They were there to keep airplanes from strafing us.

Ernie Frazier

Drugged on D-Day

For four days I'd had a daily double shot of penicillin and sulfa drugs for infected teeth, so I wasn't even too sure what was going on when we landed on the beach.

The navy bombarded the Germans. Our ships and landing craft seemed to string out forever. We dropped anchor off Utah Beach on the Cherbourg Peninsula.

A lot of guys had to wade in but our boat hit the shore so hard that our jeep was unloaded down the gangplank and didn't even get any water in it.

The harbor was full of guys who'd been wounded, then drowned when they couldn't make it to shore.

Our group was one of the first to land and we were parked off to the side. It was two days before the whole outfit arrived. We had a message center and telephone and radio. But every time we touched a key, the Germans zeroed in our signal and fired bazooka rounds so we didn't start up any of our jeeps for two days to open up the radios or put up antennas.

When we did communicate, our base unit would use encoded (cryptograph) messages and we had certain numbers assigned every day to decode the messages. One guy would receive the message then pass it to another one who would run it over to our message center.

Rounds whistled overhead

The 359th was the next to land and they had to wade in water up to their necks. Small arms fire opened up and we could hear the rounds whistling over our heads. Bombs and shells were coming in all the time, too, but we got lucky and weren't hit. Our navy had a ship a long way out in the harbor. It located the German gun that was shelling us and bombarded the area. We heard no more from that German gun.

To me, one of the biggest flops in the invasion was when our gliders loaded with troops from the 82nd Airborne tried to land. The Germans had set up posts about every twenty feet or so in every plot of open ground and many planes crashed into them. The 101st jumped in but had been detected by German radar and had to drop into a hail of machine gun fire.

I remember they carried dime store clickers (crickets) that they used to signal each other in the dark. When a guy heard one, he'd better click right back or he'd probably get shot. The crickets were found in department stores in Chicago and California about a month before the invasion.

Giant pillboxes housed a lot of Germans. Our troops would crawl up there, pour five or ten gallons of explosive down their vent pipe, then run like hell. They'd explode it with a flare or an incendiary shell. There might be 1,500 or more people in the really big ones. The doors would be blown off and the Germans would be on fire or run out to be shot.

Attached to Patton

After three days on the beach, we were attached to the Third Army under General Patton. The Fourth Armored and the 90th Division were his babies. We started penetrating inland, always into little villages where our foot soldiers had to do a lot of fighting to clean up those towns. We were told not to attack the churches and the Germans started using them as observation towers. So, we blasted them. This went on for three or four weeks, then the man with more influence over the military than anyone else, the Pope, intervened and the shelling of the steeples stopped.

The Pope was in charge

The Geneva Conference had laid down the rules and the Pope was more or less the Geneva Conference, at least one of their top officials. The Burgermeister in those towns was supposed to swear that there was nobody up in the church towers. Evidently he kept them out so we didn't blow up any more for a while.

Ernie Frazier

In the hedgerows

The 1st Battalion took the bridge at Chef du Pont and rescued a battalion of paratroopers. They took the town of Picauville. They hit us with mortars at Pont L'Abbe and we wound up in one of the bloodiest battles of the war in the hedgerows of Normandy. The mile between Picauville to Pont L' Abbe was heavily defended by the Germans. You could smell the Normandy soil.

German 88's and burp opened up on us but we went hedgerow to hedgerow, rooting them out.

The final assault on Pont L'Abbe took place on the 12th of June. The Air Corps sent in P-47's and artillery bombarded the place.

It took us probably two weeks to get out of the hedgerows. We saw lots of casualties. Our medics carried the wounded part of the way then loaded them on jeeps. They didn't take them to the headquarters medics. They took them to evacuation hospitals.

We were close enough to see small-arms fire; the battles were that close. We were ahead of the artillery batteries so they were firing over us and the Germans were firing back at them.

When we were in the high terrain of France, in a little town of maybe 150 people, a German plane zeroed in and swooped down about a mile away to lay his egg on us. One of our P-51 Mustangs was right on his tail and it fired into the German plane. That exploded the bomb in the air about ¼ to ½ mile from us. The concussion was the worst I ever felt. The roofs in town were slate and there wasn't one left after that. Anytime a shell explodes in the air, it does more damage than if it's on the ground.

The boys who threw the hand grenades had them in their hand and used their teeth to pull the pin. They would count the seconds before they threw them, wanting them to explode off the ground. I think four seconds was the amount of time they had to throw them. A lot of the guys lost hands because they waited too many seconds. You had to know what you were doing.

On the June 15 we attacked toward Le Calias. German machine guns had set up fields of fire that criss-crossed the area. The Third Battalion and the Second Battalion encountered terrific fire. Many men became heroes as they battled their way over an open field covered by a curtain of flying bullets.

The First Battalion crossed at dusk and all three battalions held firm.

We went into a defensive position extending from Coigny to Baupte, France. The first week in France, we found cognac cured in 300 or 500 gallon wooden barrels mounted on stilts. The infantry found some and drove nails in the bottom and filled their canteens. It was green cognac. I remember that. The fumes were strong so no one was supposed to smoke around it.

We went through areas that were mined. A jeep would go over them but anything bigger would set them off. A minesweeper with a big wheel on front would roll over and explode the mines.

I was a radio operator the whole time. By the time the war was over, I was a message chief.

First blankets since Normandy

This was the first time since the landing at Normandy that many of us had a blanket to use. In addition we got some hot chow, another real treat. We got little sleep. Artillery shells were screeching and screaming overhead, then exploding. The concussion shook the earth.

The weather was rainy and dismal on the 3rd of July. Our division attacked to the southwest against fanatical paratroopers and SS men.

The 2nd Battalion charged through and by-passed Les Sablons on a mad dash to the south. The 1st Battalion was in battle at St. Jores. The 3rd Battalion swept into Les Sablons, cleared out the town and joined up with the 2nd Battalion. It was raining all the time. We came to a big hill in a forest rising from the mist. We were at Foret de

Ernie Frazier

Mont Castre and Hill 122 overlooking the English Channel; where we'd first landed.

The 1st Battalion captured the eastern nose of the hill but was pushed off by the German's counterattack. The rest of the regiment got into the battle the following day. The Germans laid down heavy mortar and artillery barrages. They sent in small groups of paratroopers to infiltrate us and attack them from the rear.

Hand-to-hand

On July 11, the 3rd Battalion attacked the enemy's supply line. German paratroopers launched a fanatical attack. That resulted in the bitterest hand-to-hand fighting ever experienced by our outfit. We suffered a lot of casualties.

Our entire regimental front advanced the next day and cracked the Mahlman Line, one of the German's greatest defensive positions.

If you weren't scared you were either a damn liar or you were crazy. I guarantee you; we were concerned at all times. Most of the time we lived on K-rations that came in a little box, like a Cracker Jack box. The French and Germans had gardens. We'd dig up their onions and potatoes so we could have some fresh food. We'd find cognac and use it for cooking fuel. Sometimes C-rations were shipped in. Ten men could eat out of what we called a 10 to 1 package.

Our mail service was good and we'd usually get mail at least once a week. I'd get a letter about every Monday morning from my mom. We went by one cemetery full of white crosses, rows and rows of them. Once in a while one was missing. It made me think of Flanders Field. It was all very tidy and we were told that French ladies kept it up.

We were quartered in foxholes and never saw a tent. If it got cold at night, we'd find bombed out buildings to sleep in.

The slaughter at Falaise Gap

The most horrible thing I saw was over there at Falaise Gap. The battle was in the morning. By the time we got there in the afternoon, the place was loaded with dead soldiers and horses and cattle along with tons of mangled equipment. There was a road running along the bottom of the canyon. Germans were racing along the road, trying to escape. We had a little cub airplane spotting them and radioing their positions back to our artillerymen. They'd spot the position and tell the artillery where to fire. Finally a guy said, "Quit computing and go to shooting!" They just blew the Germans to pieces. The plane really helped because our ground communications were no good; too much interference. And if the artillery tried to calculate their range mathematically, they'd likely fire too long, then shorten up and wind up hitting our own troops. Huge numbers of Krauts surrendered. One non-com alone accounted for 800 German prisoners.

The Third Battalion was stationed at the end of the trap and had to withstand constant attacks by the desperate Germans trying to escape. Charred bodies littered the valley. We annihilated the German Seventh Army.

We heard that American Forces had entered Paris. The 358th was relieved by British Forces.

On August 26, we headed east to take the bridgeheads at the Seine River, which was close to Fontainebleau. History repeated itself; we fought over the old WWI battlefields at Verdun and Château Thierry. Air transports flew in large quantities of gas to keep us going.

We survived an armored column attack at Mairy and the infantry got into hand-to-hand combat at Thionville. The Germans fell back but blew up the last bridge over the Moselle River.

On November 9 the First and Third Battalions crossed the raging Moselle River in assault boats and launched an attack. The Germans hit them with heavy artillery fire. But, our support troops made it across the river with emergency medical supplies, ammunition and food.

Company "A" attacked Fort Koenigsmacher. They were joined by "B" Company and were trapped and shelled by German artillery for three days.

"C" Company and the Regimental Intelligence and Reconnaissance Platoon took the town of Basse Ham.

Company "A" received a supply drop of demolitions and blew the enemy from the west end of the fort through the tunnels and right into

Company "G". That little trick earned the 358th recognition as one of their greatest achievements.

They called "K" Company, the "Kraut Killers" because it was said they killed five Krauts each. They led the Third Battalion to capture Inglange. The Second captured Distroff.

The 105th Panzer Brigade launched a fierce attack but was defeated by the attached armor of Company "B" of the 773rd TD Battalion and Company "A" of the 712th Tank Battalion.

We went to the Siegfried Line to tear down all the pillboxes and blow up all the mines, but one regiment couldn't destroy it.

The Siegfried line had these big tiller bombs; about 2 1/2 feet across, and usually stacked just one deep. Our troops would take an International TD-14 Bulldozer, find the bomb, defuse it and keep going. Sometimes the bastards would put two or three on top of each other. That would fool you. I've seen a TD-14 after they exploded and two men could carry away any piece that was left.

When we located bombs, our men would load them on a truck and haul them away and explode them. It would shake the whole earth.

We fought at the Saar against pillboxes firing heavy machine guns and mortars. Then we hit Pachten and Dilligen, along the Siegfried Line.

During the fighting, we named some of the streets "88 Street" and "Purple Heart Avenue".

To Bastogne

Our outfit left on January 7th for Bastogne. It was brutally cold. We attacked Belgium through Solenz, Doncoles and Bras.

We were under Patton's command all the way. Airdrops were done the night before we got to Bastogne, a vital crossroads. The fog was heavy, the cold was wicked and we had to sleep in foxholes. I didn't take off my shoes for four days. Then I found out you had to take your shoes off and change to dry socks every day. The battles were so fierce that our infantrymen didn't have time to do that and a lot of them lost feet when frostbite and trench foot set in. A lot of our paratroopers didn't even have overshoes.

Patton straightened me out

I met Patton one time. We were at a Command Post and he walked in like he was God Almighty Himself. I was by my jeep and he came over and said, "Sergeant, ain't it cold with that windshield down?" I said, "Sir, I don't mind it." He said, "You put it up, and right now!" The next day an order came that all windshields were to be up.

Another time one of our Lieutenant Colonel's asked him, "Well, General, what are you going to do when all the shooting stops?" Patton replied, "I'm going to wear a short coat so all you sons of bitches can kiss my ass!"

I'm glad I wasn't Patton. How would you feel about it if you were going to send 5,000 men into a place where maybe only 2,000 would come back? It would have to affect your mind.

Loading Germans with a forklift

The worst mess we saw was a ten-acre field loaded with dead Germans. We had some 2½-ton trucks. A black soldier used a two-prong forklift to jab into the pile of frozen bodies and load them onto the trucks, just like firewood. If that wouldn't cause him to go nuts, I don't know why.

Some other tough battles we got into were at Bras, Neiderwampach, and Oberwampach.

Ike didn't want to be identified

I told you about meeting Patton. Well, I saw Ike once, too. His jeep came along with his four general stars showing and we all popped to pretty fast. I remember that when he got out, his driver immediately got out and covered the stars. They didn't want to be identified. Of course, he was a West Point man. I respected them a lot. The first chewing out I got at Camp Barkeley was by a second lieutenant from West Point. By the end of the war, he was a full colonel and headed up our outfit. He knew what he was doing. A lot of our 90-day-wonders didn't know what to do or how to do it.

Ernie Frazier

You never know what a man is made of until he's tested. We had one Lieutenant in "L" Company. He was a hard bastard. He spent one day in combat and wound up a mental case. They hauled him out.

The battle of the Siegfried Line was from pillbox to pillbox. We were freezing and wasted no time in rousting the Krauts. We hit Binscheid and then took Holzchen. By the time we got to Arzfeld, we had the Krauts on the run.

On the 6th of March, we crossed the Kyll River and captured Gerolstein and Pelm. That created a bridgehead for the 11th Armored Division that was racing to the Rhine.

We secured another bridgehead at the Moselle River. It was defended by Hitler's fanatical SS mountain troops; but we took it.

We reached the Rhine River on March 18th.

When we crossed the Rhine, we had vehicles and tanks coming down the center of the bridge with infantry on either side. The whole time we were crossing, the Germans were dropping in mortar rounds.

On March 28th the Regiment loaded into assault boats and forced a crossing of the Main River. and plunged on across Germany through Stockheim Schlitz, Vacha and Merkers to Bad Salzungen, which was captured on April 3rd, 1945.

The fortunes of war

Third Battalion seized Merkers, which had a salt mine, and captured a fortune of gold and priceless art treasures that the Nazis had stolen.

Our regiment captured Hof, a large city near Czechoslovakia that was defended by the SS and the remnants of the German Army on April 15th.

On April 18, we were the first U. S. outfit to enter Czechoslovakia. On April 23, we liberated a large concentration camp and rescued over a

Tech Sgt Berger awarded Combat Infantryman Badge.

thousand starving Poles, Russians and French. Then, we moved on toward Susice.

The order came on May 8th for the battalions to cease-fire. We united with the Russian Armies and began the big job of rounding up the German Army.

The "Apple Jack" remembers

When I got home I got married, went to farming and raising kids. We have two boys alive and one buried. When I was 62 one son got married and took over the farm. My wife and I moved to town. She died of cancer in 1979.

I belong to the Odd Fellows Lodge. At the Grand Lodge in Topeka there is a guy who was called "Apple Jack". In the VA hospitals they have wards that brothers, sisters, fathers, and mothers can't go into. The "Apple Jack" went into that ward every day to give each patient an apple. It got to where he couldn't afford to do it anymore so the Odd Fellows and Masons and some other organizations helped him out. What you see in those hospitals lets you know what the curse of war is all about.

CHAPTER 26

BERT EARLS

"It took me a long time before I could walk on a path. I was watching for mines."

Bert received the Bronze Star for valor on the battlefield. As an unarmed medic, he didn't feel that he deserved it any more than any one else; an opinion expressed by most of the decorated men and women I interviewed. A retired teacher, he told me his story over coffee in the little town of Bucklin, Kansas, my wife's hometown. I always wondered why these types of stories weren't trumpeted from the rooftops in tribute to our heroes that won the war. Later, during the Korean War, I enlisted in the Army and met many soldiers who'd survived combat. I found out that they seldom want to re-live it.

Trying to get into the war at age 16!

My main concern, when the Japanese bombed Pearl Harbor on December 7th 1941, was that the war would be over before I could get into it. That was typical of our patriotism back then. My parents wouldn't sign a release so I could enlist. I was only sixteen and had to finish high school before I finally got into the Army. My initial indoctrination took place in Oklahoma City and Tulsa. Later, I was sent to Camp Barkeley, Texas for basic training and instruction in becoming a medic and clerk typist. Stephen Ambrose wrote that most medics were conscientious objectors. We were not conscientious objectors and I disagree with him on that. We didn't ask to be medics. That's just what we were assigned to do.

We were sent up to Camp Reynolds, Pennsylvania for more training. In particular, we had to qualify with the M-1 rifle (I made expert) by firing from the prone position for long periods in the snow. By the time we arrived at our port of embarkation at Camp Shank, New York, I had come down with pneumonia. I would've been out in a few days but some patient contracted a disease that caused them to quarantine the hospital and I had to spend about a month in there. I wound up doing KP and typing.

One night they jerked me out of bed, took my picture and put me in a different barracks. We were on 24-hour call. They would say, "Get everything ready, we are ready to leave." That happened three or four times and then all of a sudden we found ourselves on a ship.

We went to England and landed at Liverpool during the latter part of April somewhere close to the Cliffs of Dover. They put us on a ship and left us there that night and the next day during the D-Day landings. We didn't land at Omaha Beach until after D-Day. We were replacements and weren't with any division.

Fast action!

We got into action pretty fast. After our landing, I remember a whole bunch of us walking down a road and an airplane came diving in. What did we do? We just stood there looking at it. The war got real when it cut loose with its machine gun and we scrambled for cover. It wounded and killed some of our guys up in front of me. We learned very quickly to get out of the way when a plane came by. That night they put me in a pup tent by myself. I heard a Browning Automatic Rifle go off just outside the tent. The next morning I asked somebody what that was all about and he said, "Oh some guy shot a cow."

Strange characters

They gave me a typewriter and I typed all that day. That evening they called my name and said they needed medics up at the 83rd Division. They put two of us in the back of a truck with two guys who were acting kind of strange. We were replacement medics. We weren't very far from the front lines and soon we could hear all of the shelling and sounds of battle. Without saying a word, those two guys took off out the back of the truck. I guess they had been in combat and couldn't stand anymore.

Sleeping with the dead

We got up the road and the driver stopped the truck and pointed a direction for me to go and sent the other guy another way. It was late in the evening and the battlefield was strewn with bodies. Since I was a medic and didn't know what else to do, I started checking them. Pretty soon it got dark. I needed a place to sleep so I crawled into a huge bomb crater. The next morning I got up and looked around. I'd slept all night beside two dead soldiers.

Still in Normandy, I kept walking toward where I heard the shelling until I found the aid station. They had told me I was supposed to be with the 83rd Division, the 329th Regiment, but I think they got mixed up because I was at an aid station where I don't think I was supposed to be. In fact I found out later my parents had gotten a telegram saying I was missing in action. When somebody asked me about it later, I said, "No, the army might have been missing, but I wasn't. I knew where I was."

No fear--at first!

When I first went into battle I wasn't afraid of anything and I had been told, "Hey, you're a medic, you're not going to get shot at." I learned different. We were shot at. We went out day after day for months on end. I don't know how to say it: You just do your job. You become numb and do your job, but you're scared, sure. There were some who weren't scared and I think some of them were a little bit loony.

They'd yell, "Medic!"

I guess they sent me out alone to learn what to do. I would go out from the aid station and somebody would yell, "Medic," and I would take off in that direction. I'd been told that being a medic we weren't going to get shot at and I took chances there in Normandy that I learned not to take later on. I got shot at a lot. We weren't allowed to carry guns. They tell me over in the Pacific it was different. We had white crosses on our arms and helmets. Later, they had me taking litter squads out to pick up the wounded and bring them back to the aid station. I did that all through Normandy.

I would say the most dramatic battle I witnessed was in Normandy in the hedgerows. We came in after the invasion, probably on the 27th or 28th of June. The invasion forces had landed in Normandy on the 6th of June. There was still a complete mess on the beach when we landed and terrible fighting continued all the while we were in Normandy and Brittany.

Jumping into a booby trap!

You name it, I've seen it: heads cut off, bodies blown apart, legs, arms. One time in the hedgerow—and I don't know how this happened—there must have been six or seven medics all standing around in one area when the Germans cut loose with mortars. We all jumped in foxholes. There were only two of us that didn't get hit. They had booby-trapped the foxholes. Three or four lost legs. I still *don't know to this day why so many medics got together. They were from different outfits.*

Tree bursts were a terrible thing to experience. German artillerymen timed their shells to go off when they hit the tops of trees, and boy you didn't dare get under them. I remember once in the hedgerows, I heard a yell for medics and I took off. I jumped in a foxhole and every time I would rise up the Germans would fire on me with a machine gun.

Running between machine gun bursts

I timed the bursts and I jumped and rolled over to the next hole where one of our soldiers had shot himself in the foot. His buddy asked me, "What are you going to do?" I said, "He can crawl out with me, because that's how I'm going out." I wouldn't do anything else because he made me mad by shooting himself and exposing us to so much danger.

From talking to some of the others later, I understand that the Battle of the Bulge was worse: not just the battles, but also the weather. The worst part I went through was the hedgerows. You couldn't see the enemy. We would be in one hedgerow and the Germans would be in two hedgerows ahead of you. They had booby traps in trees, foxholes and everywhere. Fields were mined. After I got out of the service, it took me a long time before I would walk on a path, because I was watching for mines.

One time I remember there in the hedgerows seeing a guy out there just wandering around with no gun, no nothing, going the wrong direction. He didn't know anything and was just like a zombie. I turned him around and headed him to the aid station. I don't know what happened to him. I would guess he was shell-shocked.

In the hedgerows we had this aid station. After that we stayed in foxholes or buildings of any kind we could find. I got one bath in September or October. They gave us a change of clothing and I think we had three minutes to take a shower. We never took our clothes or boots off since the last part of June. We all smelled the same. We didn't take our clothes off. Being medics, we never knew when we would have to go out. The guys in foxholes never took their clothes off either. They slept in their clothes.

Right between the eyes

One night I was leading our squad over a railroad track when a machine gun pinned us down. This buddy of mine wasn't over 10 feet from me, and I heard him sigh and looked over at him. A bullet had hit him right between the eyes. I could have reached out and touched him.

Twenty thousand Germans on horses, wagons and bicycles

Did you ever hear of the 20,000 that surrendered? After the break through at the Bulge and after St. Malo, the Germans left and tried to go back to Germany. There were 20,000 who wanted to surrender. They sent me down with some medics to set up an aid station. I read later that there were 20,000 Germans and us. They came in, surrendering their rifles and pistols because they were afraid of the free French. Actually it was kind of a comical thing. Here came the defeated Germans riding horses, in wagons, on bicycles, tickled to death to get out of the war. The only guys we had to treat at the aid station were two GI's who shot themselves accidentally with German Lugers.

One German asked one of the American GI's for a cigarette and the guy told him, "Yeah, I'll give you one for $100." The rest of us really didn't give them a hard of time.

St. Malo is where the German's had four or five years to build up their fortifications. They created an underground citadel of concrete and dirt. We had a heck of a time there. One of the German colonels didn't want to surrender. They sent my squad over to talk to them about surrendering. We had to walk across this big tall abutment by the ocean.

The colonel could speak English. When he came back to talk to our officers, he kept looking at me and asking, "Why don't you surrender now?" I don't know why he was asking me. Anyway, they finally surrendered. From there we went clear to Luxembourg.

Ernie Frazier

At Luxembourg, we medics were supposed to go in right behind our attacking infantry. Along came one of our trucks with two black guys. Remember, we weren't integrated yet and that was the first time I had ever seen any black troops over there. They said they were from graves registration. That seemed kind of funny because they usually didn't show up until a long time after the battle. About that time the Germans cut loose with artillery and they got in that truck and took off. That was the last we saw of them. We had a hard time figuring out just why they were there. It didn't make sense.

Luxembourg was more or less the same thing. We could see the Siegfried line. The Germans had already retreated across over into Germany then. On November the 12th I was wounded.

I was wounded twice over there. The first time I was wounded while I was in Normandy. It was just a slight wound and didn't amount to anything. It was a machine gun bullet. It hit along my chest and was really just a scratch. I've had both bullets and shrapnel hit my helmet and my shirt. I was really lucky.

<u>A Bronze Star at St. Malo</u>

The second time, I was in a jeep going out to check on a wounded guy when I heard a noise. The first thing you learn to do is hit the ground. I didn't quite make it when I jumped. Shrapnel caught me in the leg before I landed. At that time, you have to remember, I was an old timer. The other guys stayed in the jeep and it never touched them. I think it was mortar fire, but I don't know for sure. All I know is I heard the explosion. I was lucky because my guys just turned around and took me back to the aid station. I wasn't injured all that bad. When I was discharged, it was with 40% disability, which was later cut to 20% and now it's 10%, so it's not bad. I received the Bronze Star at St. Malo.

I was lucky that I was wounded before the brutal winter weather set in and lots of our guys got their feet frozen. At that time I didn't think I was so lucky, but I was.

They sent me to a field hospital where they did surgery. From there I think I went to Paris. At least they said we were in Paris. They put a cast all the way up my leg. From there I went to a hospital not far from South Hampton, England, and then was sent back to the states.

When I was down at the Army General Hospital being discharged, they offered me a corporal's rating if I would stay and do some clerical work. I told them I had all I wanted of the army.

I got a bunch of Lugers and other weapons. I lost everything when I was wounded. Some guys in the Air Force came up later wanting to offer us $100 apiece for those things and I said, "Heck, I don't want them, you can just have them." When I was wounded I lost my barracks bag and everything, so I didn't come back with anything.

I was in the army for two years. I went in June of 1943 and got out in June of 1945. I was just a private; being a replacement there was no way I was going to get anything else.

If you will look at the statistics, there are about 80,000 in World War II who are missing in action and I never heard a thing about anybody trying to find them. Now there are two or three thousand in Vietnam missing in action. I've always said Vietnam was probably the worst war we ever had. I remember all those demonstrations. People who came back were actually looked down on. I've talked to some Vietnam vets and it was a different war. We actually knew who we were fighting. The Germans were in uniform. We could tell. Our government was behind us too.

I would say the front line infantry—the guys who lived in the foxholes and did the actual fighting—got my respect the most. In a division of 15,000 there were only three or four thousand who actually did any combat.

When I was a senior, married and getting ready to graduate from college, the Army offered several of us first lieutenant ratings if we would go back into the service. I know I wasn't interested, and I don't think the others were either. That was in 1950. Korea was cranking up. Second lieutenants probably suffered the highest percentage of wounds and casualties of anyone. The medics ran a close second. While others could stay in foxholes, we had to get out and pick up troops on the battlefield. And we weren't armed.

Ernie Frazier

CHAPTER 27

STAN SUTTON

"Seven out of the 18 pilots in our squadron were killed."

In June 1941, the Great Depression still held mid-America in its grip. Stan Sutton at age 21 saw few opportunities for making a living. War was coming so he enlisted in the Navy as an aviation cadet. He went to Jacksonville, Florida, and then to Corpus Christi, Texas to train as a dive-bomber. December 7th rolled around and Pearl Harbor was bombed while he was still in flight training. By May 1942, he'd received his commission and was home on leave.

A new bride and bad tires

The battle of Midway Island was fought on June 4th, 5th and 6th while I was still on leave. My fiancée, Dolores Van Voorhees, and I were wondering whether to marry prior to my going overseas. I believe it was on the 5th that I got a telegram ordering me to report immediately to Com-air-pac. We got married that night and started out the next morning for the Naval Air Station at San Diego. Our old car had two good tires and two that weren't so good. It was impossible to buy new tires. We were afraid to try to cross the desert at Needles, California with tires that could blow at any time. I was able to locate a re-liner (a tire within a tire) and put it on. In the morning, we found it was flat so I went to the rationing board. They gave us two new tires and we made it to San Diego.

I joined Torpedo Squadron 10. It was one of the first squadrons to have the TBF, which was the Avenger airplane. Most of my training was on two passenger planes. The TBF, a torpedo plane, had a pilot, turret gunner with a 50-caliber machine gun and a radioman with a 30 caliber. We could carry one torpedo or a 400 or 500-pound bomb along with 2,000 pounds of detonating product. Our bombing would be considered light bombing as opposed to divebombing which meant coming in at a steeper angle.

Within six weeks, orders came for us to leave but we didn't know what our destination was. Alaska? Maybe. Actually we were placed on a troop ship, The USS Republican, and sailed for Hawaii.

At Kaneohe Bay we practiced field carrier landings for about a month and then headed out to sea. We'd seldom seen an aircraft carrier up to that point but now we had to qualify landing on them. We actually qualified because the wind was blowing from the south. If we had not qualified, we would have been returned to land and stayed there. About half our squadron was there and we all qualified. Some of the boys brought down by ship later didn't qualify. But, the group I was in was on our way to combat.

Bombing Guadalcanal

We went down to Fiji and spent three or four days taking on provisions before going on to New Caledonia. That became our homeport and we would go out of there on a carrier.

We island hopped all the way up to Efate and Espiritu Santo and on to Guadalcanal where our troops were fighting a fierce battle. We spent two tours bombing the area, relieving our Marines.

The United States had us more or less waiting until they got more ships in the area. All we had in the South Pacific at that time was the Enterprise and the Saratoga. We had no CVEs, the small carriers, in the area. While at sea, our combat air patrol would shoot down at the fighter squadron that was guarding the Japanese fleet. We'd shoot down a Jap plane about every day.

For a while we operated with the HMS Victoria, a British aircraft carrier that was in the water with us. Our planes would go out on search parties every day, 200 to 300 miles, to see if we could spot anything. We'd fly about 1,000 feet above the ocean, as it was the best distance for visibility, and fire on any enemy aircraft that we could find. In addition, our combat air patrol was over our fleet all the time at about 20,000 feet.

Mostly, we were bombing up in the Solomon Islands and I only had the opportunity to fire on enemy aircraft three or four times.

Seven of our eighteen pilots killed

We had both marines and army soldiers fighting there. The majority were marines.

We bombed Bougainville, which was about 300 miles from Guadalcanal and Kolombanagara where the Japs were trying to build an airfield. We bombed the hell out of it with dive-bombers, torpedo planes and fighters. Seven out of eighteen pilots were killed from our squadron alone. One of them, George Schunke from Michigan, was shot down and made a forced landing on Bougainville. He never got out of the airplane.

A terrible death

The Japs must have caught him before he got out and planted a grenade in his belly and blew him up. We got the report later about him.

Dave Feldenthaul was a nice Jewish kid from Shreveport, Louisiana that I roomed with for a while. He was always asking, "How far is it to Shreveport?"

He disappeared and we never found out for sure what happened. His plane probably went down in the ocean.

Another kid—named Keyes—from Wichita, Kansas ran out of fuel when making an approach to the carrier and ditched in the ocean. A destroyer picked him up about 1,000 feet behind the carrier. His stomach had ruptured and he died after they got him back to the carrier.

Landing empty!

I had my closest call when we flew back from a nighttime mission and I ran out of fuel. I had to wave off (circle around the ship) because of a foul deck. I made it around and came back and landed empty on the carrier. There wasn't even enough fuel in my tank to taxi any further.

There were 18 pilots and about 80 planes in our squadron: a torpedo squadron that I was in, a scout bombing squadron, and a dive-bombing and a fighter squadron that were interchangeable.

We were all on pins and needles until we'd get in the air. Then we were cool, calm and collected. When the mission was over, we'd unwind and kind of fall apart a little bit.

Our intelligence people provided maps for us to use in locating targets. They had spotters—a lot were Australians—or natives from the region. Also, our army had a P38 that would go up high every day and photograph the area.

Anderson Field on Guadalcanal was one of our fly off points. When we came in there we could hear gunfire just off the airstrip. We were on the front lines, just beyond the battles that were being fought on the ground. One of our guys bought a Thompson sub-machine gun and went out for some target practice. It wasn't five minutes until someone was on his ass saying, "There'll be no firing in this area." I could see that some of our guys in battle just a few yards from us would be unnerved if they heard shots from behind. One pilot in our outfit, Fos Blaire from Pennsylvania, was shot down and spent 24 hours in the water. The navy rescued him with one of their coast watchers. Somebody had spotted his life jacket and radioed back the location.

A brother killed at age 19

Later I came back to Pearl Harbor. My brother was a gunner on a dive-bomber and his ship—I think it was the Bellwood—had just docked there. We had two days of liberty together before I was to come back to the mainland. We stayed up all night over in one of the hangers. We got a fifth of booze apiece and had a great visit. A short time later, we got word that he was killed in the South Pacific. He was declared missing in action and we never knew what happened to him. It was 1943. He died at 19. I was 23.

Back in the states I was assigned as a combat instructor on torpedo planes in Jacksonville and Miami, Florida. After the war ended, I was sent to Croswell, Michigan to form a squadron.

I got out a little later but stayed in the reserves where I had a Tac Squadron 56.

I did a lot of flying after the war for a construction company and as a crop duster and managed a municipal airport.

Recalled for Korea

In 1951, I was called back to active duty. The Korean War was on and seven or eight of us guys were called back to instruct pilots in fighter tactics even though we weren't fighter pilots. It was no problem for us.

I didn't go to Korea but trained pilots and instructors who were training pilots in Memphis, Jacksonville, and Pensacola. By that time I was a Lt. Commander and went through helicopter school. After that, I sat on a Comair Atlantic Court Martial board at Norfolk.

Afterward I returned to Jacksonville. The navy wanted an older man with no jet plane experience—me at 33—to serve as the guinea pig on a two-passenger jet, learning to fly under instruments. It worked out just fine.

I loved the Naval Air Corps but could see I probably wasn't really going anywhere in the navy, so I decided to pack it in and return home to my family.

Back home I flew for several years and helped build the Kansas Turnpike. In 1956 I bought a Coca Cola franchise and ran it for 23 years. Currently I'm employed as a real estate agent.

CHAPTER 28

M. J. COMBEST

"I was a Kriegie."

The diary of Lt. Merwin J. Combest, a Kriegie, was started after he'd been imprisoned in Stalag Luft 1, Barth, Germany. Krieg is a German word for war. Prisoners of war were known as Kriegies. There were some 2,000 American, Polish, British, Belgian, Yugoslavian, French, New Zealand, Australian, South African, and Canadian officers incarcerated there, some as long as five years. Russian officers were there but for reasons unknown to the prisoners were separated from the others.

Lt. Combest lived to return home to his beloved wife, Twilla and their daughter Signe. Tragically, he died less than two years later in an airplane crash. Dirk, his new son, was ten months old. Now in his 50's, Dirk provided me with a brief commentary of his own and a copy of the diary his dad compiled while a prisoner of war.

Dad was the co-pilot on a B-24 bomber that had taken off from their base in Italy on their eighth bombing mission. The crew of eight young Americans—two pilots, a bombardier, navigator, nose, tail, and two turret gunners—were soon flying high over Austria. There,

German anti-aircraft batteries opened up. Flak ripped the plane and it began to careen out of control. The Pilot screamed for the men to jump and six men leaped from the plane. Two of the gunners stayed in their seats. They had been killed in the barrage. Dad floated down and saw that he was going to land right in the middle of an anti-aircraft battery. German soldiers were ready and he was captured immediately.

The diary covers the last two months of his imprisonment. The Russian (Joe's) armies had moved within eighty miles of the prison. The prisoners were living on meager rations, which is reflected in the Lieutenant's preoccupation with hunger. The guards enforced their rules and prisoners were being shot. The diary--only selected passages are featured here--reflecting the anxiety, fear, hunger, and hope experienced by Lt. Combest during his ordeal.

He added portions of letters that various prisoners received from home. I've interjected some of those throughout the diary as a means of exposing the unbelievable ironies resulting from captivity and the pitiful lack of understanding and empathy that many of their loved ones displayed in light of the prisoner's circumstances.

Those excerpts, written mostly by wives and sweethearts—at least the prisoners thought they were their loved ones—would have been hilarious if they weren't so tragic.

The Diary

March 8, 1945: I wish I had started this a year ago but I didn't so I'll start now. We are having cold and dreary weather. I think that I've been shivering steadily all winter. We don't get enough coal to keep the room warm more than for a day or two. When I get back to the states I'll never let my stomach even begin to get low on food. You never know when you may have to do without it so eat while you can. I thought we didn't have enough to eat when we got a Red Cross parcel every week but we haven't had a full parcel since the first of February and that was more like a quarter at a time.

Letter to Lt. J. M. from ex-wife

" James: I'll be glad when you get home so I can make our divorce final. I've been living with an Infantry Captain for some time. He is really swell."

The Red Cross man was here last week and instructed our ration man not to issue more than one-half parcel at a time even if we get a supply in because the Germans don't have the transportation to get it to us since the Russians are so close. (C'mon Joe!) They're only 80 miles away now. I never in my life thought I would go so hungry for so long. I didn't think I could stand it and I'm still not sure. We're getting one meal a day—about a half-cup of German stew, which is rotten stuff. But, I'm sure glad to get it. Pop used to say I would eat a lot of things and like them some day. I'm damn glad to get this stuff but I don't like it.

Letter to Lt. P. T. from home

" Son, we are not sending you any parcels. We hear that you can buy all you need in the stores near your camp."

Nesbitt has had it as far as I'm concerned. I've given him candy and gum and biscuits, etc., and also one of those big Argentina chocolate bars out of my two packages along with some coffee. He got a package the other day and didn't offer me a bite.
March 11, 1945: The food situation is still no better. I had 4 very thin slices of bread, two boiled potatoes and fifteen spoons full of stew today. I didn't know you could live on so little but we've been doing it for two weeks now and didn't have much more for the past month.

Letter to Lt. B. S. from a sister

"I am so worried over Adolph, the cat. I took him to the veterinarian yesterday and he said his diet was insufficient."

Ernie Frazier

March 12, 1945:   Our intelligence officers advised us to start making knapsacks to prepare for our evacuation. We expect the Jerries to march us out soon but they haven't mentioned it yet.

I've been counting our money again. With our savings and what I can borrow, I could go into farming, which may be the best considering all the angles.

Letter to Lt. J. A. from wife

" Darling: Sorry I can't send you any money but I'll send a wallet the first chance I get."

March 14, 1945: Scoubo got a package from home. What a break for him. It came at just the right time. Shuman got six more cartons of Luckies today. That makes 24 cartons he's received. I bought a carton for 4 slices of bread. It's a really good deal because in another month the value of cigarettes is going up again. Even if rations come in regularly, which isn't likely, the most we can get is three packs a week.

Nesbitt got another package today. That's two in two weeks right in the middle of the famine. He still hasn't offered me a thing. Tomorrow I'm going to give him a chance to offer me something.

March 18, 1945: Things are getting ROUGHER. The Jerries shot two of our men today. One, an American, died. The Englishman is still alive. They're killing us with the slightest excuse. We're supposed to stay inside during air raids but one man stuck his head out the window. The other was washing clothes and went out to hang up his stuff. He didn't know an air raid was on. A year ago we'd stand out in the middle of the compound during an air raid and razz the tower guards by yelling "Rostock", or "Berlin kapoot!" We certainly don't do things like that anymore.

Letter to Lt. A. R. O. from sweetheart

" My darling, I'm sure they are treating you very well because they tell me so here in the USA."

I'm a pilot and prefer to fly when I get out, but there'll be an awful lot of pilots after the same jobs. If I could fly until I'm about 40, I could save enough money to invest in farming and live comfortably the rest of my life. That's my life plan. If I could only live it I would be happy, I think.

Letter to Lt. H. B. from mother

" Son: If you need any money let me know."

March 21, 1945: We had a few bites of barley for breakfast this week. It wasn't much but every little bit helps. I feel like I'm about to starve to death. I'm the weakest I've been since I had my tonsils out and lost so much blood. The least exercise wears me out all day.

Letter to Lt. G. H. K. from wifie

" Dear Bill: I went to the Red Cross the other day to find out what I should send you. They told me that you probably could send me packages as you have so much food and clothes over there now. They also said you could go to school and learn a trade."

March 25, 1945: Boy the news is hot. I believe we have a good chance of getting home in early summer after all. We are getting lights now until 10:00 p.m. The weather is beautiful and I've been sunning myself.

Letter to Lt. M. C. L. from wife

"My Darling Husband: Do you get to town very often while a prisoner of war?"

April 1, 1945: Good times are here again. 70,000 Red Cross and 2,000 personal parcels are now in the camp. The famine is over. From the sound of the news, we won't be here much longer.

Ernie Frazier

April 3, 1945: Max Schmelling, the German heavyweight boxer, is in the compound on a public relations tour. Everyone is gathering around to get his autograph.

Some mail is coming in. I got a letter dated 44 days ago and that's the best service I've gotten.

April 5, 1945: The mess hall burned down yesterday morning. We all turned out to form a bucket brigade but we couldn't slow it down. It was completely gone in an hour. We salvaged a lot of wet bread. We toasted it and for once had enough bread to eat. It's another Saturday night, my 59th I believe. That's a long time to spend in prison.

Letter to Lt. L. B. P. from an Aunt

"Honey: I'm enclosing a calendar. Thought it might come in handy as it has several years on it."

April 14, 1945: I hope the snapshots that Twilla mentioned in her letter a couple of months ago come in this batch of mail as I don't expect any more until we're liberated. Also, it's just as well that Signe won't say "Da" because I don't want her to be saying that to every man who comes along. It looks bad.

Letter to Flight Officer J. R. C. from wife

" Dear John: I gave your golf clubs to a German Colonel, a prisoner of war here in Canada. I hope you don't mind."

Note: John did mind, wrote back and told her to get his clubs back and to ---! with the German P. O. W.

John's country club immediately canceled his membership for ungentlemanly conduct!

April 15, 1945: Every day I expect the American drive to stop, but it's still going. If they keep it up, we should be out of here in just a few days. I've been here so long that I just can't feature the fact that it is 'possible' for us to be liberated soon. I'll sure be disappointed if I don't get home to Twilla and Signe soon. I've never let my optimism build up so high before and it'll be an awful let down if we don't get out shortly.

Letter to Warrant Officer from wife

"Dear John: I am going to file for divorce. Mother and I have talked it over and since you've been gone so long (over four years) we decided this was best."

April 20, 1945: The American drive stopped three or four days ago but the Russians are opening up. We hear there are terrific battles west of town and we could hear artillery fire all night.

April 24, 1945: Twilla's birthday. I sure wish I could be with her. I love her so much and I really miss her.

Letter to R. A. F. Sergeant from wife

"I have been living with a private since you are gone. Please do not cut off my allotment as he does not make as much money as you."

April 26, 1945: I put my name down for a set of Wear-Eaver aluminum cookware today from a guy that'll get me a 25% discount and priority. I've signed up for so much stuff I can't even remember it all. The main thing is this; If any good deals come out of this place I'll be in on them. If not, I don't have to worry and will just disregard it. I ordered a couple of books on Kriegie life and records of songs written and played here by our orchestra.

A month ago I said that a man could live very well without sex. Now that I'm back on a regular diet with a fresh supply of vitamin pills, the old urge is right there again. I guess I haven't aged as much as I thought.

April 29, 1945: We heard the Russians are 50 miles southeast of here and may roll in any minute. I never would have believed the Germans could hold on this long.

I bet $50 on Reeder vs. Griffith in a boxing match today. Griffith was a Golden Gloves champ in Chicago but Reeder beat him in a match last summer. Hope I win.

Ernie Frazier

We got all the records featured on the Hit Parade. We adopted the number one record, Don't Fence Me In, as our theme song.

April 30, 1945: The war doesn't lack much of being over. The Jerries have been moving out all day. Only a few are still here. The Flak school is only about 1/4 mile from here. They blew up all their equipment and then blasted the airport. Jerry soldiers and civilians broke into our Red Cross parcels that were stored in the flak school so we went over—no guards accompanied us—to rescue them.

We're not legally free just yet but our own C. O. won't let us out anyway. It's for our own protection. We thought the German civilians would make an attack on this place, but they are doing just the opposite and are trying to get on the bandwagon at the last moment.

We expect the Russians to get here tonight or tomorrow. We dug slit trenches outside our windows today just in case the Russians let a few stray shells fall around the area.

May 1, 1945: The camp was officially turned over to us last night at 11:20. I lost $20 by forty minutes. (The prisoners placed bets on when they would be liberated as they did many things during their imprisonment to pass the time.) The Russians are about 3 kilometers from here and Colonel Zempke is in contact with their liaison officer. The Colonel is a good C. O. He had everything planned out and organized ahead of time so that when we took over everything went like clockwork. It's sure good to see that white flag on the flagpole instead of the Nazi flag. It'll be even better when we get the American flag up.

We got to listen to the British Broadcasting Company's version of the news tonight. When they mentioned the Baltic Pocket, we knew they were talking about us.

It'll probably be a week before we get shipped out of here. I think going home will be just like coming to life after you've been dead. I don't expect to be home to see Twilla for about a month. It'll be the slowest month in history, even longer than the fourteen months I've been here.

Letter to Lt. from father

"Dear son: I knew I should have kept you at home and joined the Air Corp myself. Even when you were a kid I expected you to end up in prison."

10:15 p. m. That was a false alarm about the Russians being here this morning, BUT THEY'RE HERE NOW! WHOOPEE! GOOD OLD JOE! He finally came through. There will be no sleep tonight. What a day!

10:25 p. m. The radio just announced that Hitler is dead. My God! What a day! They're playing Don't Fence Me In. We'll be together on our wedding anniversary, honey! We can't fail now!

Letter to R. A. F. Sergeant from fiancee

" Sergeant: You can consider our friendship at an end. I would rather be engaged to a 1944 hero than a 1943 coward".

May 3, 1945: They just played The Star Spangled Banner over the public address system. Right here in the very same place that we have been under the heel of the Jerry B- - - - - - d for so long.

The Russians moved in force yesterday morning. They are TOUGH BOYS and I don't mean maybe. Watching them occupying a territory is an experience that you can't imagine. It's not hard to see why the Germans flee before the Russians. Colonel Zempke was going to keep us in camp to keep us out of trouble, but, a Russian Colonel rode in and gave orders to let us out or he would bring in tanks to tear down the fences. They don't argue. What they say goes and they are all drunk most of the time. And when they take a town, they TAKE IT! No kidding. They're more like a Guerrilla band moving in than an army. The Germans are terrified and I would be, too.

When they turned us out, I went to town and found a beautiful model of an ME-109. I tried talking to a Russian in the street to see if he'd be interested in buying it. He took it and looked it over. When he saw the German insignia, he slammed it down on the pavement and smashed it. I smiled and said "Komarad" and got the hell out of there.

The Russians are looting everything in town and it's really a mess. If anyone says anything to them about it, they quiet them quickly and permanently. They're tough! I'd hate to have them on the other side. Yesterday at 2:00 they said they wanted us out in six hours. We had a big hubba hubba. We were supposed to just follow up behind the front lines on our own. We finally got them to let us stay until some American planes come for us.

Lt. C. P. N. from Letter to a girl he met and dated only once two years earlier

"I am going to spend the summer with your folks. They are fine and all your relatives are very kind. All the girls around are worrying about the man shortage and being old maids. But, maybe we can beat that when you get home. YOUR LOVING FIANCEE."

I milked a cow yesterday and had fresh milk for the first time in eighteen months.

The Russians wanted us in town yesterday so they could display 8,000 Kriegies being liberated but a few boys got killed and today we are restricted to the peninsula. I prefer to get along with them because you can't tell if they're in a good or bad mood. Some of our boys showed up at the wrong places and they won't go home because of it. The Russians are short tempered. When they start shooting, they just fire in a general area. If anybody is in the way, that's just tough. The average soldier didn't even know we were in the area.

Letter to Lt. J. C. E. from wife

" Dear J: Please have a picture taken and send it to me."

There are five or six of the worst concentration camps within five miles. Our doctors are working out there every day. We won't get to see the camps, and I don't want to. I won't describe them here but it's easy to see why these Russians are so tough. They weren't front line troops, but are guerrilla bands and terrorists sent in to clean up. If I taveled with them for a while I would torture every German I could find.

Letter to Lt. V. H. from his wife

" Dear V: When and if you do get back, I'd like a divorce. I'm living with a cadet at Santa Ana, California and I'd like to marry him. He is a wonderful fellow, and I know you will like him."

One camp was dug in '39, presumably as an air raid shelter. Our people found a dungeon where 27 men and women were shackled to the wall for one to three years. The stench was terrible and they had to wear gas masks to go in. When the captives were brought out into the fresh air most of them died immediately.

Letter to Lt. W. J. E. from wife

" Dear W: Sorry to hear you are a P. O. W. We thought you were dead."

May 6, 1945: I may be leaving the wrong impression of the Russians. I kind of like them myself. They're eager to please the 'Amerikancki'. They're just like a big clumsy puppy playing with a little kid. They are supplying us with fresh meat and bread. If you ask them for something they don't have such as milk, eggs, or anything else, they'll hand you their gun and motion you to go get it.

Letter to Captain S. W. C. from wife

"Dear S: It must be nice to be able to play golf again."

May 7, 1945: BBC just announced that Stalag Luft 1 had been liberated and next of kin are being notified and we're told every day to prepare for evacuation. Our airfield is ready and we don't know why they haven't come for us.

Ernie Frazier

Letter to P. O. W. from woman who sent a him a sweater through the Red Cross

" I am sorry to hear that a prisoner received the sweater I knitted. I made it for a fighting man."

We had a Russian stage show today with three beautiful girls, or at least I thought so. It's been a long time since I've seen any beautiful women.
May 9, 1945: The Russians gave us 500 cows and tried to give us 1,000 pigs but we couldn't handle them. So, we got them anyway. If the Russians want to give you something, you have to take it.

Letter to Lt. from his father (a complete letter)

" Dear son: Hello! How are you? We are all well. With love from all, Dad."

Letter to Lt. C. B. C. from cousin (another complete letter)

"Dear C: Keep 'em flying!"

May 13, 1945: At 9:00 a. m. this morning we boarded a B-17. Six thousand men were evacuated today so the air was thick with planes. I thought when the news reported that a city had been leveled that was just a figure of speech, but I was wrong. Munster is terrible, almost nothing left there. Cologne is worse. I don't think it'll ever be a city again.

Letter to a Lt. from his wiie

" Darling: Suppose you are close to Frankfurt and Cologne. We have a man here in the office who has lived near these places. He says they are beautiful and has told me many nice things about them."

We landed in France, were loaded into trucks and came to Rheims where we got a typhus shot, ate supper and waited around for our next flight.

May 14, 1945: I got hauled about ten miles down the road where I got a shower and new G. I. clothes.

I expect to go out to Le Havre this morning.

Letter to Lt. B. L. from wife

" I find it difficult to live on your $200 allotment each month."

***

Additional Reading

In 1946 Lt. Morris J. Roy, authored a book about the prison, <u>Behind Barbed Wire</u>, which was published by Richard R. Smith, New York. Since the Reich could not work the prisoners in Stalag Luft 1, the captives had to find ways to occupy their time. Remarkably, they turned out a daily (underground) newspaper full of war news, produced a variety of plays for their own entertainment, operated a library which was patronized by many, organized a glee club, wrote music, arranged boxing matches, ball games and other sporting events, created a sort of arts and crafts show which exhibited their handiwork, and made clocks and clothing. They wrote and illustrated their book and it was all done behind barbed wire while under the strict eye of their German guards.

<u>Welcome To P. O. W. Camp Stalag Luft 1, Barth Germany</u> is the title of a non-copyrighted cartoon book created by Flight Sgt. Budgen of the R. A. F. and Squadron Leader B. Arct, a Belgian flier attached to the R.A.F. It was lithographed by Edwards G. Broughton Company, Raleigh, North Carolina.

This excerpt from an old newspaper tells of some of the events that occurred after the war: A prisoner of war medal was recently awarded to Twilla Kraus, Ransom, for her first husband, the late Merwin J. Combest, for his service in World War II.

Ernie Frazier

Excerpt

In 1944, Combest was a Second Lieutenant and serving as co-pilot of a B-24 bomber in the 15th Air Force Division based in Italy. In February, that year, he was shot down over Austria and reported missing in action. Later in April1944, the family was notified that Combest was taken prisoner by the Germans and held in Stalag Luft 1, Barth, Germany. In April1945, the prison camp was liberated by the Russians and he returned to the United States in June1945. Combest died in a plane crash April 21, 1947 while serving in the Army Reserves.

CHAPTER 29

GEORGE QUASENBARTH

"Sometimes we had to scrape out body parts so we could repair a tank."

    The majority of military personnel are unsung heroes who provide support services for the combat units. George was a support soldier, the man behind the man behind the gun who kept everything working. He and his comrades toiled outside in freezing sleet and snow, sometimes under enemy bombardment, to repair disabled tanks, trucks, artillery pieces, and other equipment. Without them, the Allies would have never won the war.

Ernie Frazier

__Watch repairmen and blacksmiths__

I was drafted in November of 1942, took 14 weeks of basic at Ft. Riley—part of it was in the medical corps—and then was assigned to the 9th Army Division and wound up studying engineering at the Colorado School of Mines. After my time there, I was sent to Camp Cook, California to join the 11th Armored Division.

I was put into a combat ordinance outfit. Our job was to overhaul and keep the division's equipment operating. We had guys that could fix watches. Then we had blacksmiths with old time forges, anvils and hammers. Some of our people had worked on racecars at the Indianapolis Speedway and others who'd worked in automobile factories. They were a skilled outfit and could fix just about anything.

I was in Company A of the 133rd Ordinance. We serviced combat command, which consisted of a battalion of tanks, a company of infantry and a company of artillery.

We shipped out to England. The first thing General Patton told us when we got there was, "We didn't bring you over here to fight. Your job is to keep our stuff rolling because it's worthless if you don't."

While we were in Patton's army, I never met him. They said he was a stickler for fuel. Guys said, "Don't ever pour gasoline to start a fire to keep warm. Patton will get on you in a minute."

I did see General Eisenhower once. He was standing in a jeep that pulled off the road so we could go by.

We crossed the English Channel on about the 17th of December and landed in Cherbourg in a storm. One of our ships broke an anchor chain and had to go back to England for a new one. I slept through the whole crossing because I'd been driving a truck for about 24 straight hours.

Once we landed, we pushed on to Paris. About all I remember was one street called the Champs-Elysees. We got into trouble when one driver got to looking around and ran into the trailer in front of him and we had a wreck right there. I didn't even get to drive down the Arc de Triomphe because we turned off toward Lyon.

Combat came on Christmas Day

It was Christmas day, 1944 and we encountered our first enemy fire. We were parked in our trucks along the street when the Germans opened up, killing several Frenchmen that were on bicycles nearby. One of our guys got missed by six inches while he was sleeping in his truck.

They made me a parts clerk, which meant I ordered and supplied repair parts to the units that needed them. Huge trucks and other equipment were used to haul or drag in big stuff like tanks or tank tracks.

Spearheading Patton's Army

Even though we were in the repair business, we became the spearhead of Patton's Third Army and went right down the road with some of the other infantry divisions. Sometimes our troops would break through the enemy lines, we'd all push through, then the Germans would re-group and come back. A lot of fighting went on all around us and we had to keep on repairing the equipment. It was a miracle that our outfit did not get one man injured by enemy action, even though our vehicles got shot up and sometimes we were only missed by inches. Sometimes the guys working in the tanks would have to scrape body parts out so they could make the repairs.

We'd go by the woods and less than 400 yards away our troops would be locked in battle. As we passed by we could hear machine gun and rifle fire. Overhead, artillery shells were being lobbed into the area.

Ernie Frazier

We had a company commander, Wilbert Rayburn, who was really on the ball. Whenever we stopped, the first thing he had us do was to fill our gas tanks so we'd be ready to roll at any time. One night in Belgium, I had just come off guard duty and was sleeping in a saloon or café about 10 feet away from a plate glass window. I woke up suddenly, could hear glass tinkling, and rolled over to get my gun. A V2 rocket had missed us by about 200 yards and the concussion blew out the windows. The first thing I heard was the command, "Company, be ready to roll in five minutes!"

I grabbed my bedroll and in less than ten minutes we were rolling. We heard that about ten minutes after that another V2 hit—right where we'd been.

Welding at night is illuminating

From the time we left England, we were working and moving day and night with no time off. Our main job was to weld what we called "duck bills" on the tank tracks to make them much wider and longer to support them in the mud and snow. We were out there with electric welders that illuminated us for miles.

While the fighting troops would get a little time off, maybe a couple of weeks of R & R which they certainly earned, we got no time off and that's when we worked the hardest to get their equipment repaired.

Every man in C Company 21st Infantry was killed

We moved on into Belgium. The fighting was fierce at St. Vith and Houffelize. In one battle, every man of C Company 21st Infantry was killed. Another company, I think it was the 42nd Tank Battalion, lost all of their tanks.

Sleeping outside in rain and snow

People wonder how we kept clean. We didn't. If we found water anywhere and had the time we might give our clothes & ourselves a quick rinse. Mostly we slept outside in the rain or snow in a wet sleeping bag and that provided for all the cleaning we got.

Praise for the cooks

I was really impressed with our cooks. It was bitter cold in Belgium but they usually had warm meals cooked up for us and we seldom had to eat rations. Even when we were being strafed by enemy aircraft and diving for cover from bombs or rockets, the cooks would be out there working their heads off day and night to keep us in good food. Unfortunately, the cold forced us to decide whether to eat our oatmeal or drink our coffee first, knowing that one would be frozen before we could get to it.

Many amputations for frozen feet

Frostbite hit a lot of the guys. Many had no overshoes and their boots and socks got soaked. They slept in their clothes, if they slept at all, without a change to dry socks. Their feet began to freeze. Amputations were frequent. Nobody can understand the terrible conditions we worked and fought under unless they were there.

Some suspected that the quartermasters were shipping our wool clothing home and selling it back to the French. So, it wasn't getting to us. That was one of the big things I understood that Patton was looking into at the time. We kept as warm as we could by wearing what we called our Form 32. That means we wore all the clothes we had all the time.

We got up to the Ardenne Forest. We weren't the first people to fight there and we saw hundreds of graves holding World War 1 soldiers who died there. Now it was our turn and a brutal battle occurred there along with several others in the region. We were held back, maybe 2 to 5 miles from the front and set up in the freezing cold and mud to do major overhauls on our tanks that got hit. We put on tracks, overhauled transmissions and every thing else. Artillery shells were zooming overhead but we kept on working.

Ernie Frazier

A guardian angel

We must have had a guardian angel overlooking us. At night we'd have to drive out and scrounge repairs from our supply units or other tanks. Lights were forbidden, as they'd draw enemy fire, so we traveled with our "cat eyes" on. They'd only let you see about 25 feet. We'd be moving along and suddenly come face to face and be looking down the gun barrel of one of our own tanks. I'd ask, "Where are we?" They'd say, "You just came out of no-man's land." They'd say they hadn't been up there yet. They didn't realize that they'd got ahead of the whole outfit. They got lost and were just now coming back, looking for their unit.

Corpses stacked like firewood at Bastogne

The 82nd Airborne followed us in trucks up to Bastogne. Then they got into the battles there. They'd been at Omaha Beach somewhere on D-Day. Bastogne was one of the great battles of the war and the troops on both sides paid a bitter price. We saw German and American casualties all the time. Since it was freezing cold, corpses were stacked up like cordwood on the north side of buildings and stayed frozen until our American graveyard detail came along to bury them.

While we didn't get the publicity of D-Day and some other battles, the 11th Armored Division was in constant ground warfare for over five months. I believe that our tanks provided the artillery support for the 82nd Airborne when they attacked Bastogne.

At Remagen

We supported the infantry in the battle at Remagen and another battle when we crossed the Rhine. One of our half-tracks was mounted with an anti-aircraft gun and a plane came over our no-fly zone. Our crew shot it down. It was a B17 with a British crew on board. They didn't know they were flying in the wrong spot.

One memory I have is of a comedy that almost turned into a tragedy. We were in a big cow pasture that served as a German airfield. There was a big hanger there that housed about every kind of German aircraft. All that was needed to get them in the air was gasoline. It was about 9:30 at night when a Hinkle attack bomber came in to land. One of our guys opened up on him so the German turned on his lights and returned our fire. A .50 caliber machine gun was on the back of my truck and I thought about manning it, but changed my mind. I figured, "If I get to my gun, I'll probably just get mowed down. If I knock the plane down, it'll fall right down onto me and all the trucks behind me."

I just ducked down behind the engine block. About 30 feet away one of our cooks was working on a little platform on the back of his truck, baking bread. I had to laugh!

A cook in a rage of anger

The cook was in a rage and was shaking his fists at the aircraft and screaming at the German. Bullets were flying everywhere and he just stood there. What saved him was a small building that prevented the airplane, with its fixed guns, from swooping in for a good shot. Then, one of our guys hit the plane. It pulled away for a short distance and we saw a big old ball of fire when it hit the ground.

Another time a Messerschmitt 109 came down to strafe us. Our guys fired and it fell about 100 yards from me, skidded about one half mile and blew up.

The Germans began surrendering en mass then, as they knew they were losing the war. I was sitting with a .50 caliber machine gun watching for Germans when a sergeant from infantry came along and said, "That's my job." He took the .50 and started firing at the roofing tiles on a nearby building. After he destroyed about one half of the roof, the Germans came out with their hands in the air.

There were many times when the Germans surrendered even though they had enough ammunition to conduct a major battle. They just decided to quit, and we took lots of prisoners.

We were down in Austria when the war ended but we didn't know it, and spent another day in combat.

Ernie Frazier

Liberating Mauthausen death camp

After the war ended, we were sent to help liberate the German death camps. Mauthausen was a big one. Our division commanders told us that more prisoners went through there than anywhere else. We went into camps looking for German soldiers. There were big rows of barracks full of prisoners. They were just skin and bones and we couldn't tell whether many of them were dead or alive. The Germans had dug huge trenches, probably 100 meters long, where they would stack a layer of corpses, cover them with dirt, then stack more rows covered with dirt on top of them.

We saw the gas chambers where thousands of prisoners were gassed and the incinerators with big cast iron doors that opened to receive coal and the corpses for cremation.

We talked to one civilian within two miles of the prison gate. He knew others who'd gone over to see what was going on in the death camps and they were never seen again. He said, "We knew that something terrible was going on over there but we had no idea what it was." He said that everybody who went over there was caught by German sentries.

Churchill, Stalin and Roosevelt determined the new political boundaries. We were 50 miles too far east, encroaching on the Russian sector so we had to withdraw. The German people got down on their knees and begged us not to leave them to the Russians. When they saw we were leaving them behind, they all got out and started down a road heading west.

The Russians

The Russians came in and took everything. Our company commander had to go back over to a large German machine-gun factory that was full of lathes and other tools. He came back and told us, "You know there is nothing left there except the empty building. The Russians stripped it clean and only a row of bolts was left sticking up out of the floor."

When we went down through the Ruhr Valley where the Germans mined coal, we saw shafts off to the side of the main mine shaft where *people had dug holes and were living underground. We went in there and it was just like a house above ground with bedrooms and everything else.*

When you talk to the guys that fought in the jungles they say it couldn't be worse. But if you talk to the guys who were freezing to death, they have the same opinion. Either way it's pure hell.

CHAPTER 30

CARL KURT ZACHARIAS

"With the name of Zacharias, I didn't last long as a member of Hitler's Youth."

Dr. Carl Kurt Zacharias, a compassionate and caring physician, spent much of his life healing others. As such, he doesn't meet the stereotype of the single-minded, brutal German soldier. His story provides a rare look into the psyche of a frightened youth who was pressed into service by the maniac, Adolph Hitler.

He could have been an American boy. It was his misfortune to have been born under the long shadow of Adolph Hitler.

Greek, German, or Jew?

I was born in Hamburg, Germany in 1921. My father was a seaman who became a harbor policeman. After the First World War, Germany was not allowed to build any new ships. The few old ships they had were called floating coffins. Many of them didn't come back from their first journey.

My name was of Greek derivative. The Stein-Hardenberg, (a pseudo government) became Prussia in about 1848 and then became Germany. At that time Germany was about 320 little principalities. After the Napoleonic war they wanted to have a united Germany and it didn't exist until 1871. They all had family names. Zacharias was used as a first name; you know from the Bible, there was Zacharias and his wife Elizabeth who were the parents of St. John the Baptist. Most children had Christian names at that time. They were either Catholics or Protestants but they were all Christians. One of my ancestors had a first name of Zacharias and we used it as a family name. We don't know for sure, but that is my assumption.

Germany had been a democracy

Hitler came to power in 1933. He joined the Nazi party in 1919 or 1920, which, until 1933, was not strong at all. They were just kind of a rabble group. Germany became a democracy in 1871; however it was a monarchy-driven democracy, much as England still has. The Kaiser used to be the Prussian King. When I was born, Germany was strictly a democracy. The Kaiser had been ousted. People didn't know what to do. They had never had that opportunity to vote for president, so the communist party candidate, Frederic Ebert, became president of Germany at that time. Nobody took him seriously and they all did more or less what they wanted. Of course, that was not very fruitful. Eventually, Germany had a new government about every six weeks and that didn't work. Adolph Hitler was smart enough to realize this. He put all his members into uniforms and made strict rules.

If you didn't agree with Hitler, you disappeared

When he came into power, the first thing he did was disband the German Parliament and they just took on ermaechteongsgetez (Jesus' power). That gave him extra power. From then on, the people could only say, "Yes, yes, yes," and that's all. If they didn't, they disappeared. We had a few neighbors who we didn't know were communists, because people kept their political opinions to themselves. Hamburg was considered mostly communistic. These people disappeared and never came back. We assumed they were killed at concentration camps.

They thought we were Jews!

They assumed my father had a Jewish name and he was put on unpaid leave until he had proof that he was not Jewish. That took him several months. He had to go to several churches and get the documents copied. It wasn't like now where you copy them in the Xerox machine. When he came back, somebody else had taken his position as a policeman and he was then transferred into Germany's special police, working in weights and measures. He had to do this and he was so depressed his whole life, because he had been a captain with Verminlenia and now he was nobody. It wasn't easy for my dad. My parents got married in 1906 and in 1907 they had a baby girl, which was born dead. My brother was born in 1909. Afterward came World War 1 and my dad was in that. When I was born Germany was in a deep depression. I remember my parents talking about that. My father got paid every hour because the value of the money decreased so fast. They printed billions of marks, little pieces of paper that you couldn't buy anything with. My father would get paid and then my mother would take the money to the closest grocery store and buy some food for us. If she was lucky, they had it. This was a very bad time for Germany.

Joining the Hitler Youth

I grew up in a very loving family. I had no problems at all. My brother was 12 years older than me so I was actually treated like a single child. I was 12 years old when Hitler came into power in 1933. My brother was a Boy Scout and they had meetings in our house. I was so impressed with this that when I was 8 years old in 1929, I insisted that I be allowed to join the scouts. When Hitler came to power one of the first things he did was outlaw the scouts. Interestingly enough he copied the uniform for the Hitler Youth exactly from the Boy Scouts--100%. If we wanted to be together as *friends, we had to join the Hitler Youth. We had no choice and I joined the Hitler Youth when he banned the Boy Scouts.*

I loved it because we learned to sing and we hiked every weekend if we had a chance. I remember one of the hikes was about 25 miles. For 10-year-old boys, that was an awful lot, and I did it.

That didn't last very long because we were split up and I was assigned to another outfit. I was in high school at that time. High school in Germany was something different than we have here. We had to pass an examination to get into high school. I was a high school student and could snub the ordinary people, you know. I laughed whenever they said something In the Hitler Youth we had meetings once a week and were told about all the Nazi history and occasionally the leader would tell us about German history and that Frederic the Great was a homosexual and Goethe was a Free Mason and a philosopher. Of course I had learned differently and I laughed about this "bull shit" I called it, and I was not afraid to say this out loud.

Expelled!

I didn't last long as a member of Hitler's Youth. They thought Zacharias was a Jewish name and booted me and within six months or so I was kicked out of the Hitler Youth. I found that wonderful because I didn't have to go to the meetings anymore. What they were teaching in the Hitler Youth was completely different than what I had learned in school or in the Boy Scouts. I was more interested in girls and this way I had time for them.

I was not allowed to join the Nazi Party or any organization. The law stated that if you wanted to practice medicine as a physician, you had to be a member of the Nazi Party. I would not be able to practice medicine, which was my goal. I didn't take that too seriously, however. I thought this situation was not going to last forever, and I was right. It didn't last forever. Hitler always talked about the Thousand Year Reich, and some people believed him.

In 1939, I graduated from high school and was drafted into the German Labor Service. You had to serve in it, especially if you had graduated from high school and were planning to go to the university.

Ernie Frazier

We had to write down what we wanted to do. I had written down that I wanted to be a doctor. We had to prove ourselves in the labor service. I found that 6 months in the labor service very enlightening because we had to do the most arduous and hard manual labor you could imagine—digging ditches in the swamp—and having to move 8 cubic meters of soil every day. Eight cubic meters is 8 tons and eight tons is an awful lot and I never could do it. There was a tall man next to me in the group who was a butcher's apprentice and he did it for me. He had muscles like nobody's business. I enjoyed him very much, because we were so very close. We were people of different backgrounds you know.

When the war broke out and Germany invaded Poland in September of 1939, we were shipped to East Prussia to be ready to be brought into the war as pioneers (construction people). The war ended with Poland very soon and we weren't needed any more. I was discharged from the service and allowed to return home to study medicine.

Studying medicine

Hamburg had been hit by a very few bombs, but the university had been severely damaged and was closed. This was in 1939. England had declared war on Germany when Hitler invaded Poland, so I couldn't go to England to study. I was studying on a stipend and went to the governing office to get a certificate that relieved me from having to pay tuition at any university I chose to attend. There was a big poster there that said, "The University of Prague wants you." They asked me which university I wanted to study at and I said, "I will go to Prague." I had no idea what it was like. I went to Prague and it was fantastic, absolutely wonderful.

An infantryman in Hitler's army

On the other hand, the war situation did not go as well as anticipated, so in April 1941 I was drafted into the army. I was 20 years old and had only completed four semesters at the university. In Germany, after four semesters you have to pass the first examination, and then you have to study another six semesters before the last examination.

All of the buddies in my company, except two or three, were medical doctors freshly graduated from medical school. We were 120 men, now in the infantry. Hitler had no use for people who went to the universities. I was sent to Therisenstadt, which was a small old Austrian fortress. (I think right now it is in Czechoslovakia, or it used to be Terezene.) The guy who killed the Austrian crown prince (which triggered off World War 1) was imprisoned there. He was 18 years of age and could not be condemned to death, so he was imprisoned for life. He died at Therisenstadt in 1926 of tuberculosis.

This was where I was trained. It was very old, but somehow cozy. It didn't have the modern German barracks. We had 16 men in one little room and three bunks, one over the other.

We knew more about poison gas and other things than the instructors and we always made fun of them. When we had lectures and the instructor would say something which was obviously not quite right, one of us would raise his hand and say, "Corporal, this should be so and so." They didn't like us, but they treated us decent. I must say that.

Hearing Hitler speak

When we were finished with our three months of training at the end of June, we were sent to East Prussia. Of course we didn't know we were to be infantrymen. We were issued new uniforms and all looked nice. In the middle of the night we were shipped away on a train. We arrived two days later in East Prussia at the time Hitler was giving a speech. It was pitch dark on the parade ground and we sat down on the dirt with our packs and with no weapons, just uniforms, and Hitler said; "Now we will have to attack Russia." A few hours later we were put on trucks and off we went. By sunrise we were in a village in Lithuania. I remember that very clearly. Lithuania was part of Russia at that time. Hitler had divided Poland between Germany and Russia. Half of the original Poland is still Russia. It has never been given back to the Poles, even though the Balkan nations have become independent.

Ernie Frazier

The village was almost deserted. I had no idea as to what had happened there. On one side was a big slope, about 300 feet almost straight up. On the other side was the village. The truck stopped—we were in three or four trucks—and we all got out.

Our officers deserted

The corporals and sergeants who had brought us there said, "So long boys," and off they went, leaving us alone without an officer or anyone in charge. And we had no weapons. We didn't know what to do but we had one private first class in our unit and he took over. He said, "Let's assemble and go." As we did this, a Russian tank appeared on the top of the ravine and tried to get into position to fire on us, but he couldn't do it. They cannot shoot down, you know, so the tank finally backed up and we walked away. About a half an hour later we were on a country road and came upon a Russian tank that was burning with a Russian soldier hanging out of the turret. He was sizzling like a steak. It was terrible—our first impression of war—and everybody wanted to run away. Our thoughts were, "My God, what have we gotten ourselves into." We had no weapons, nothing.

Finally we got to a first aid station where they were taking care of wounded German soldiers along with a whole bunch of Russian soldiers who had been wounded and were now prisoners. Our private first class went to the commanding officer. We were put under the command of a captain who then took us over and marched us into a forest where we spent the night.

A bass drum flies through the air

All of a sudden a regimental band came marching by and we heard "Oompah, oompah." It was unbelievable. Then, the Russians opened fire with artillery and grenades. A shell hit the band. Everyone started running and I can still see the big bass drum flying through the air.

We had been given emergency rations, which were in a little can, and were given orders to eat it. We hadn't eaten anything the whole day. The awakening was so dramatic that it is indescribable. We were suddenly at war.

From that time on, it was that way every day. We'd fight the Russians in the morning, they'd retreat, and then we'd dig in. They would determine our positions and fire their artillery in on us.

Summer clothing and the Russian winter

It was in September and was very, very cold. We didn't have winter clothing, just our summer uniforms. I remember one morning a solder had his hand frozen onto his rifle. We had a tarp to put over our foxholes. Nobody did that because it was too time consuming. We were exhausted after walking so many hours and being shot at. We dug ourselves in. It was tough. 120 men started out and when I was wounded on the 6th of September (three months after we went in) there were only 12 men left.

Reaching the Czar's palace

After many marches, our unit arrived within sight of the Czar's palace, Peterhos, which stood in front of Leningrad. We were that close and we slept right there. I was now machine gunner #1.

I remember one time, I couldn't dig myself in with my equipment because the ground was so hard, and I had my ammunition box in front of me, so I put up my hand, and said, "Come on, shoot me through the hand," but nothing happened. I wanted out. I was not a hero. I don't think anybody in my company was a hero. We did what we were told to do, but that was all. In the German army, they used iron discipline to keep you in line.

Under fire with no toilets

Of course there were no toilets and the ground was so hard you couldn't dig a slit trench. Once, while lying down under fire, I pulled my pants down, defecated in my shovel and threw it out. What a stupid thing. You never think about those necessities. Several times I had diarrhea in my pants because I couldn't quickly get them down. It was terrible. We were practically reduced to animals.

Loving a Russian girl gets you executed

We were not allowed to fraternize with the Russians. One of the soldiers in our outfit had fallen in love with a Russian girl and was making love to her. We were not allowed to do that and he was immediately shot dead on the scene. That was in a town that was burning. The Russians had abandoned it.

The machine gun we used was an air-cooled, .30 caliber weapon. When I was machine gunner #3, I carried the ammunition—900 rounds. That's an awful lot of weight. When machine gunner #2 was killed, I advanced to #2. A new man took over as #3.

We received replacements because we had lost so many men. I remember how my machine gunner #1 was killed in Russia. We were in the Baltic nations. The Russians were just over a little hill, firing on us with heavy machine guns. Our #1 was getting the machine gun ready to work when all of a sudden he keeled over dead. He'd been shot right through his helmet. I got orders to retrieve the weapon. I crawled out to my dead comrade, grabbed the gun, and came back. Fortunately, some of our artillery had silenced the Russian machine gun. Otherwise, I probably would have been killed, too. It was a very dramatic experience.

A lot of tragic things happened. Our company commander had been wounded and sent to the rear for treatment. When he returned, we attacked the Russians in the forest. There was a little clearing in front of us and apparently there was a sniper sitting in a tree. The captain was right beside me. I heard him say, "Oh," and he rolled over dead. He'd been shot right through the heart. Why the sniper didn't shoot me, I don't know, but the captain had his insignia on and now he was dead. Later on the Germans quit wearing their insignia.

Another time, we were fighting to get into a Russian village that was heavily fortified with rolled up wire, and we couldn't get in. We were standing there and one of my buddies got his right eye shot away. He began running and screaming. That was the realism of war. It was terrible, absolutely terrible. He died after moaning and groaning and raving madly with pain. We took the village, but at what cost!

As I said, when I got wounded on September 6th, we had only 12 men. We were so far apart, that I couldn't even see my neighbor. Our line was stretched that thin. We had headquarters and were still a company of soldiers. We had many lieutenants come to serve as our company commander. They were reservists, untrained for battle. They'd be in battle for half an hour and then they were dead. It didn't take long. They did stupid things. As an infantryman, you automatically learn to take cover. You don't walk upright. The young lieutenants walked upright. Bingo! They were killed. So we had a sergeant who took charge of everything.

The battalion commander was a dentist, Doctor Lange. He was a regular reserve major and got the Knight's Cross for conquering Riga, Harvatone and Latvia. The poor guy always had diarrhea because he was always scared. I don't know what happened to him. He didn't get killed while I was there.

We formed a hedgehog

Tremendous battles went on every day. We got some sleep at night. We formed what we called a hedgehog, the little animal that has bristles all over, with an igloo in the center and guns pointing out in all directions. We all would take turns. I was on every two hours because we had so few men. I remember lying behind my gun, and every time my head would fall onto the gun, the hammer would wake me up. We didn't get much sleep.

Shot! I was glad!

I got shot through the right chest when I was not moving and that saved me. I was cleaning my glasses and was shot at by somebody in the tree. We got used to finding out where the bullets were coming from. We were lying in an oat field. The oats were just about three feet high and you can't shoot from there. You had to get up on your knees. I was up on my knees, and was looking, and wham, something like a 2 X 4 hit me over the shoulder and knocked me down. My right arm was paralyzed and boy, was I relieved. People with chest injuries had to be sent home to Germany. Most died, but I was sent back and lived. The trip took about three days.

The entry wound was a little bullet hole. The exit hole was a little larger. They put in a tampon (a plug) to keep it open in case it got infected. My arm was paralyzed so they put it in a sling and sent me home.

We were only 12 men at the front and when I came back, there were soldiers all over the place. They had figured out how to stay away from the "Iron containing air," they said.

I was sent home to Bavaria. There was a village called Muenenerstadt and the townspeople assembled there. There was a little girl who got a bunch of flowers and came to greet me. She screamed when she saw me. Of course I hadn't seen myself in the mirror for six weeks and was covered with mud. I never took off my helmet and my hair was so matted, it was terrible. I had been in my uniform all that time and stunk to high heaven. Of course, in the hospital we were bathed and taken care of. We had good food and a nice clean bed. It was absolutely wonderful.

Refusing to execute a fellow soldier

One morning while I was convalescing they called us out and we counted out 1-2-3, 1-2-3. Every third man had to step forward and we were 12 men. We were ordered to be a firing squad and execute a German soldier. He had shot himself through the knee because he wanted to get out of the war. I went to the company commander and said, "Sir, I can't do it. I just can't do it. I can not live with myself, knowing I had definitely killed somebody."   "Oh," he said, "You might get the fake bullet." "No," I said, "I can't do it." "Well," he said, "let me see, if I find a volunteer to go for you." He called for volunteers, and three guys stepped forward. So I thanked God that I didn't have to do that. I figured, "If the guy is already so scared as to shoot himself to get out of the war, I don't want to have to kill him." I had been scared too. I knew what these people were feeling. If I had the guts, maybe I would have shot myself through the hand. The poor sucker. If nobody volunteered I would have had to do it.

When I recovered from the injury, I was sent back to a reserve company. That's the way it was handled with the wounded that recovered. It was just around Christmas time. I was sent home for three weeks through Christmas, and enjoyed that very much. My parents were very happy to see that I was sent back.

Then I was sent back to Russia. My father took me to the train at Grand Central Station. For the first time in my life I saw him cry because chances were good that he would never see me again. But I made it and he didn't. He died in 1945.

All the glory of war had disappeared. When I saw that Russian tank burning and the soldier hanging out of the turret, sizzling like a steak, any illusions of grandeur disappeared.

Running with a sewing machine and pooping your pants

One of our soldiers had to carry a sewing machine to repair our boots. One time I had to carry it over an open field. I had it on my back and was struggling to carry it along with my machine gun and ammunition. The Russians opened fire on me and I could hear bullets striking the sewing machine. If you poop in your pants at that time, it wouldn't be unusual.

I saw hundreds of people killed. Every morning we had to clean up the mess. When one of our comrades was directly hit by a grenade, there was nothing but mush left. We had to identify him and wrap him up in a tarp.

The whole highway from the German border to Leningrad became a burial ground.

There were crosses beside crosses all the way. My wife, Anja Hackenberger, had a brother who was killed there. Our dead were brought to the road and buried right there. Nobody knows it anymore. The guy who shot me saved my life.

It's a glorious feeling when you have driven the enemy back, but when you have to run away, it causes mixed up feelings. It matures you very quickly. When I finally came back home from the war, I'd been a combat soldier as well as a prisoner of war and was only 24 *years old. I think I had the mentality and experience of a 50-year-old man.*

I don't think I killed many people. Usually we were just shooting in the direction where the Russians were. They would come yelling, "Hooray, hooray," the Germans would yell, "Hoorah." Most of the Russians were drunk. I never saw one up close.

One time we were on the River Lauga. The Russians were on the other side. Apparently a Russian soldier had been seriously wounded and was crying out "Moi Vaga, moi Vaga," (My God, my God). I will never forget that. He finally went silent and apparently died.

We never knew how many losses the Russians had. Whenever they retreated, they always took their dead with them and we never found anything. They must have had a lot of dead people to drag back.

According to my friends, the sniper who shot me got shot himself and was left hanging in the tree. That is the only Russian I knew of killed by my company. He had tied himself to the tree so that he would have two hands free to shoot. He was left behind, but otherwise the Russians would take everybody with them. That's a big chore if you are retreating. The people attacking go forward and others have to clear the battlefield. This was something they had to do. Very seldom did we see Russian soldiers wounded or killed.

The Russian woman

I once made a prisoner of a Russian woman. We were in the forest and suddenly it got dark. The shooting stopped because you can't see anything and you might kill your own buddies. Everybody digs in and sleeps. I slept through the night, and in the morning when the sun was rising, I heard somebody crying. It was just about 20 feet from me and it was a Russian woman in uniform. She had a rifle hanging over her arm and had tears running down her eyes. She came to me and surrendered. I took the rifle and banged it against the t-bolt that broke the butt off and then threw the rifle away. I didn't know what to do with her, so I said, "Well, go on back." She did. I don't know what happened to her. She went back beyond our lines to our side. If she had gone back the other way the Russians would have killed her. Stalin did not allow any prisoners among the Russians. Anybody who became a prisoner of war of the Germans was a traitor and they were immediately killed.

The Russians must've been very disciplined. I don't know whether they were well trained. I doubt very much that they were. So many of them were apparently illiterate and believed everything they were told.

Captured Russians pray to God

When they surrendered to the Germans and were not immediately shot by the Germans, they would fall on their knees and pray to God and thank him. They had some very well trained political commissars in their company. They were hated by everybody in the Russian army. When we had them as prisoners, the Russians would point them out to us and they were separated immediately from the others. I don't know what happened to them after that.

Three of us once had to control over 100 Russian prisoners. They could have overthrown us easily. We didn't have much ammunition. The Russians are a very proud people. They surrendered and that was it.

The hatred against the Germans was understandable, and the Germans knew that. Whenever the Germans had a chance to run away from the Russians, they would. Sometimes they couldn't. The stories from the Germans who were surrounded by the Russians, and made prisoner, are not very pleasant to listen to.

To the east of Leningrad is Lake Peipus. It was frozen and had a railroad on the lake. The Germans would fire artillery, make holes in the ice and destroy the railroad tracks. Overnight, the Russians would move the railroads a little bit on the ice and the transports were able to move again. That was how they kept Leningrad connected during the wintertime. When that was gone, they really suffered.

The Russians love their country more than anything. You can tell that when you have a Russian immigrant in the United Stated. They never lose their love for Russia and the Communists made use of that. Stalin tried to. He called it the Patriotic War Priority, and a lot of

Ernie Frazier

Russians believed him. It took quite a few years before they found out what kind of person Stalin was. He had his own mother killed.

Hitler and Stalin were allies and they divided Poland up like it was a piece of meat. The part that Hitler gave to the Russians is still theirs. Poland had to be compensated with a big hunk of German territory.

The German people right now have no hatred for anybody. They just want to be left alone.

One of my sons wanted to know about my experiences in the war and I said, "Well I went into the war thinking about how heroic I could be, and it was bull shit." You get all that heroism out of you.

Hitler misjudged America

I think one problem of the Nazi's was the misjudgment of America. I have a book by a German Secret Service man who wrote, "Hitler never took the Americans serious." He said, "They're not going to be fighting. They can't. They don't know how to fight," and was he ever surprised." The book is by Galenth, and it is call "The Service." He had many conversations with Hitler about that. You see, Hitler called Roosevelt a Tibetic. It is a disease in the final phase of syphilis. He would never recognize that he had polio. He made fun of him. A good politician doesn't do that to your enemy.

Hitler's speeches

Hitler's talks were always the same, and at the end of the talk something dramatic would be mentioned, so you would listen to the end. When Germany occupied Czechoslovakia or when they occupied Austria, he always had a big speech. Sometimes his speeches were two hours long. You would sit there and yawn. It was Hitler's birthday in April and we had to listen to a speech. There was one of our sergeants sitting there with a saber between his legs and all of a sudden he fell forward. He was sleeping and the saber came out of the sheath. He picked it back up and the company battalion commander didn't say anything, because he was one of his few, trusted sergeants. He probably didn't think much of Hitler either.

Back to Russia

I was sent to Smolensk, a city about 100 kilometers (60 miles) behind the lines. We treated all the wounded soldiers there. I was assigned to the laboratory. My main job was to arrange for blood transfusions. Mind you, this was at a time when we had only three groups of blood types. We didn't know any more, and it was very difficult sometimes to identify blood types because they weren't clear-cut like now. I was head of the blood transfusion division of the laboratory even though I was a low-ranking dogface at that time. I did get promoted to private first class.

At about 10:00 p.m., the soldier's broadcasting from Belgrade, Yugoslavia, would play the song Lilly Marlene. The soldiers would be brought in and they would cry hearing that song. When I talked to our friends in America later on, they said they also played Lilly Marlene and cried. It was such a touching melody, you know.

I was sent home after 20 months to continue my training in medical school because the losses in the medical corps had been so enormous and they needed replacements. I graduated from medical school in March of 1945. Hitler was almost dead and nothing was functioning right anymore.

We knew the Americans were coming, because the little town where we lived, Sankt Andreaberg, had the Americans in camp around it. They bombed us and fired artillery into the town, destroying about 50 houses. However, no resistance was mounted. We hid in our cellar during the bombardment. I was not married but was living with my mother-in-law and my wife to be. Suddenly the shelling stopped. About an hour later we came up out of the cellar and looked around.

Zacharias surrenders

An American lieutenant came into the house. I saluted him and gave him my sidearm, a revolver, and he said, "Well the war is over for you. You can do as you please." He was very nice, very nice, I must say. Since he said I could do anything I wanted to, I got rid of the uniform because that was all I had, and borrowed a suit from a friend who wasn't home yet. He was a soldier about my size.

But that didn't last very long. Ten days later the occupational troops came and we had to report again, because anybody who was harboring a German soldier was liable to get 20 years in prison. When I reported to the authorities, a lieutenant was sitting there that spoke German. He wanted to know when I ran away. I told him, "I didn't run away sir, I surrendered to the Americans, but I didn't run away." He just laughed. I gave him my soldier's identification booklet and dog tag, which he threw in the corner. There was already a mountain of papers there. I don't know why, but four American soldiers with rifles came in and took me away into the cellar of another house, then turned around and brought me out.

Facing a firing squad

They made me stand against the wall and brought up their rifles. I thought, "They are going to shoot you." I was absolutely cool and calm. I had resigned myself to that fact, when they abruptly left. They just had fun with me. They didn't do anything to me. I didn't poop in my pants either. At that time I would have expected almost anything. I became a prisoner and was shipped to the Rhineland to a real big prison camp. There were about 120,000 German soldiers prisoners there. I wasn't kept for very long. In June I was released to go home.

We didn't get much to eat in prison camp because word had come out about what the Germans had done in the concentration camps. They didn't treat us too bad, but all we got was about four crackers and a teaspoon full of milk powder every day for several weeks. We all had hunger edema and our legs would swell up. Then we got another commander for the compound. Things changed overnight and we started getting good food and medication. The food was nice in comparison to what we had in the German army. The German army had butcher companies that did the cooking. They had field kitchens, but if they didn't have anything to cook, we didn't get anything to eat. The Americans had C and K rations and that's what we got. By then, we had all developed the dysentery. We had no facilities but a slit trench and people would fall into the damn thing at night. That was all changed. (There is a book written by a Canadian author, called "All their losses." He describes the whole situation very clearly.

Escaping the Russians

Apparently Roosevelt and Stalin had made a deal in Yalta whereby America would hand over a certain number of prisoners to the Russians. When we were discharged from the American prison, we received our discharge papers and were sent on a freight train into the heart of Germany. We arrived in Eisenach at about 5:00 a.m. and were marched up to a modern German barracks. As we came into the parade ground, I saw Russian officers standing there. My two buddies beside me said, "We don't belong here. Let's turn away." We turned around. While the others were marching in, we marched out. We wondered, "What are we going to do when they shoot us?" We decided, "They won't shoot." We said we are the Americans, and walked out. We escaped and all the others were shipped to Russia. That was the first time and the only time I did something Germanic, but it saved my life I'm sure.

When I came home from prison camp I weighed 123 pounds and was 6 feet tall. That is not very much. My wife said, "Only your boots kept you upright."

The Russians did not treat the Germans very well, and they had their reasons. The Germans did not treat the Russians very well either, you know. I think it was very fortunate that when the war ended I was taken prisoner by the Americans. They are very nice people.

When the war ended, the universities were all closed. I wanted to go back to medical school but there was no way to do this, so I joined a local physician so I could stay in touch with medicine. Then in 1946 or 1947, the universities were opened again. I re-enrolled in college and studied two more years. Even though I had finished medical school and been made a doctor, I knew nothing, so I went back and became a real doctor.

Ernie Frazier

Anja was a patient at the last university I attended in 1944. We started a relationship and I fell in love with her. In 1946 we finally married. She was forced to work in a factory, like many women, and was assigned to a job in a factory that made guidance systems for torpedoes in Cologne. When the bombing got too bad there, the factory relocated to the Hartz Mountains in the center of Germany. She was sent there, got sick, and was sent to the university hospital where I was.

A physician

In January 1945, I graduated and became a physician and was assigned to a small hospital in the Hartz Mountains. Anja lived in another town about 10 miles away. Because I was a physician, my superiors said I could go home every night, but had to be back to work at 7:00 in the morning. This went on until March or April. The assassination attempt on Hitler had taken place and Himmler had ordered that if you suspected another soldier to be a deserter, you could kill him right away. The SS in particular was trained that way. The word was around there were SS troops in the Hartz Mountains.

German officers desert

I had never seen one, but one night I was walking home through the woods (I knew the way and didn't follow the roads) and heard somebody moving nearby. So, I stopped and stood behind a shrub. Along came an admiral with another high ranking navy officer and several sailors walking through the forest. They came closer and closer, and finally I stepped out of my hiding place and the admiral said, "Oh thank goodness you are not SS." I said "Admiral, where's your ship?" You are very bold in a situation like that, you know. He said, "Oh we were on an official trip and our car got destroyed so we had to walk."

I suspected they were all deserters.

The hospital where I was working had only sick and injured ordinary soldiers as patients. By the time the war ended, we had nothing but officers. This admiral, of course, was treated well. Here in the middle of Germany, in a forest, was an admiral. You could tell because they had light blue stripes on their pants. We realized that he and his men had run away from the navy. That was very common in those days because everybody figured they would be killed and many of them did get killed. The naval commander, General Admiral Donitz, was killed at Nuenbeck. He had been put in command of all of Germany at that time. He was in prison in Nuenbeck, Austria. I think he was hanged. So it is understandable that people tried to disappear.

Shortly afterwards they had the finance reform in Germany. I worked at the University Hospital in Frankfort without pay because they had too many physicians who wanted to learn something. When the money was changed, the Reich mark had the value of 10 to 1 to the German mark. We could exchange 600 Reich mark for 60 German marks. As an unpaid physician, I didn't get anything. After two or three months we were broke. The University Hospital had a blackboard that listed open positions for doctors. I visited several but didn't like what I saw.

An American doctor

I found out that the American Consulate wanted to have an English-speaking physician so I applied and got the job. I worked at the U.S. Public Health Service for about three years, until 1952. I was now an American doctor.

But, we'd lost everything. My parents lost their home in the bombing and while Anja's house was still standing, nobody was there. Her mother had left and some other people moved in. They had to. What else could they do? They had lost their homes. When Anja's family finally had a chance to go back there, everything was removed. You wouldn't know this if you went to Germany now. They have recovered too much.

I remember when I was a medical student in Prague, we were discussing Hitler and we said, "If Hitler ever makes war with Russia, we're finished." We didn't think he would do it, but he did. So, the thinking people were known as charlatans and dilettantes. But, Hitler had the power to kill you. If you were sworn in as a recruit you had a

Ernie Frazier

choice, either swear an oath of allegiance to Hitler or get killed. In the war, if we didn't follow orders, they could shoot you right away.

The most important thing to me was to realize the horror of war. While Germany was still successful and we were heroes, it was all right. We would put up with a lot of horror, but when the war turned bad for us and we had to run away, it was terrible. We were really scared to be the last one in the group that was retreating and you look back all the time.

CHAPTER 31

RUBY BRADLEY

"I was a pretty good thief. We stole food for the children."

Ruby Bradley was an army nurse captured in the Philippines by the invading Japanese. While the majority of the stories in this book resulted from personal interviews with each veteran, her story is reprinted from an Associated Press article that appeared in the Hutchinson (KS) News on Sunday, Feb. 10, 2001.

Reprinted with permission of The Associated Press
PRESTONBURG, KY –

Ruby Bradley ignored her hunger in a World War II prisoner-of-war camp, opting to give most of her food to children who also were being held captive.
In the midst of the gloom, she and other nurses also set up a clinic to care for the sick and wounded and to comfort the dying.
Now, Bradley, who is 93, is one of the nation's most decorated female veterans, is the one who is weakening, and others are proudly stepping forward to help.
"It's hard for me to imagine what she's been through," said Leigh Ann Hamilton, a physical therapist who works with the retired colonel each day. "I get goose bumps just thinking about it."
Sometimes Bradley does, too.
She will never forget the night a U.S. Army tank crashed the gates of the Japanese prisoner-of-war camp, freeing her after three years of captivity.

"We had heard rumors that American soldiers were close by," she said. "Then, that tank came through. It was the best Saturday night performance I've ever seen."

Bradley, now living in a nursing home, said nothing has ever matched the excitement she felt in the moment that the tank cleared the wooden rubble and she saw troops following on foot.

The scene ushered out what seemed like an eternity of short rations, largely rice, for the Army nurse who was imprisoned at the Santo Tomas Internment Camp in Manila, Philippines.

Bradley can no longer walk, but her memories are sharp. She wept as she recounted the hardships and violent deaths of fellow prisoners who tried to escape.

"She has made a lot of sacrifices in her life," Hamilton said. "She put duty first, and never married, never had children. It would be so easy to be intimidated by her, because of her extensive knowledge and experience. She won't let you. She is really appreciative of every little thing you do for her."

A native of Spencer, W.Va., Bradley moved into the Prestonburg Health Care Center earlier this month after a small personal care home where she lived in West Virginia scaled back its patient load.

"All the nurses here are absolutely in awe of her," said her nephew, Charles Bradley. "They really do give her special treatment."

A black-and-white photograph in her room shows Bradley as an attractive young lady in the uniform of the Army Nurse Corps. Next to that hangs a shadow box filled with medal and ribbons once pinned on her chest. Thirty-four medals in all, including two Legion of Merit medals, two Bronze Stars, two Presidential Emblems, the World War II Victory Medal and the United Nations Service Medal. She also received the International Red Cross' prestigious nursing honor, the Florence Nightingale Medal.

Bradley insists that she was never sick during the time that she and her nursing colleagues battled disease, starvation and crude conditions to care for other prisoners, both soldiers and civilians.

A vintage photograph shows Bradley and other nurses, all thin and frail, riding in the back of a truck, smiling and waving as they were driven out of the compound after their rescue.

Bradley said her earliest nursing experiences were taking care of animals on the family farm in Roane County, W.Va. After a stint as a teacher, she became a nurse in 1933. She joined the Army Nurse Corps as a surgical nurse a year later.

When the Japanese bombed Pearl Harbor on Dec.7, 1941, she was a 34-year old administrator serving in the Philippines at Camp John Hay in Bagulo on Luzon Island, 200 miles above Manila. She was captured three weeks later.

Bradley was moved to Santo Tomas in Manila on Sept. 23, 1943. There she was among a group of imprisoned nurses who became known to captives as the Angels in Fatigues. Not only did they provide medical treatment for prisoners, but they were adept at stashing food for the little ones.

"I was a pretty good thief," she said. "I would take food and put it in my pockets for the children."

While the children ate, Bradley shrank. She weighed about 80 pounds when the American troops arrived on Feb. 3, 1945.

For the next five years, Bradley enjoyed peace. Then came the Korean War. A month after its start, she was overseas again, working as a combat nurse in evacuation hospitals, an assignment that expanded her collections of medals even further.

Bradley gladly shares her experiences with people who ask, and lots of people ask.

"I've got a long list of questions," said Valary Sykes, an occupational therapist who has been helping Bradley regain strength in her weakened hands so that she can write again. "She's lived through things that we can't imagine. Things that movies can't capture."

Bradley wouldn't change any part of her life. The experiences, she said, have made her appreciative of the small things, especially food.

"I haven't missed a meal since 1945," she said. "I eat everything."

Note: Ruby also appears in Elizabeth M. Norman's excellent book: *We Band Of Angels*.

CHAPTER 32

WILLIAM W. (BILL) CARLIN

I had to write, "Your husband was killed in action."

I was in New Mexico interviewing war veterans in November 2001. Bill Carlin drove in from his ranch and met me at the VFW post in Hobbs.

When we met, I saw that he was small of stature and appeared to be about 80 years old. He had very bright, expressive eyes and a firm handshake. He wheeled in an oxygen tank. It had a hose running to his nostrils to aid his breathing.

The VFW was closing early so I offered to drive him to my relative's house where we could talk in private. He said he'd drive himself, disconnected the oxygen tank and placed it on the back seat and got in the driver's seat and reattached the hose. I followed as he negotiated his way through traffic.

I knew right then that I had met an extraordinary man.

War on the horizon

In September 1940, I was living in Pontiac, Illinois and decided to join the Illinois National Guard—the 33rd Infantry Division, Headquarters Company, 65th Infantry Brigade.

It was activated in early 1941 and we left immediately for Camp Forrest, Tennessee, about 100 miles southeast of Nashville at Tulahoma. I was in the brigade headquarters that served two infantry regiments, the 129th and the 130th. I went in as a PFC since I'd been trained as a radio operator. We got our basic training there, and then, in April or May 1941, prior to Pearl Harbor, went on large-scale maneuvers. They were staged in Tennessee, Arkansas, and Louisiana and lasted until November.

I remember what I was doing when Pearl Harbor was bombed. I had a gal in Nashville and I was at her house for a fried chicken dinner. The news came over the radio and an announcement followed ordering all military personnel to report to their units at once. I waited until the last train at 6:30 p.m. When I got back, my outfit was already packing to leave. We left the next morning, part of the two regiments ordered to guard the Tennessee Valley Authority Dams down around Chattanooga, Hiawasee and other towns.

My job was as a radio operator and we could communicate—in a rather primitive way compared to the communications of today—with operators stationed at all the dams.

The organization of Army units changed dramatically after Pearl Harbor. The old divisions were square divisions consisting of four infantry and one artillery regiment. Afterward, they went to triangular divisions of the three infantry regiments.

Commissioned

I ended up in a cavalry reconnaissance unit and attended three months of radio school at Ft. Benning, Georgia. My grades were good enough that they promoted me to sergeant. I went back to my unit. We didn't do much and in July 1942 I decided that if it was going to be a long war I might as well get as much as I could out of it and put in to go to OCS. I qualified and went back to Benning for three months of Infantry OCS and was commissioned a second lieutenant in November of 1942, with an MOS of 0200—communications officer.

My first assignment was at Ft. Knox, KY with the Headquarter Company of the 49th Armored Infantry Regiment of the 8th Armored Division.

I was there until January of 1943, and was transferred to Camp Campbell, KY, 3rd Battalion Headquarters, and 56th Armored Infantry Regiment as communications officer. We became the cadre for the 12th Armored Division that was being formed and made into combat teams.

In May 1943, I was promoted to 1st Lieutenant. Another officer outranked me; he became the battalion communication officer and I went to Company B of the 56th Armored Infantry Battalion as platoon leader. It wasn't long until I became the company commander.

So, in late 1943, I took over the company. They needed replacements because of the losses we'd taken at the Kasserine Pass in North Africa. I remember one night they called for 1,200 men and 100 officers to ship out the next morning. In the meantime, they were going to send us to Indio, California for desert training. But things changed. That's why we wound up at Camp Barkeley, Texas. My job was to get the men ready for combat. There were normally 180 men in an infantry rifle company but we had 250.

To the armored infantry

There is quite a bit of difference between a regular infantry company and an armored infantry company. The ordinary rifle company is allocated two Jeeps. In the armored infantry rifle company, I had five jeeps, 18 half-tracks, three towed 57-mm anti-tank guns with weapons carriers, a lot of machine guns and Tommy guns, and several trucks to haul ammunition and other supplies. It amounts to an armored infantry company and a tank company teamed up together as a combat team.

Our job was to break through the enemy, circle the wagons and hold our position.

The men in 1943 and 1944 weren't "milkshake" soldiers. We worked them hard. We alternated their work days, one week in the field and one week in camp. The non-coms run the company. If a sergeant told a man to do something and he refused, he might just get knocked on his rear—and nobody said a thing. No one in those days ran to mamma or to his congressman.

The only two good jobs in the army as far as I'm concerned are company commander and first sergeant.

I felt that I was pretty tough on the trainees. You don't train a horse by being gentle with him. Discipline—following orders without question—was what we stressed. You can't run a military operation without it.

As soon as our training was completed in 1944, we were alerted and sent to New York. We were to ship out to France, but the orders were changed because they activated Patton's 3rd Army and he took all of the vehicles that were waiting for us in France. So, we landed at Liverpool, England. We went on down to Salisbury and it took us about two months to get new equipment together. By then, D-day had come and gone and the troops were fighting up at the Hurtigen Forest. That was the battle prior to the Battle of the Bulge.

We convoyed through Rheims and ended up at the 7th Army sector in the area of Sauerloten and Bining, France. The region was occupied by our troops so we didn't get into any combat at that time.

Our first action came on December 5th at Bining and Rohrbach, close to the German border. Our 4th Armored Division had been fighting for about two weeks to take those towns. They were pulled out to go north—they were part of Patton's army—and we came in to replace them.

We were in the attack mode. Our mission was to take the high ground and continue north to Germany. We took Bining fairly easily, and then took Rohrbach, which wasn't too bad. However, we ran into the Germans right after Rohrbach and they really gave us a good clobbering.

Ernie Frazier

A terrible loss of life!

Twenty-three of my men were killed the first day. We lost our battalion tank commander; he had his head shot off. Fifteen of our tanks were knocked out. I was the only one out of the five officers in our company that wasn't killed or wounded. They shelled us with anti-tank guns—88's that doubled as cannons. Those were unmerciful weapons. They could blow a hole through our tanks so you can imagine what they did to our men. The Germans were good with mortars, too, and dropped hundreds of rounds on our positions. They exploded when they hit, killing or maiming everything within range.

We defended our position the best we could that night, and then a regimental combat team of the 44th Division came in to relieve us.

People wonder about my reaction to being in the middle of a fierce battle. Actually, you're so wound up that you have little time to worry. We just had to go right on and make a 4:00 a.m. attack on the high ground a couple of days later.

I'll never forget that because there was a lieutenant and his wife who lived next to us in Abilene when we were at Camp Barkeley. He was killed in the battle.

Our outfit was pretty well shot up. We were running out of men and were scattered all over the place. The 92nd Cavalry was on our left to reinforce a low-lying area, and our unit was to take the town of Uttweiler, just across the German border.

We brought our artillery and cannons in and bombarded the town from about 300 yards. In the afternoon we went in, took the town, and then fell back and held the hill until Christmas day.

In frozen foxholes on Christmas

The temperature on December 25th was way down and the ground was covered with snow. We'd been in foxholes and everyone was about half sick. Early in the afternoon, I could see Germans—a lot of them—coming out of their line of foxholes, advancing on our position.

I got on the radio and called for artillery. They zeroed in on the Germans. I directed their fire and that led to me getting my first Bronze Star.

My job was to run the company. However, I carried an M-1 rifle because the enemy patrols would try to infiltrate our lines at night and attack us in our foxholes.

Some soldiers wouldn't shoot

One fact a lot of people don't know, but it's an established fact: A lot of our infantrymen never fired their rifle. They would freeze and just couldn't bring themselves to fire. People are kind of like cows. When they were hunkered down in a foxhole, they didn't want to rise up to shoot.

On Christmas night, we knocked that attack down. We were supposed to be relieved by the 100th Division but the Battle of the Bulge was going on and they didn't show up. At midnight, we came out—the ones of us that were still standing—and began walking. I walked five miles carrying a heavy machine gun.

A stable for a hospital

When we got back, I was feeling pretty rough. I was sent back and spent a month in a hospital in France with an ulcerated tooth and pneumonia. The general hospitals were full so we went to what we called E-Vacs. The one I went to was an old French stable. It had an outdoor john. It didn't matter how bad off you were, if you went to the toilet, you went outside.

When I went back to my unit, I found out that it had been in a hell of a fight. My company and Charlie Company were practically decimated at a place called Herrlisheim.

The corps commander had made a mistake with his intelligence reports and we lost a complete tank battalion.

Only 21 Americans survived out of two battalions

After the last attack, B Company of the 56th Infantry Battalion wound up with 11 men and C Company had 10.

When I got back to take over the company, they were south of St. Marie Auxmines. That's the town where they executed Private Slovak. He was the only soldier executed by our government during the war. He deserted three times.

Our outfit was being replenished with green troops who'd had little training. They were taken out and got to fire a few shots on a rifle range and that was about it.

We got orders to move down to the Colmar Pocket in February of 1945. That's one of the area's where Audie Murphy fought. He won the Medal of Honor just on the west side of Colmar. We went through Audie's outfit on the way in.

The C. O. writes to his men's widows

It was in that time period that my responsibilities as a company commander really hit me. That's because I had to write the letters home to the families of the men that were either killed in action or wounded in action. I'd write these notes to mothers, fathers, wives and sweethearts. The worst part was, they would write back, wanting to know all of the gory details. Of course, I usually didn't know all of that, and, if I had, I wouldn't have told them anyway.

When you get up in the morning, you wonder: Will I be alive at sundown? I wonder what will happen to me today? Will I become a bundle of junk, or whatever you want to call it.

Fighting with the Goums

When we went through Colmar, we were joined by the French Goums. Those were the Moroccan troops fighting with the French. The Germans feared them as much as our old cavalry had feared the Sioux and the Apache. The Goums had a habit of sneaking around on night patrols. They'd catch a German soldier and cut off his ears and hang them on their belts.

We were about a mile out of Colmar when we really got belted. We found out later that we were fighting the German 6th Mountain

Division that came out of Norway. They were tough cookies, tenacious, just as bad as our own paratroopers.

We teamed up with the 109th Infantry Regiment. They were part of the 28th "Bloody Bucket" Division that got themselves chewed up royally, the same outfit that Private Slovak was in.

An unexpected thing happened. We were hiking up the road when a soldier from the 109th came over and said, "Hi ya, Bill. What'cha know?"

He was the kid that lived across the street from me in my hometown and was a sergeant in the intelligence platoon, (2nd Battalion, 109th Infantry Regiment.) We walked together for about a half-mile. I never saw him again until after the war.

Right after that, I got clobbered. We got to fighting in the timber. Our platoons got separated and my old friend, Salvador Galiardi said, "Bill, we'd better get the platoons together before nightfall or we'll be in a hell of a shape."

I said, "That's right. I'll go this way and you go that and we'll round 'em up."

A bazooka shell hits the jeep

I remember starting to cross a field and thought I heard a round coming in. It was about 2:00 p.m. The next thing I recall was it was about 1:00 a.m. the next morning and I was in an aid station. I didn't know my own name or anything else. My jeep driver had been killed, blown to pieces by a Panzer Faust, which is like our bazooka. However, I hadn't been in the jeep at that time.

What put me down was a piece of shrapnel. It hit my eye socket. They sent me back to the hospital for observation. They patched me up, saved the eye, and within two days I'd recovered enough to go back to my outfit.

Soldier shoots his buddy

A horrible thing happened. I sent out a patrol and told my men to be watching for other patrols that would be coming back. No unnecessary shooting. Well, one of the patrols did come back and one of my men, just a kid, yelled out, "I see 'em! I see 'em," and he let her go, hitting one of his friends in the head.

Now maybe you think that I didn't have something on my hands. The kid went nearly crazy over what he'd done. We had to get him out of there and practically had to tie him up to restrain him. He went to an aid station and we never saw him again. These are the things you never talk about very much. In this action I got my second Bronze Star.

Running with Patton's army

After Colmar, we joined Patton's army to join the run to the Rhine up through the Palintate. There was the Battle of the Bulge, The Rhineland, and Central Europe, all major campaigns.

The Germans began setting up roadblocks and we had to fight our way through those. We called in aircraft to strafe their columns. We got involved in a hit and run battle with the Germans, then took the town of Speyer.

Communications during the battles broke down pretty bad. It almost becomes every man for himself. That's why I have the greatest respect for the non commissioned officers. They are the backbone of the infantry, the glue that holds the men together. I remember back at Camp Barkeley, our First Sergeant was an old-timer. We had a lot of 2nd lieutenants just out of regular college ROTC, which didn't prepare them for much of anything. The old Sarge would tell them, "Lieutenant, this is just your first enlistment. Don't get excited."

Best friend killed

It was tough and I was really affected by the death of my buddies. We were in a firefight in Germany and my best friend, who was my best man at my wedding, was trying to help a wounded soldier onto a tank. A sniper shot my friend in the head, killing him on the spot.

A few days later, I lost two other friends—platoon leaders—one from A Company and one from C Company of the 56th. I wrote home to my wife and told her, "Just send flowers. That's all."

Their wives were still living in Abilene, Texas, outside of Camp Barkeley.

These are the things that bothered me for a long time. In fact, they still do.

Responsibility

Leading troops into combat is an awesome task. I was aware that a lot of enlisted men hated their officers, but somebody had to take the responsibility. Responsibility is the key word. Few people really want it. The only lieutenants we got that had much military training were those who'd graduated from military schools. You know, when the Korean War started, they commissioned the entire graduating class from New Mexico Military.

Afterward, I was relieved of my company, which I was happy about, and was assigned to Combat Command B as Assistant Communications Officer. That's where I stayed until the end of the war. I got decorated a few times while I was over there: Two Bronze Stars, a Purple Heart, the Combat Infantry Badge, a commendation for fighting in the Battle of the Bulge, and several other medals and ribbons.

You know, they said the only reason you got a Purple Heart was because you forgot to duck!

Released, then back a year later

I got home from Europe in December 1945. There weren't any civilian jobs available around Hobbs, New Mexico. So, in less than a year, I took the opportunity to go back on active duty. I had to drop down a grade and went in as a 1st lieutenant. They sent me to Ft.

Ernie Frazier

Bragg, NC, where I took over as the company commander of an infantry basic training company.

Japan

From there, I was shipped to Japan to be a Company Commander in the 27th Infantry--the famous Wolfhounds of the 25th Division. Our economy was in bad shape and the military was being downsized. Our weaponry was so old and obsolete and worn out that we didn't have a machine gun barrel that hadn't had the rifling shot out of it. Our ammunition had come in from the South Pacific with the 27th. I was about half afraid to go down to the ammo dump. The hand grenades had all gotten rusty and you never knew when a pin would fail. Our supplies and equipment were in such bad shape that we had jeeps jacked up on blocks because we couldn't get valve cores for the tires. Some of us pitched in and went down to a Japanese store and bought a bunch so we could air up the tires and get around. Troop training was pathetic. You could imagine what happened to them when they were sent to Korea.

In Japan, I coined the remark, "Milkshake soldiers." General Douglas McArthur was a Prima Dona if there ever was one. In Tokyo, he lived like royalty. The training for our regiments was nothing more than a social event. It was just like it was in Honolulu prior to Pearl Harbor. Incidentally, the 27th was at Pearl Harbor on December 7th.

I spent two years in Japan. Considering everything, I enjoyed it a lot. I'd go back again today. In fact, I've kicked myself over the years for not making a career of the army.

Recalled for Korea

I was called in June of 1950 for the Korean War and I became a staff officer in the G-2 office of the 2nd Armored Division at Ft. Hood, TX. Later, I was sent to the Post Headquarters in Fort Hood, Texas, as Assistant Director of Intelligence. I won't talk much about that but will tell you that I had an atomic energy clearance and worked with

people out of Sandia Base in Albuquerque, New Mexico, on various classified projects. I was mostly a desk soldier during Korea.
I spent a total of 12 years in the army.

After I got home, I worked with an oil company until they sold out; then I went to farming and ranching.
My wife's parents were old-time pioneers that homesteaded a sizeable ranch outside of Hobbs, NM. Her mother, Thelma A. Webber, is still living. She's real active with the College of the Southwest, which is remarkable because she just had her 95th birthday. The college named a dormitory after her. Also, she maintains a private museum at the ranch that is stocked with antiques and collectibles from the ranch.

CHAPTER 33

HARRY FUKUHARA

" I didn't want to go on the invasion of Japan. My family still lived there."

The story of Harry Fukuhara is a classic case of truth being stranger than fiction.

He was rejected for service in the U. S. military due to poor eyesight and was confined to a Japanese internment camp because of his Japanese ancestry. When the U. S. Army needed Japanese interpreters and interrogators, they inducted him without the mandatory physical exam or basic training. Ill equipped for combat, prohibited from becoming an officer even though his Caucasian counterparts were automatically promoted, and facing the distrust of his fellow soldiers, he nevertheless went into combat against the Japanese forces in the South Pacific. Meanwhile, his three brothers were serving in the Japanese army. He knew when the U. S. dropped the atomic bomb on Hiroshima. His mother lived there.

A renegade in Japan

My wife, Tariko (Terry) and I have been married almost 53 years. We have four children and eight grandchildren.

My parents were both born in Hiroshima, Japan. An older brother brought my father to the U. S. in the early 1900's when he was only 14 or 15 years old.

My father worked as a houseboy in Seattle, Washington where I was born on January 1, 1920. Later we moved to Auburn, Washington where I attended school from the second through the eighth grades.

We only spoke English at home. My father became ill and passed away when I was 13. The immediate family I was raised in consisted of my parents and two younger brothers and me. My older brother and sister had been living in Japan and came back to the U. S. in about 1930. During the depression my mother felt she could not carry on in the States. Against my strenuous objections, since I did not want to go to Japan, she took us there in 1933. I was kind of a renegade. I refused to go to school and ran away from home. Unfortunately, I couldn't speak the language and had no money. Japan is an island nation, with few places to go. I finally met some Nisei friends and decided to go to school. When I got in, I actually enjoyed it, but my grades were mediocre and I finished in the lower half of the class in 1938. We graduated in March and I left in April to return, alone, to the United States. My older brother and sister were willing to stay in Japan and my two younger brothers did whatever they were told.

$15 a month in California

I did odd jobs in the Seattle area, mostly seasonal work and had no roots; but no one was telling me what to do. I moved around and wound up in Los Angeles. I needed money and a place to live, so in January 1939, I ran an ad, seeking a job as a houseboy. I got a job in

Ernie Frazier

Glendale, California for a couple that wanted me to keep an eye on their two boys. It paid $15 a month plus room and board with one weekend off each month. They were very nice to me and I stayed there until sometime in 1940. Their neighbors, the Mounts, were schoolteachers without any children and I went to work for them as a cook and houseboy until two or three weeks after Pearl Harbor. They offered to adopt me when the war started and our people were getting put into detention camps.

I was off on Saturdays and Sundays so I found other odd jobs and made money on the side, mostly working for gardeners, earning $5 a day. My social life was about non-existent. I had a few Caucasian friends and that was about all

My sister had returned to the States, married, and was living in Seattle. She and her husband separated so I told her to bring her baby and come to the Los Angeles area and we could all live together. We knew that we would be sent to an internment camp soon. That was a most difficult time for me. Up until then, I only had to worry about myself. Neither of us had any money. A lot of defense jobs were available but the government wouldn't hire Japanese-Americans.

No one would rent a house to us so we moved in temporarily with some Nisei friends. They shut down their business, knowing that they would soon be sent to the camps. We did find a Nisei lady whose husband had died. She lived alone in her house in Glendale and was lonely and afraid. She offered us a place to live. We moved in, but the neighborhood people didn't like that. I had to leave there after about two weeks because the grocery store wouldn't sell me anything. They didn't hold anything personally against me but said the other customers didn't like them selling to me. I was strictly an outsider. Incidents of that type continued from about February until May and it all kind of piled up on me. I was bitter and became very antagonistic. The Mounts were the only people that I could go up and talk to. If it weren't for their counsel, I might have gotten into some serious trouble. They were always there for me.

A gardener for interred Japanese

By that time, I had my own gardening route. I also ran another little business where I picked up—mostly on consignment—all kinds of stuff that the Japanese who were being interred couldn't sell, and hauled it out to various vacant lots and sold it. I had to move my location regularly so the police wouldn't catch me.

Work-wise I had more than I could handle. A lot of gardeners were leaving for Denver or Salt Lake City and they left me their equipment and customer lists. I kept the good customers.

After the evacuation of the Japanese-Americans to the internment camps, certain areas became off limits to Japanese; Los Angeles was one of them. I'd have to circle around there to get to my customers. Curfew was 9:00 p. m. and our travel was restricted to five miles, making it very difficult for me to operate. I came in late one night-- that was when I still lived with the Mounts--and the air raid warden who was our neighbor turned me in. I knew him but he said, "Well, you are violating curfew laws so I've got to turn you in." I told him I was working very late and had a hard time traveling back home. He didn't accept my excuses. I understood and didn't hold it against him.

I was living with the Mounts and a couple of times a months I'd go do the gardening for another family. I forgot their name, but they had a big house and were nice people. That's where I was working on December 7, 1941. The lady came out and told me that she just heard that the Japanese bombed someplace.

I said, "Is that right?" I thought she was just making conversation.

Japanese attack

She came back out about 20 minutes later and said, "Oh, it's terrible. The Japanese bombed Pearl Harbor. American soldiers have been killed and battleships were sunk!"

I thought maybe it was the Pearl River in China that was bombed. The Japanese were fighting there.

She told me, "No, it's in Hawaii," and said that I probably should go home.

Ernie Frazier

She paid me and I went back to the Mounts'. That bothered me and I told the Mounts that those people had always been nice to me; now they suddenly sent me home and didn't want me back. The neighborhood was all white people and I said, "Maybe I should just move out."

She said, "No, this is your home."

The neighborhood people didn't say anything about that arrangement.

One time they had a practice alert. I was over playing cards with a friend named Ed Arbogast and some others when a knock came on the door and I answered it. An air raid warden came to see if any lights were showing through the windows. He saw me and got all shook up. He told me that I was Japanese and shouldn't be there.

Ed decided to get me back home before I got into real trouble so they stuffed me in the trunk of a car and away I went back to the Mounts'.

U. S. orders Harry to internment camp

It wasn't long until our orders came to report for internment. On May 1, 1942, my niece, sister, and I joined another family and left in my old truck for the Tulare Assembly Center, a temporary internment camp. After we arrived, I had no use for the truck and was going to abandon it. A Mexican fellow asked to buy it and I said, "No, I'll just give it to you," and handed him the keys. However a short while later, I received a check for $50 from him. It was a lot of money back then and it made me feel a lot better about my fellow man.

I came down with the valley fever, a lung disorder that affected young people. I was 22 and was one of the oldest in the hospital. I wasn't really very sick and slipped out one night to go to a dance. A doctor warned me not to do it again, but I did it anyway, and he kicked me out of the hospital. I didn't know how bad the valley fever was until years later. I still have a scar on my lungs.

In August we were moved to Gila River, Arizona.

I had all kinds of problems in camp, which I could have avoided if I behaved myself. I joined Nisei and Kibei organizations. The Kibei side was bad because they were bringing in rumors such as, "The

Japanese are going to land in Mexico and get us out of camp," and a lot of anti-U. S. stuff that sounded good to us.

In November of '42, I was supervising the audit section but I didn't know anything about auditing. The chief auditor said he'd teach me all I needed to know and said, "Go out and hire the people we need." They needed 20 girls and I thought, "Gee, this is a great job!" And I went out and hired 20 girls. I was the only male in there. Soon we added 10 more girls. It was a lot of fun.

The military came around, looking for Japanese linguists to go into the Army. They wouldn't draft Japanese-Americans. If we wanted in, we would have to volunteer. I explained that I'd flunked one physical and was a 4-F. I didn't know that we'd been re-classified to 4-C.

No physical exam or basic training

They said their job wasn't to give physicals. If I passed a language test, I'd be accepted. So, I went into the army without a physical exam. A friend of mine from Santa Maria, California was there. We volunteered and went in together.

We were told to leave Gila quietly; no going away parties because of the anti-American sentiment in the camp. Twenty-six of us left a couple of days before Thanksgiving for induction into the army at Ft. Snelling, Minnesota.

We took no basic training and on December 1 were sent to linguist school at Camp Savage, Minnesota.

Additional students came in—about 400—which made up the largest class they'd ever had.

In March, they wanted some linguists, so they picked 50 of us that were doing well and were split into teams of 10. I told them I had no basic training. They told me I'd get it eventually. (Later, when we made our first enemy landing, I was really unsure of myself. I didn't know how to clean a gun or fire one. I didn't know anything about combat.)

Other students were sent to Camp Shelby in June for basic. We didn't but our team did well and was promoted after three months.

Ernie Frazier

We were sent to San Francisco for shipment overseas. We had to wait a week or so until the ship was ready. Then they sent us to Angel Island, a former immigration center taken over by the military.

Meeting German sabateurs

Every morning we had to march around the island for exercise. On the first or second day, we saw other soldiers marching around the other way. They were German prisoners under American guards. They saw us, assumed we were Japanese prisoners, and waved to us.

We found out that some were from a German sub that surfaced and others from a freighter that was sunk in our waters.

When our ship was ready, we shipped out for Australia; a trip I'll never forget. It took 17 days and I was so seasick. We weren't traveling in a convoy and had to zigzag all the way across.

We couldn't let anyone know we were in intelligence work. Other soldiers on the ship thought we were cooks. We were all NCOs and none of us knew how to cook. I was detailed to cook for a while, which consisted mostly of opening cans. I was so seasick that I vomited all over the table. It was really bad.

The Military Intelligence Service

We landed at Brisbane, Australia and were assigned to the Sixth Army. Our team of 10 men was assigned to Sixth Army Headquarters. Our team leader was the first MIS (Military Intelligence Service) guy to get killed in action. That was on June 23, 1944. We're going to have a memorial service for him on June 23, 2002.

Sixth Army was spread out and couldn't accommodate us so we were sent to ATIS (Allied Translators and Interpreters Service.) That's where the linguist's pool was. It was part of an organization under General MacArthur's headquarters. Since it was an organization of our allies, it was made up of Australians, Dutch, Chinese, and British, who were mostly officers. The Nisei were enlisted men.

We took training on translating and interrogation. I was on the translation team. After several weeks, we were sent to Sixth Army Headquarters at Camp Columbia, Australia. We shipped out from there to New Guinea to Good Enough Island.

We were there for a couple of weeks. Regimental combat teams were being organized to begin MacArthur's strategy of island hopping. We went to different units. Unlike Europe, our units were small because we were operating in the jungle. A regiment would be the nucleus of the regimental combat team.

There is an island close to New Guinea called Great Britain Island. That was where we joined the 112th Cavalry Regiment, a gung-ho National Guard unit from San Antonio, Texas. They hadn't been in combat but did have some jungle training. They didn't know us and we didn't know them. It was an odd situation because they had never seen any Japanese before and didn't know why we were joining them. They said they never took prisoners and wondered why they needed us as interrogators? We had to sort of sell ourselves to them and explain why they would benefit by our presence.

Issued a gun he couldn't shoot

Sometime after the 15th of December 1943, we boarded landing crafts (LCMs). The army didn't have enough so they borrowed some from the First Marine Division, a veteran outfit that had landed on Guadalcanal. That's when I was first issued a gun. It was a Thompson Machine Gun and I didn't know what to do with it. I took it back. It was too heavy for me and they gave me a carbine. There I was with no training and no confidence. I just followed along and did what the others did.

The Texans were a close-knit unit. Many had been in the National Guard for a long time and were in their 40's. We didn't have much time to get acquainted so we were considered outsiders. Our higher-ranking officers transferred in from outside the unit. We came under the S-2; the intelligence unit.

There were four of us linguists; Terry Musitawa, our team leader; Ben Nakamuro who lives now in California; Howard Ogawa from San Jose, who died a couple of years ago; and me. We were all bi-

lingual. However, I was the only one that was new to the army and without basic training.

The smell was terrible

Two bodyguards were assigned to protect us. We lived out in the jungle without tents, just hammocks with mosquito netting. It was a terrible assignment for our guards because they had to stay with us 24 hours a day. For a while I slept with another guy. Boy, I tell you, it was terrible. It was hard to bathe and we all smelled so bad we could hardly take it.

A Lt. Botting was assigned as a linguist and acted as our representative to the staff. He was transferred after a few weeks and our team leader took over. An Australian officer in the S-2 also looked after us, so to speak. We were all-new to the operation and didn't know what to expect. The type of training we had as linguists was to obtain documents or information from prisoners that would support the operation. Before we made the landing, we were told where we were going and to expect opposition. All they knew that Japanese soldiers had been on the island for quite a while and that the area we were landing at had been a coconut plantation that belonged to the Australians. That's all we knew, so we tried to gather any information we could, analyze and report it to S-2, and explain how it would be of value to the U. S. forces. In the meantime, we asked that they apprise us of the situation so we could adjust our mission to support the fighting unit. We received very little information because they didn't have any. We had a few Australian maps and knew we were going to cross a channel called the Bismarck Sea.

The night we boarded the boats, we were told that we'd have one final hot dinner. We hadn't had one in a long time. It was like the "Last Supper." We had turkey and ham and everything. Rations were issued for us to eat for the next three or four days.

I had a lot of things in my pack so I threw out dictionaries and other things I didn't need and put the food in.

Into combat with a typewriter

A lieutenant gave me a portable typewriter and said, "You carry this."

I thought that looked funny, a soldier going into combat carrying a typewriter.

Our group, the headquarters group, was put onto the small landing crafts. We had a jeep and a trailer and eight or ten people aboard. All of a sudden, we hit a storm. They knew a typhoon was coming but it didn't matter; we had to go in anyway. Our boat was the next to last landing craft. We landed but the storm got so bad that the last craft couldn't make it in. They jumped onto our boat, doubling our numbers. It was so crowded that you couldn't even sit down.

Typhoon!

The typhoon really hit and water began coming up over the sides of our boat. It was getting dark, we were seasick and started throwing up all that great dinner we'd eaten earlier.

The waves washed all the vomit out to sea. I was sitting down when the guy in charge of the boat said, "Bail the water out," because there was so much pouring in. All we could do was scoop it out with our helmets. I was terribly sick and scooped up a couple of times; then my helmet went overboard. I didn't even care. All I remember is thinking, "Boy, this is a terrible way to fight a war, being sick all the time."

We couldn't see any of our boats or anything else in the dark. No lights or smoking were allowed. I must have passed out because when I woke up about 4:00 a.m. it was real quiet and the sun was up. There were about 15 landing crafts circling around the island, waiting their turn to land.

The signal came for our boat to land. I was worried and excited, not knowing if we'd be fired on or what. But, for a while, it wasn't exciting at all. However that soon changed. Some of our planes were flying overhead. A Japanese plane came over, dropped down and started strafing us. We had a couple of machine guns on our ship. All of our ships, including our destroyers, opened fire.

I was scared but there was no place to run to: no place to hide. I tried to get down under the jeep but someone was already there. The attack was over in a matter of seconds. Then, another Zero came over, but his attack wasn't as scary as the first one. My glasses were splashed over with salt water, making it hard to see that there was blood all over me. I thought, "I must be shot!"

I saw another guy was covered with blood. When he and I tried to get under the jeep, a guy behind us got hit and it was his blood that was all over us.

It's quite an experience. Without any training, I had no idea what to expect.

Unloading in deep water

Our turn came and we went in for the landing. We were told that we would probably have to wade in when the boat stopped. It lurched to a stop, was stuck and couldn't move. We were ordered to get off the boat. I looked and saw nothing but water everywhere. We were carrying a lot of equipment so we fastened flotation bladders under our arms to keep from sinking. In front of me was one of the bodyguards.

The guy in front of him stepped off the boat and sunk down, out of sight. I thought, "My gosh, what's going on?"

We were actually stuck on a coral reef. The Australian maps didn't show those reefs and it made a big difference in a landing whether the tide was up or down.

The guy that went under never came back up. I knew how to swim and I wondered if I shouldn't get rid of my equipment.

A sergeant, a big guy, said, "Hold onto me," and I did just that. I had a carbine, which I hung onto, but I think I threw the typewriter away. Somehow, we made it to the shore. I still remember that the lieutenant came up and asked me, "Where's that typewriter?" I said, "Oh, I think I must have lost it."

He was so upset. He said, "I'm signed for it and I've got to pay for it!"

I laugh when I tell the story today, but it was no laughing matter, then.

After that, believe it or not, it was all-new to me and I enjoyed the experience. We got strafed and were bombed night after night. We had no radar on our anti-aircraft guns. I volunteered for patrols and went out with the navy on PT boats. I went out on everything. Our mission was to take a peninsula. The whole thing was a coconut plantation that the Japanese had taken. We were to hold it. What had happened was the First Marine Division had gone around us and hit another part of the island named Cape Gloucester. That was the same division that landed at Guadalcanal.

Decoys

We were used as decoys in the landing and were to send out recon patrols. We were there from the middle of December until March 1944 and only took one prisoner in all that time. He was wounded and couldn't tell us much. But, we got our documents.

G-2 realized that when you can't see the enemy your intelligence must gather information. Of course, it was just as bad for the Japanese as for us, but they were already there. They were dug into caves or tied up in the trees.

It wasn't like Europe where you could talk to civilians or have planes overhead taking aerial photos. Nor were we taking a lot of prisoners. Consequently, our intelligence provided scarce but much needed information. It had to be information that was perishable, something that could be used right away, not two months later. A lot of documents we found were important and were sent back to headquarters for translation. We found out about their strength, morale, supplies and logistics. We got information that would help our air force in identifying targets all over Japan. Our army and marines wanted immediate information, such as what was in front of this unit, how many soldiers, what kind of equipment do they have, what kind of weapons, and how is their food supply.

Prisoners that were stragglers or sick didn't have current information. They'd been left behind when their troops went on without them.

Ernie Frazier

Natives on the islands could supply some information, but it was unreliable because they had neither written language or numbers and couldn't tell you, for example, if something was between numbers 10 and 15. When they said there were a lot of Japanese soldiers, were they talking about 15 or 100? They didn't understand measurements or distances from one point to another. We used our fingers to explain numbers to them, but when we got past 10, they had no concept.

I worked with an Australian warrant officer who, when he was a civilian, had a job in that area. He knew the plantation well. He handled the natives that we used on patrols. They were good and I went out with them.

They liked rice. I'd eat it along with the fish they caught by damming up a little stream. Sometimes we'd throw a grenade into the sea. It would explode and about 50 fish would float to the surface.

The natives didn't mind wading in deep water when we went out on patrols, but I thought it was terrible. When they got tired, they'd just lean against a tree and sleep. That was something I couldn't do. They were very simple but good people.

Sometimes we'd sing some Japanese songs and the natives would join in, singing the Japanese "gagooka." They sang it without an accent, just like they were Japanese. If they sang it in English, it would be with an accent. We knew they had made some Japanese friends who taught them the songs. They questioned whether I was an American or a Japanese soldier, but it really made no difference to them.

We had to explain to our chief of staff that the natives would kill the Japanese rather than take them prisoner, and we had no prisoners. So, our General sent down an order to capture some.

Before we got there, the Japanese had lookout stations around the island.

Night patrols

I went out on night patrols in speedy PT boats that would go 50-60 miles per hour. There were manned by three naval officers with several young sailors, volunteers that would go home in six months, that weren't afraid of anything. I was 23 and the oldest one there.

The boats went out in pairs. They'd speed in to torpedo Japanese ships in the harbor and then try to escape. Our men enjoyed it. They went up the river one night, saw lights and assumed that the Japanese were there. They decided to take me out to see if I could get into a conversation with them.

I was seated in the very front of the boat and was told, "When you see the light, start talking to 'em." I made up a little scenario of what I was going to say based on the documents we had about the units in the area. We didn't know who was there at the time and assumed it was just an outpost. I was to convince them that we were a Japanese ship bringing in supplies and they should signal us so we could land at their location.

We went up the river very slowly as our wake could be spotted by Japanese airplanes overhead.

We pulled into the area but I didn't see any lights. I began talking over a megaphone in Japanese. It was real quiet so voices would carry.

A narrow escape!

I was talking and looking around, trying to see lights or hear someone talking back to me. All of a sudden, the boat I was on, the front boat, opened fire. We had one cannon in the back and two machine guns. They made a terrific racket and I couldn't move. Our boat reversed and tried to back out but hit a coral reef or something and we got stuck. Our boat was made of wood and we carried thousands of gallons of gasoline. Our guys said that the Japanese opened up on us, but I didn't see or hear them firing. If they hit us, even with one bullet, it would have blown us to pieces. In a way it was a lot of fun and real exciting, but I was so scared I didn't know what to do. I was just holding on and couldn't go anywhere. The boat behind us also opened fire.

We finally got loose and got out of there. I said I'd go out again but our superiors said, "No," because we linguists weren't supposed to go out on those missions.

Ernie Frazier

I talked to other guys that went into Rabaul and other islands that hit the Japanese ships with torpedoes, and then escaped. It was fantastic, what some of them did. PT boats are what took MacArthur out of the Philippines.

Bombarded!

After we made our landing, I was with Misutari, following him, when planes dropped down to strafe us with machine gun fire. Actually, it was one of our fighter planes firing on us. We jumped into a bomb crater that had a lot of water in it but its sides were all loose dirt. Bombs exploding nearby practically covered me with that dirt and I didn't know whether I was hit or not. My ears hurt because of the dirt being blown into them. It was hot and humid. I didn't see much fighting from where I was. There were no front lines.

The next day, up at the plantation, we had no water so it was brought up in five-gallon cans. Someone told me to get in a jeep and go for water. I went down to the beach, unarmed and alone, and found a couple of water cans. I looked around and a G. I. was standing there pointing his weapon at me.

Mistaken identity

He thought I was a Japanese soldier. I tried to talk my way out of the situation and told him I was an American soldier. He was confused. He didn't expect a Japanese soldier that could speak English. I talked for a long time before my bodyguard came looking for me, knowing that I had taken off alone. Even he had a hard time convincing the soldier that I was on their side. Later I asked the soldier why he didn't shoot me. He said, "I don't know."

My bodyguard was a nice guy about 19 or 20 years old. He wanted to go back to his combat unit and they let him re-join them.

I heard later that he went out of his mind and had to be medi-vaced out of there.

I was a T-4 at the time, a technical sergeant with a T under the stripes.

Bombed for 60 nights

We got bombed almost nightly for 60 nights. Most of the headquarters people headed into a big tunnel when the bombing started and stay until morning.

We went in there a couple of times. It was terrible. You could hear the bombs dropping so Misutari said, "Let's go up and see what's going on."

We were told that we couldn't do that, so we sneaked out. After that, we stayed out of there. We couldn't dig foxholes in the coral rock, so we found a coconut tree next to a cliff. We put up a nice tent and would sit up and talk all night long. Bombs fell around us, not very close, and mostly fell into the ocean.

In March we were told that we were to return to 6th Army Headquarters or go to Australia. Misutari was going with me but changed his mind and went to Australia. I went alone to 6th Army Headquarters to train the Niseis that were coming in. Then I went on two more landings. I came down sick with malaria and on June 20th was sent to Australia for treatment. Misutari was sent back up to take over another team and was killed on the 27th of June. He was only on his new assignment for a couple of days. It's ironic. If he had gone back to 6th Army with me, like he originally planned, he wouldn't have been killed. It was also tragic that his father was in an internment camp when Misutari was killed.

We didn't have all the sophisticated technology that is now used to gather intelligence. Japanese speaking Nisei were very valuable in gathering documents and interrogating prisoners and civilians. Before our landings, we relied on Australians, missionaries and plantation workers who'd stayed on in New Guinea for our intelligence.

Even though the navy or marines wouldn't accept Niseis, they needed them so they borrowed them from the army. In fact, Niseis were on all the marine landings in the South Pacific and even rode in B-29's when they were on bombing raids.

In May 1944 we made a landing at Itabe, New Guinea. It had been bombarded for days by our forces and we met no opposition. The Japanese had no weapons to fight our air force or navy so they all took off for the hills. Our navy had sunk all of their supply ships and nothing was getting to them.

They had just left before we arrived. They had no refrigeration but they had skinned a buffalo or cow and hung it up in the sunshine. It was covered with flies.

There were six of us linguists. We carried socks full rice, as we were tired of our dehydrated rations; and we had mishoshitu, biboshi and beef. We had nothing fresh unless we traded some documents to the navy for food. They'd give us a few fresh eggs. One would feed five or six of us. Once a chicken was cooked up and served to our general. He ate a small piece and gave the rest of the meat to his staff. When they were done with it, they made soup out of the bones and that's what we got.

In April, I was at Itopi and we had prisoners come in. Somehow the Japanese soldiers had been surviving up in the hills, but they needed salt. They couldn't live without it so they'd go down to the ocean to find some. The natives would find them and turn them over to us. The MP's brought in two prisoners. One was a big guy. He was very anti-American and non-cooperative. We didn't have an interrogation room or even a tent so we just talked to them out in the yard.

Miusaki was interrogating the big guy. He suddenly came over to me and said, "The prisoner I'm talking to keeps looking at you and asking about you."

Neighbor from Japan becomes prisoner

I looked at the prisoner and said, "I don't know who he is."

Ten minutes later Miusaki came back and said, "He asked if your name is Fukuhara."

That got my attention so I went over and looked at his P. O. W. tag. His name was Matsura.

I said, "My gosh, I know Matsura. We were neighbors in Japan for four years!"

He stood up and was much taller than me. He hadn't eaten much for a long time and was real skinny. I'd left Japan in April 1938. He said he left in February to join the Japanese army.

He'd been in six years and was a master sergeant. He swaggered around and had a beard and wasn't very co-operative. The MP's had rifles and were watching him all the time.

He wanted food so I brought him some along with some cigarettes. He started hinting around about how he could escape. I told him, "No you can't do that. You're a prisoner."

He was with me about 45 minutes. I guess he hoped I'd look the other way and he'd take off. I didn't see him again, but when the war ended in 1945, I went to look for my family in Hiroshima. I found Matsura's parents, which was remarkable since they were near the epicenter of the atom bomb blast. I told them that I'd seen their son still alive. They wouldn't believe me because they hadn't heard from him in years. He'd gone to China and then to New Guinea.

In 1989 I went again to Japan and looked up Matsura's home place, but he had moved. I left word with some people that I was staying with my cousin, and that evening Matsura called me and we had a reunion. The Japanese reporters got a hold of our story and wrote it all up in the paper. They identified me as the enemy!"

I still hear from Matsura every year.

We didn't form too many buddy-type relationships like the 442nd or the 100th. They were actual units whereby we were only attached temporarily to various units. That's why I think the Presidential Unit Citation we were awarded was the only thing the intelligence people had in common. It is the highest unit citation that you can get. There's a difference between individual and unit citations.

Fourteen of the guys went over with Merrill's Marauders and spent 14 months together, fighting behind enemy lines all the time they were there. They developed a very close relationship.

In my team, there were ten of us and we were split up a lot of the time. We never served together as a team in combat. After Misutari was killed, I was promoted and took his place. We joined the 33rd Division, a National Guard unit from Illinois. We were sent to the island of Morati, a jungle island north of New Guinea that belongs to Indonesia.

That was in 1944. In January of 1945 we landed on Luzon in the Philippines. Our division was sent north with several other divisions to take Bagiuo, the summer capital of the Philippines. General

Ernie Frazier

Yamasihta, had moved his military headquarters there. I think we took Bagiuo in June of '45. Then we went down to the lowlands in the Philippines to prepare for the invasion of Japan. Even then, when I went to other units, guys would transfer in and work with me for a while, and then be sent elsewhere so we didn't get too close. We don't have big reunions like the other units.

The story of the MIS during wartime is exciting but fairly brief. Our work extended far beyond the war but it's not something to talk or write about because you don't go out and sacrifice your life or anything like that. However, the MIS was more active after the war than during it.

Other soldiers from regular outfits were allowed to rotate home on the point system. We linguists were considered indispensable and were not allowed to go home even though we had more points accumulated than most of the others. In July I got a hold of a couple of team leaders; Masiomoto, who passed away a couple of years ago, and Pat Macy. We got some time off and went down on a personal basis to Manila to see if we could get some high-ranking officers to exempt us from going on the Japan invasion. We saw Colonel Mashbeard, who controlled all the linguists. I told him I didn't want to go because I had family in Japan and wouldn't feel right about landing there. Also, it was very painful to consider that I might be taken prisoner by the Japanese someday.

He was very understanding but he politely told us it that that would be impossible to exempt or transfer us since there weren't enough linguists. He said the landing would be larger even than the Normandy invasion and they needed us all. We began to realize just how important that operation was going to be. He promoted a bunch of us to officers, giving us battlefield commissions without requiring that we go to school. Initially, when we completed language school, all Caucasian graduates became officers. None of the Nisei's were authorized to be officers. Now, they realized the significance of our contributions and authorization came down to promote us.

My family was at Hiroshima

Just a couple of days later, the atomic bombs were dropped and the war ended. It was excruciating to hear that Hiroshima was bombed. My mother and three brothers were living there. My happiest experience was when I found out they had survived, although one brother died later from the after effects of the bomb. I also found out that my brothers had all served in the Japanese Army.

When we went in to occupy Japan, we were surprised that we met almost no guerilla fighters or other resistance like in Europe.

During the occupation of Japan, I was covert all the way. I had one official covert job and I used that as my cover as I was in the liaison business. No one knew about my second job except for the people I worked for. Some people knew me from my covert status. I always used my own name, not a fictitious one.

There are varying degrees of operating undercover. It was very difficult, as the wives didn't know what was going on. Sometimes they would try to write about their husband's undercover activities, but they only knew part of it. Probably the agent never told his wife or anyone else about his activities.

The degree of sensitivity of the project we were working on determined who knew what we were doing. Our headquarters were in Hawaii but we maintained offices in Japan. We had bi-lateral projects where we worked with our Japanese counterpart in Korea, Vietnam, Taiwan, Thailand, the Philippines, and other places.

Counter-intelligence was pretty much on the surface. A lot of that was conducted with our counterparts. We supplied the funds and techniques and the Japanese agencies did most of the groundwork. As they became economically independent, they contributed funds.

Positive intelligence entailed getting information out of China, Russia, North Vietnam and North Korea. We had a joint interest with Japan in those efforts, as they too were interested in what was happening in those countries.

Over the years, I'd be interviewed by Japanese news media that wanted to know what I did with the Japanese government and what agencies I worked with. I could only tell them that I worked with

Japanese intelligence agencies. But, I could not tell them what we specifically did.

Not many books were written on our activities. Reporters put out articles that were usually incorrect. We didn't bother to correct them because we always had to protect our source of information. Much of the time the writing was negative.

In a covert operation, we had no counterparts; it was strictly a U.S. operation. We didn't tell the Japanese about them but they knew what we did because they would uncover some of the stuff we were doing. They'd come to me and ask, "Is this one of your American operations?" I always had to reply, "I don't know but I'll check it out." My job was to run and protect the operations. Even if our Japanese allies uncovered the operation, we considered it had been compromised. By the time they came to me they had investigated it so thoroughly that in about 99% of the cases I had to admit, "Yeah, it's ours."

There were all kinds of intelligence organizations operating in Japan and Germany; the Chinese, the Russians, the South Koreans, and the Japanese who were working all of them. Some really big operations were going on and it became quite complicated.

We had Russians who gave themselves up to us. They'd come to us and we'd turn them over to our Embassy and the C. I. A.

When things went smoothly, I didn't get involved in the operations. I had no need to know what was happening. I'd get involved when a problem occurred, such as when the Japanese or other countries would get suspicious of our activity. We had to be real careful to avoid publicity, get certain people out of the country, and protect ourselves in general to avoid embarrassment.

People still call me and ask for details of what I had done. I tell them I just don't remember.

All Japanese people expected to die

Conditions in Japan were terrible after the war. Their major cities were bombed out. There was no food or medicine nor industry. Nothing. When Japan surrendered, it was a surprise to the people because they all expected to die, fighting to the death against the allies. My brothers and my mother expected to die. They didn't want to but figured it was the only way out. When the war ended, they went along with the surrender; they decided to go along with it. But, they were frightened; they'd been told that the Americans would torture and rape them. It didn't happen. Today, Japan is like the United States; most of the young people don't know what happened in Japan during the allied occupation.

I'd say the most significant legacy of the M. I. S. was that they served in the U. S. armed forces, which wasn't the easiest thing to do. After December 7, 1941 the U. S. passed a law against drafting Niseis. When we volunteered into the army in November 1942, they wanted Nisei linguists, as there was no one else available. But, the law prohibited that. All Nisei's had a D classification: undesirable aliens. For those of us in internment camps, the only way to get into the army was by volunteering, not by the draft. I was actually 4-F for physical reasons. There were about 5,000 Niseis in the army prior to Pearl Harbor that had their guns taken away from them when the war started. That really hurt because disarming a soldier was about the worst humiliation he could suffer. Within the next few months, half of them were discharged. It was termed an administrative separation. It was for the convenience of the government. On one side, they wanted everyone to come into the military. On the other side, they were kicking the Niseis out, all because of their race.

The U. S. is a a better place to live

In my opinion, the United States is a much better place to live than before the war. All of us Niseis expected to meet racial discrimination and racial profiling. The government is now much more supportive of minorities and there are lots more of them than in the past. In 1941, we had no support in the federal, state, or local government that would come out and speak in our behalf. Churches and schoolteachers were about the only groups that would speak up.

I'm proud of the Nisei who did much after the war to bridge the cultural gaps between the United States and Japan during the occupation of Japan.

Ernie Frazier

Harry served as a Japanese language interpreter, interrogator, and translator from April 1942 until August 1945.

CAMPAIGNS/ASSIGNMENTS WW II:

May '43—ATIS, Brisbane, Australia
Sep '43-Jan '45—SW Pacific, New Guinea, New Britain, Dutch New Guinea, Moratai
Dec '43—Landed on Arawe, New Britain with 112th Cav. Regt)
May '44--Wakde-Sarmi Operation, Dutch New Guinea with
. 163rd Regt., 41st Div.
Feb-Sep '45—<u>Luzon, Philippines</u>
Jul '45—Near Bagiuo, Luzon with 33rd Inf. Div.
Sep '45-Jan '46—<u>Occupation of Japan</u>
Sep '47-Jul '54—<u>Occupation of Japan</u>

I stayed on active duty in the United States Army for 29 years and retired with the rank of Colonel in October, 1971. I then became a Department of the Army Civilian and served with the 500th M. I. Bde. in Japan until retiring in October 1990.

Author's acknowledgement: I thank the California Civil Liberties Educational Program for allowing me to utilize excerpts from Diane Masuda's February 4, 2002 interview with Harry Fukuhara.

CHAPTER 34

CLAY DECKER

"Our own torpedo sunk the Tang, killing 78 men. Nine of us went to a Jap prison."

This is the story of the sinking of a U. S. Navy submarine, the Tang. It achieved a prominent place in Navy history when its crew plunged into the dark depths of the Formosa Straits. Nine of her crewmen cheated death. They survived, only to face a worse fate: long-term imprisonment and torture at the merciless hands of the Japanese.

Every man aboard was an American hero. Clay Decker was one of the few that survived to tell the incredible tale. His quick thinking and action at the bottom of the sea saved lives and earned him a Silver Star. Talking with him was almost like being there.

I'm one of the nine survivors off the sunken submarine, Tang, a WW II sub named after a tropical fish

I was born and raised at Paonia, Colorado, on a cattle ranch. I grew up and got married. We had a two-year-old son and I was going to college when I decided to join the Navy to fight in WWII. I'd heard about their warm beds and good food. I like marching but didn't really care to become a foot soldier.

I went to boot camp in Farragut, Idaho in December 1943, and then on to torpedo school in Norfolk, Virginia. Upon completion, we could serve as a torpedo man on P. T. boats, destroyers, aircraft, or submarines. I volunteered for submarines and was sent to submarine school at New London, Connecticut.

Ernie Frazier

We trained on an "O" boat for three months and had to jam a lot of information about the boats into our heads. After completing submarine school, I was assigned to the Tang, a submarine built at Mare Island, California.

The submarine service is all volunteer. Back in those days, like the flyboys, we got extra pay. It wasn't a lot but every little bit helped.

Most of the lads coming in were 17 or 18 years of age so, at almost 22, I got the nickname of "Dad", a name that has stuck with me to this day among my old buddies.

I was fortunate, I believed, to be assigned to the Tang.

O'Kane

Our skipper was Captain Richard Heatherton O'Kane, a future Medal of Honor winner, who'd been put in command when the Tang was commissioned. I was a member of the commissioning crew.

When we'd come in off patrol, fellow submariners would say, "I don't know if I want to go out on the Tang with "Killer O'Kane."

I'd stop and correct them right then. "Dick O'Kane is a married man with two youngsters. I have two youngsters and I don't want to die any more than anyone else and he doesn't either."

The way it worked out, he was one heck of a good submarine skipper. Prior to coming to the Tang, Dick was the executive officer under Mush Morton on the Wahoo. It had just completed five runs and had a whale of a record.

To those of us on the Tang, Dick was a man you had to respect. He ran a tight ship but he always gave you a reason for his policies. For example, he wouldn't allow beards. We'd ask, "Why not?"

"Men," he answered, " if something happens and a pharmacist's mate has to sew up a six inch gash in your face, I don't want him to have to fight two inches of hair."

I was stationed in the forward engine room on the Tang. Dick would come through for a white glove inspection. You had to respect him because, if you did a good job, he'd thank you for it. It was all teamwork, working with Dick. The Tang had a great record and we sunk nine ships on one patrol.

I always thought that pilots had to be the most closely knit units in the military services. But, if you think about it, a pilot goes out with his crew on a bombing mission and then comes back and lands. The officers go one way and the enlisted men go another. Not so in a submarine, the average patrol is 60 days. Some lasted much longer.

Living arm-pit to arm-pit

We'd come in from patrol after sinking three or four ships, and taking a lacing from depth charges. After it was all over, the officers didn't get very far from us. We ate the same food, and while we didn't sleep armpit to armpit, we were still right there together. The head (lavatory) was shared by everyone. So, I changed my mind and came to believe that submariners were the most closely knit outfit of all services.

Of course, if you get 80 to 100 men together, whether it's in a submarine or any military post, you're bound to find a couple of bad actors—guys with big mouths or not as tidy and neat as they should be—and we had one or two of them on the Tang. I just ignored them.

We arrived at Pearl Harbor around the holiday season in 1944. Our first patrol out of there was successful and we spent some time in R & R at Midway Island.

The two main factors determining the patrol time are the fuel and ammunition. A third one would be if you ran out of chow!

Our second patrol was in April 1944 at the battle of Truk Island. We carried 24 torpedoes; six tubes forward and four tubes aft.

It was considered a successful patrol even though we never got to fire a torpedo. Two other submarines were to rendezvous with us near Truk. They didn't show up. I can't recall their names. We heard that they successfully fired all of their torpedoes.

Truk Island was loaded with ships. We knew that our Navy was going to make a big bombing raid on the harbor. They really wanted to do a number on 'em. I think it was the Fifth Fleet, Admiral Halsey's fleet that went in there.

We arrived as the sole submarine with the task of rescuing survivors that were shot down.

Truk was a large mountain with a big airfield and waterfront. The only way our planes could come in without being spotted and shot at miles away was to come over the mountain, and then dive right down for their run on the airport. They were on a direct line with the sea and, bless their hearts, a lot of them were shot down. They'd scoot out and drop in the water and that's where we came in.

Rescuing downed pilots

It was hairy and many times we picked up those flyboys by going down to periscope depth, and then tying a rubber raft to the periscope shears. We'd go into shallow water—it was scary— pick them up and head out to deeper water, away from the shore batteries that were firing on us.

We picked up 22 fliers on that patrol and the Tang was awarded their first Presidential Unit Citations. I've been told that each and every man serving on the boat at that time was considered to have received a Presidential Unit Citation. For the record, the Tang wound up being the holder of two of those citations.

We had a crew of 87 men on the Tang. The additional 22 men really cramped our sleeping arrangements so we had to go to "hot bunking" which meant that after you spent three or four hours in your bunk, one of the flyboys would be ready to crawl in when you crawled out.

Admiral Nimitz was in charge of the Pacific Fleet but our immediate boss in charge of Sub-Pac was Admiral Lockwood. His orders were for us to get those fliers back to Pearl Harbor as fast as we could.

Going back to Pearl meant two weeks of R & R for us at the Royal Hawaiian, which we enjoyed very much.

Torpedoes malfunction!

On our third patrol we fired all of our torpedoes except one. We had a miserable time with torpedoes running erratically. Captain O'Kane brought the one torpedo back so Admiral Lockwood's experts could check it out.

We had torpedoes that would hit the target...thud! No explosion! Duds. Others that were right on target would go underneath the keel and wind up exploding on the beach!

Except for those malfunctions, the patrol was successful.

Dick O'Kane was selected after the war to the committee to go to Japan for the war trials of the Japanese that mistreated us in the prison camp. He also went to the Japanese Department of the Navy and checked their archives. He discovered that many of the sinkings that we recorded with our superiors, had not been credited to us. After he verified dates, latitude, longitude, time, etc., we wound up being credited with 36 ships that we sank on only five patrols. Many ships made 12 or 14 patrols and didn't sink that many.

We were known as the "silent service." We feel a little bit neglected and didn't get a lot of recognition for what we accomplished because of that. A small percentage of our submarines sank an overwhelming percentage of the shipping in the Pacific; more than our surface craft or our aircraft. The submariners did it with a lot less personnel. Those are known facts.

The Tang was in the 300 class and known as a thick skin boat. However, on the pressure hull, the skin was still less than one inch thick. When you dive you "put pressure in the boat." I'm wearing two hearing aids today that were caused by those changes of pressure.

When we took the Tang on a shakedown cruise out of San Diego, we were to dive down to 500 feet. I don't remember why, but we got down to about 600 feet and did all right. We could handle that much depth.

When sitting on the bottom and the screws are turning, even at one knot, they are quiet enough that sound detectors won't pick you up. When you go into silent running, everything is shut off; ice machines, air-conditioning...everything. Talk about hot! You can sit without moving a muscle and just bend your head forward; the sweat will run off of you due to the compression and heat. It's really hot even though you're under several hundred feet of water.

Our third and fourth patrols were also successful and we sank some ships.

Our fifth patrol was successful as far as sinking ships were concerned. But, it wasn't successful for us individuals.

The Tang was sunk by it's own torpedo, 78 of our buddies died and nine of us survivors were captured by the Japanese.

Ernie Frazier

Years later I attended a meeting of ex-prisoners of war in Denver where we were asked how we became a prisoner. I shouldn't have let it bother me that much, but when I stood up and introduced myself and said, "I was a submarine sailor and went down in a submarine that sank itself with its own torpedo," people at the banquet kind of laughed, and that bothered me. I didn't like that because that's the way I became a P. O. W.

On our final patrol, the fifth one, we cleared harbor security and opened our orders. We were going into the Formosa Straits, which lay between the Chinese mainland and the island of Formosa; now known as Taiwan.

The dreaded Formosa Straits

Submariners used to hate to patrol the Formosa Straits. Why? It was probably the shallowest water in the Pacific Ocean.

When a submarine dives and opens the vent valves on its ballast tanks, it takes on negative buoyancy. The flood valves on those ballast tanks are opened and locked open. We're down here, let's say at 200 feet, and believe that the Japanese could set a depth charge to go off at 200 feet. A depth charge is like a 55-gallon drum with one half loaded with TNT and the other half empty; however, it takes on negative buoyancy when it hits the water and begins to sink. At a prescribed depth, it explodes.

We were very, very fearful, especially in shallow water, that if a depth charge went off beneath us, it could blow the water out of our ballast tanks and give the boat positive buoyancy. That would pop us up to the surface like a cork and we'd be sitting ducks.

The water in the Straits just wasn't deep enough for us to drop below their depth charges.

We weren't looking forward to going into the Formosa Straits, but we got there and spent three or four days with no success; we didn't see any targets nor fire any torpedoes.

Finally, at about 2 a. m. on October $24^{th,}$ our radar screen recorded a "pip". That "pip" turned out to be a convoy of Japanese ships. We later found out that they were headed toward the Leyte

Gulf in the Philippine Islands. You may recall that American troops returned to the Philippines shortly thereafter.

There were 35 ships in the Japanese convoy, steaming full bent toward the Philippines. I recall that we sunk nine of them. The reason it was good hunting was because we were on the surface firing; but it wasn't anything like big game hunting. When we'd fire a volley, no one told the torpedo men, "Just shove another shell in the chamber." No. That boat has to be level and steady because the boys had to use block and tackle to load those torpedoes into the tubes. After the firing, you clear away and give the boys time to reload and get ready for more action.

We had done that twice. Figure that there are 24 torpedoes; we fire six forward and four aft, that's 10, then we re-load and do it again. That's 20. Then we re-load the final four, all in the forward tube.

Battle stations!

We were called to battle stations submerged. I had been named the ship's bow planesman and was back on the throttles in the forward engine room. I left the throttles and went forward to the bow planes. The action was on the surface. Even after we fired 20 torpedoes and loaded the last four, the ships in the convoy were in such a rush to get to the Philippines that they weren't zigzagging to avoid us. Usually there would be two ships abreast in a convoy; they'd zig for a number of minutes, then zag. The job of the fire control party on a submarine is to go up in the conning tower and determine what type of ships we were encountering; one stackers or two stackers, etc. We wanted to know where the water line was in relation to their keel so we could set our torpedo run to hit the target as close to the keel as possible. If you hit above the water line, even if you blow a big hole, they still have watertight compartments and can isolate that department; they're still in business. If you strike him at the keel, bingo! You break his back and he isn't going anywhere.

Ernie Frazier

A shooting gallery

On this occasion, all the ships were in a line and it was like a shooting gallery for the Tang. We fired most of our rounds and one of the ships we hit was a troop transport. Later in the prison camp, when we called each other by our first names, Dick O'Kane told us, "Looking through my binoculars, I figured there were about 5,000 Japanese troops aboard that transport. I could see it was loaded with Japs and I had one torpedo left."

In previous patrols, O'Kane never called for the submarine to stop dead in the water to fire a torpedo at 700 yards. We always had three or four knots at least on the screws.

However, O'Kane completely stopped the boat 700 yards from our target. That reminded me of when I was hunting for big game and only had one shell left in my rifle. I'd steady it against a limb. I'm sure that Dick was thinking of something like that when he stopped the submarine; he only had one shot left.

We'd been told that we were going to Australia and were all looking forward to that. We said, "Yeah! Fire one more torpedo and we're on our way to Australia!"

The errant torpedo danced like a fish on the water

We fired the last torpedo. O'Kane and two lookouts were on the bridge watching with binoculars.

They followed it about 300 yards out of the tube. Suddenly, it came up out of the water and was dancing like a fish. It dropped back into the water, had a hard left rudder on itself, and came right around our port side, circling straight back to us. I was sitting right there and could hear Dick on the bridge, pounding on the deck, screaming, "All ahead full! All ahead full!"

He wanted some knots on that screw. If we'd had two or three knots, we could have cleared the path of the torpedo as it made its circular run. But, we didn't have the knots. The torpedo hit the Tang at the maneuvering panel, which is just at the hatch where you step into the aft torpedo room, and exploded.

We talked about it in the prison camp and Dick would say, "Damn! If I just had two or three knots on the screws!"

Carnage aboard the Tang !

Dick, along with his lookouts, First Class Botswain's Mate Liebold and First Class Radar Technician Caverly, were blown clear into the water. Fortunately, the water was full of debris from the ships we sunk. They grabbed onto some to stay afloat.

Immediately, we began to sink. Men started coming down from the conning tower to the control room. The normal way to do that is to grab the ladder, or just slide down the rail, which some guys did. However, now the water was gushing in and everybody in the conning tower was petrified. We had men that dove head first through that hatch in the deck going into the control room. True, it wasn't a long way to drop but one man hit the steel deck and broke his neck; another broke his back and there were two with broken arms.

When the hatch was open, it's connected to a lanyard with a piece of wood fastened to it. Guys coming down would slip their fingers over the lanyard, grab the wood and pull the hatch shut. The last lad down had broken his arm at the elbow when he hit the deck and it was just flopping around. With his other hand, he reached up to grab the lanyard. But it flipped up on him and got caught in the gasket that sealed the hatch, which was about as big around as a coffee table. He got it closed and dogged down but the lanyard was stuck in there and we wound up with a pretty good stream of water pouring through the hatch.

We were listing at about at a 45-degree angle. The conning tower was about 30 feet beneath the surface. In the conning tower were an officer, Larry Savatkin, who turned out to be one of the survivors, and a radio technician, a heavy set Italian boy named Andriolo.

The hatch was open and they knew they weren't far from the surface. Larry told the boy, "Come on, let's dive down and go out the hatch. We'll be on the surface in no time."

Ernie Frazier

Andriolo couldn't swim

They didn't have a life jacket or a Momsen lung, or anything. Andriolo confessed to Larry, "Oh, I don't think I can do it. I can't swim."

Larry said, "You don't have to. Just hang onto my shirttail and let's get out of here!"

Larry claimed later that Andriolo grabbed his shirttail so he ducked down and started swimming out. All of a sudden, Andriolo released his grip.

Larry told us, "As soon as I started out, he let go and I kept going."

So, four men, Dick O'Kane, Bill Leibold, Floyd Caverly, and Larry Savatkin, wound up on the surface of the water.

Eighty-seven trapped underwater in total darkness!

The rest of our crew of 87 was still on the Tang.

Later in the Japanese prison camp, Dick O'Kane was very interested in hearing about our experiences while trapped underwater.

He'd worried about us and told me, "I tried my best to swim back to the hull. I could see the bow sticking out."

I don't know what he could have done about it if he got back to the sub.

Down in the Tang, I was facing the port side. My back was toward the bulkhead of the radio shack in the control room. To my left was the stern planesman. Our stern planes were real big in the WW II subs. The ladder coming down from the conning tower was to my right.

When the torpedo hit, it rocked us, but I hardly moved—maybe six or eight inches—because when I went forward I was compressed against the stern plane and the bulkhead. I didn't get a scratch, not even a bruise.

The explosion plunged us into total darkness. Two men holding cups of coffee, George Zofcin and Jessee Da Silva, were standing at the hatch to the galley that opened to the control room and the radio shack. Jessee became one of the nine survivors.

All killed aft of the control room ! Others horribly injured!

As soon as we were hit, they stepped through the opening and closed the hatch. The hatches swing forward to aft. So from the control room, it swung back. They dogged it down right then. That meant, every man that was aft of the control room was either killed outright from the burst of the torpedo or drowned in a matter of minutes because the boat was instantly flooded.

The remainder of us were in the control room. Remember, one man had a broken back, another a broken neck, two had broken arms, and one man's leg was bleeding badly, making it difficult if not impossible for them to escape.

Incidentally, I became a qualified submariner on our second patrol. Our submarine had better than 5,000 valves and lines. To qualify, we had to learn why they were there and what they did. A qualifying officer would take you through the boat, point at a valve, and ask, "What's that valve? What does it do? Why is it there?" We had to know if it had to do with water, electricity or other functions. Did a line carry air, or did it carry hydraulic oil? Those were things we had to know. What we didn't have to know was what went on in the radio shack except for turning on the radio and sending an S. O. S. message.

We also had to know how to turn on the radar and identify a pip and, as a motor machinist's mate, I had to know how to load a torpedo into the tube, open the outer door, and fire it.

In my qualification, I remembered that the chart desk was in the middle of the control room. Immediately below that was flat table with the gyro for the submarine. The torpedo knocked out the hydraulic system and the electricity, but we had emergency battery lights, and we turned them on.

There was a flood valve and a vent valve on the ballast tanks. When we went on patrol, we opened the flood valves and locked 'em open. The flooding and draining of the ballast tanks was accomplished by opening or closing just the vent valve.

Ernie Frazier

I knew that, at our 45-degree list, there was no way we could go forward. We had to go through the forward battery department before we could get to the forward torpedo room to get to the escape chamber. Working against a 45-degree angle, you would have to have a hydraulic jack to open the hatch to the forward battery compartment. Even if we could have gotten to the forward torpedo room, we would not have been able to get out and do any maneuvering in the escape chamber at that angle.

Clay's earns the Silver Star

Dick O'Kane awarded me the Silver Star for the action I took next.

I pulled myself up on the chart desk, turned over on my back and threw my legs around a big control lever that was just above me. I extracted a release pin and that allowed my body weight to pull that big lever down over the chart desk.

That maneuver opened all of the vent valves on all of our big valves tanks forward and gave us negative buoyancy. The Tang went straight down and we felt it settle and rock on the bottom.

Now, we were down at 180 feet. The next thing was to take inventory of our injured people and see if we could help them.

The injured cannot escape!

We had 31 or 32 people in with us. Of that number, only about 21 or 22 were physically able to attempt an escape. The others were hurt so bad that they felt they couldn't begin to get up into the escape chamber to try for an ascent to the surface.

Some of our officers were with us; Henry Flanagan, our torpedo officer, was up in the forward torpedo room; Ensign Enos, who was present when we put the Tang in commission, was aboard. He was a great guy. We called him baby face. He looked so young for being an officer. We always wondered why he wasn't getting promoted; then he did something that might have been the reason. When we started making our trip up to the torpedo room, I got to the Skipper's quarters in the forward battery compartment and saw Enos with a metal waste paper basket. He was getting all the codebooks to destroy any of the vital material that the Japs might get their hands on. That was smart thinking except that he put the books in the basket and set it all on fire!

I thought, "Oh, my God! That's asinine! We don't have enough air as it is! We can't be burning anything down here!" So we got that fire stopped.

Our next move was to take up the deck covering the batteries and dump the code papers into the battery acid.

A terrific fire at 180 feet down!

After we all got up into the forward torpedo room, a terrific fire broke out in that forward battery compartment. Later, we tried to remember what caused the fire. We couldn't remember what Enos was doing back there. Our objective, when we cleared the control room, was get to the forward torpedo room through the forward battery room and in the interim, we got rid of the code books. The question was, did anybody close that hatch from the control room to the battery compartment? We were walking around in water that was coming in to the control room from the conning tower If that hatch had not been closed, it's reasonable that salt water would come up into the control room, dump over into the forward battery compartment, and start a fire. Salt water and sulfuric acid don't mix. That would cause the fire.

Plotting the escape

We got to the torpedo room and began organizing groups of four men each who would attempt the ascent together in the escape chamber. Behind us, through a big glass in the hatch, we could see the flames. It was so hot that the paint was melting on the bulkhead.

We still had air. Chief of the Boat, Bill Ballinger, who was not an officer, said, "Men, I'm going to be in the first wave. Who wants to go with me?"

Well, this Dutchman got right on his coattail. I said, "I'm going with you, Bill!"

Ernie Frazier

I'm sorry I can't remember the names of the other two lads, but I got in the first wave of four to make the ascent from the forward torpedo room by climbing up into the escape chamber.

One lad I was so glad to see in the torpedo room was Motor Mach First, George Zofcin. He was my compadre in the engine room and due to make Chief after our fifth run on the Tang. I was due to make First Class. He contacted me when we put the Tang in commission back on Mare Island. He said, "Clay, I understand you have a wife and son two years old. I have a wife and son."

He'd just bought a $6,200 row house that overlooked a hillside in San Francisco, and was wondering how he was going to pay for it.

He said, "I understand your wife is working at Kaiser Shipyards in Richmond, California. How about your family staying with my family while we're out on the Tang? Your wife can bring in some of the beans and my wife can stay home and take care of the two boys." I thought that was a perfect set-up.

Lo and behold, now here he was in the torpedo room.

We got some brand new Momsen Lungs out of the cabinet. We tore them out of their cellophane wrappers and George started helping me get one on.

Two disappear!

While we were doing that, a couple of guys, First Class Motor Machinist Mate McMorrow and a Chief Torpedo man named Wheatley, pulled a bad stunt that cost them their lives.

Doggone it, while Ballinger was trying to get the first wave and second waves organized, these two dudes crawled up into the escape chamber, closed the hatch, dogged it, flooded it down and went out of that chamber! They hadn't put a lung on or put out the buoy or a doggone thing!

We didn't know what happened to them. They weren't up there when I went out on the first wave with Bill Ballinger. We went through the proper way, with our Momsen Lungs on. We flooded the trunk down and built up the pressure, opened the hatch and let out the buoy.

McMorrow and Wheatley were not to be seen. The opening in the deck on the escape chamber was 3 feet square. It was pitch black. We theorized that if they didn't have the line tied to the first rung of the ladder on the escape trunk, and had no line to hang onto, it would take a miracle to hit that opening. Picture this; if they didn't hit it, they got hung up 180 feet below the surface in the super-structure. That's outside the pressure hull but underneath the deck. We talked about it a lot in the prison camp. There are possibly a dozen skeletons trapped in that super-structure.

<u>Beginning the ascent!</u>

The way the escape trunk works is that you have four men standing together, chest to chest. It's that tight. You have the escape door going to the sea, which swings aft. You come up through the hatch through the torpedo room, close and dog down the hatch, let water come into the escape chamber and rise to the top of the hatch door. Now your head is in an air bubble. Our pressure gauges were working properly. You build up the air pressure to exceed sea pressure by five pounds. You then open the hatch to the sea. It's scary! When you open the door, your thinking, "My gosh, we're at 180 feet. We're at the bottom of the sea!"

The water does rush in a little bit. The air bubble won't let it come up any higher than your chin, then settle down about your chest. You have your mouthpiece in and your nose clamp on. There's an airline that you use to charge your lung. You test yourself by submerging a couple of times to see if everything is working.

Bill Ballinger handed me the line with the buoy, which was a little smaller than a basketball, and said, "Clay, for our information, when that goes out count the number of knots that go through your hand."

I recalled when we went into the escape chamber during training, we'd stop at every knot and inhale and exhale every fathom, every six feet.

So I did count the knots and could tell when the buoy got to the surface because the line was jerking in my hands; it was riding on the waves. I told Bill it was working all right. Simple mathematics told us we were right on the nose and were at 180 feet.

Ernie Frazier

We were loaded for bear. Those of us that were making the ascent had access to .45's and ammunition. Also, we heard the Formosa Straits were loaded with sharks so we all had shark knives. We took pieces of line and tied our pant legs down at our ankles and filled our pants with c-rations.

We were only about a mile off the Formosa coast, close to Fuchou, China. We wrapped our shells real tight in what we called gosling paper and stuck 'em in our pockets.

Admiral Momsen developed the Momsen Lung. It's a simple device. There's a little canister in there with soda lime in it. You exhale carbon dioxide into the soda lime. It absorbs this free carbon and expels free oxygen.

The big factor is this; no two people have the same body chemistry. I may have the capability of breathing free oxygen longer than you. None of us had any problem at 100 feet at New London, but here we were at almost twice that depth. Some of the guys were worrying about the ascent, because if you breathe free oxygen long enough, you'll get a bubble in your blood stream; it hits your heart and you're gone!

Bill Ballinger and some of the others were talking about that when we were making up our waves of four. He asked the guys, "What alternative do we have?"

Talking about alternatives, here's one that all submariners have discussed; torpedo tubes. We used to call them water shots. We'd flood the torpedo tube, open the outer door and, poof! fire a water slug, hitting it with 2,500 pounds of air. It's interesting because the boat reacts the same way it would if you fired an actual torpedo. The thought ran through our minds, "Hey, would we be able to put a lung on so we could breathe while underwater, crawl into a torpedo tube, have someone flood it down, open that outer door and hit us with the water shot!

Well, it could be done but would probably split your head open if you tried it. So, there was no real alternative.

When George Zofcin was helping me get the clip off my lung, I told him, "Let's get a lung on you, now."

He said, "Clay, I've got a confession to make to you."

I said, "George, what the hell are we talking about. Confessions? Now isn't the time for any confessions. Let's get out of here!"

He said, "I can't swim."

Well, I remembered us frolicking on the beach at the Royal Hawaiian and realized, that's right; George never did go into the water.

I told him, "Look, George, you'll have your lung on. Close that mouthpiece properly. It's like a Mae West and we've got the buoy we can hang onto. Let's give it a shot!"

He said, "Tell you what, Clay, you go with that first wave and I'll come up with the next wave."

George Zofcin helped me put on my Momsen Lung on. It had a rubber relief valve at the bottom that was about the length and width of two fingers; reminiscent of "raspberries," the noisemakers that we blew into when I was a kid. The relief valve would let air out but wouldn't let water come in.

The Momsen Lungs we practiced on at the 100-foot tower were on racks. You might go over to get one, and heck, some guy might have just used it two hours ago. But, hey, getting a brand new lung out of a cellophane package was a different ball game. It's got the mouthpiece and nose clamp. That escape valve on a new lung was folded shut and secured with a wire clip to keep dirt out.

In the prison camp, we discussed the training class where an instructor came in and showed us how to take a new lung from its bag and remove the clip. I had to confess, "Hey, I was either sleeping that day or they actually didn't demonstrate the clip removal in my class. I certainly don't remember ever doing that."

George reached down and pulled that clip off my lung. That saved my life.

Bill Ballinger charged my lung and I put the mouthpiece and nose clamp on. The mouthpiece had a valve right under it. When you get to the surface, you take off the nose clamp and turn the valve before you take the mouthpiece off. The lung then becomes a life preserver, just like the old Mae West we used to strap on.

I started up and stopped at every knot, inhaling and exhaling. Bubbles rose up from the relief valve because my lungs were full of air. As I ascended, both the internal air pressure and the outside pressure decreased. So, the lung is constantly expelling extra air.

When my head popped up at the surface. It was daylight and I was thinking, "Oh boy! I made it!"

I reached up to take my nose clamp off, wiped my hand across my face and was shocked to see that it was a mass of blood! I spit the mouthpiece out and wondered, "What the hell is going on?" Maybe I panicked. In the meantime, salt water was flooding my lung because I hadn't shut my valve. It wasn't any good at that point so I threw it away. Fortunately, the bleeding stopped after a very short time.

The navy interrogated me about the incident after we got out of the prison camp. I told the lad that was questioning me that I had no pain or stinging sensations or the bends from coming up too fast.

He said, "Probably what happened to you was this: You came up, checking every knot and inhaling and exhaling like you were instructed. But, you probably came up a little faster than you should have and ruptured those superficial blood vessels in your cheeks and nose."

I wasn't on the surface for a minute until Chief Bill Ballinger came to the surface just about an arm's length from me; screaming and bleeding! He was wearing a lung but didn't have his mouthpiece in or his nose clip on. The man was drowning. I could have reached out and grabbed him; the guy that really helped me to get out of that rascal, but something told me, "Don't do it!"

My navy interrogator told me, "Clay, it's a good thing you didn't reach for Bill. A drowning person can pull a horse under water. If that man touched any part of your body, you wouldn't be here talking to me today."

I guess I did the right thing. In discussing Bill's tragedy, all we could figure was that he failed to remove the clip from the exhaust valve on his lung. "If that was the case," the interrogator guessed, "I'd venture to say that he didn't get more than 50 or 60 feet when the lung burst on him."

He'd certainly panic when that happened and he'd get rid of the mouthpiece and nose clamp.

On the surface

In our first wave of four, I was the only one that made it out successfully. The other two lads in my group never made it to the surface. They probably didn't reach out and get a hold of the line to follow it properly to the surface, missed the opening and their bodies got hung up down there. That's what we thought happened.

No bodies at all surfaced on the next wave of four. None.

The next two people that surfaced were Jesse Da Silva and Walt Flanagan, from the third wave. The two men with them didn't surface even though they had the lungs on. They must have missed the line and ventured off one-way or another. You'd have to panic if you did that because it was pitch black down there. You wouldn't know whether to go right or left or backwards or forwards, or what.

I immediately asked Jesse, "How about George Zofcin?"

Jesse told me, "Clay, right after you got up into the trunk, George went over and laid down on a bunk in the forward torpedo room."

George hadn't even made the attempt to escape.

We calculated there couldn't be more than five hours of air left in the sub because of the fire in the battery compartment. It would be a simple death. You simply go to sleep and that's it. There'd be no pain.

Two more men, Hayes Trukke and Pete Nowatzke, suddenly surfaced and joined Flanagan, Da Silva and me. Now, there were five of us, alive, on the surface. It was morning. The tide was coming out from the mainland and we could see the China coast. The stuff we carried was weighting us down so we undid our pants and got rid of it all. Fortunately, we didn't see any sharks.

The buoy had handles around it. It was tied to the boat by a line on a spool. Picture a small basketball with five men around it. On the surface, you could hang onto it with one hand and swim with the other.

Trukke and Nowatzke were pretty husky lads. They said, "We're going to make a try for it."

They stripped down, pulled off their lungs and shark knives, and took off swimming. They didn't got 15 or 20 yards until they came back and said, "There's no way you can swim against that tide."

About that time, bingo! Here came another man popping up, right up the line. He wasn't in as bad of shape as Bill Ballinger, but he too was drowning. It was Larsen, our first class pharmacist mate.

If we were on shore, we could have laid him down and pumped the water out of him. But we had to handle him in the water the best we could. We don't know if he had the same problem with the lung that Ballinger had or not. His lungs were full of water and he was gasping for air. We were trying to hold him and he was vomiting air and water. We'd take turns holding on to him and turned his valve so the lung would operate like a Mae West.

We were in the water four or five hours before we rescued.

Rescued…by a Japanese destroyer!

A Japanese destroyer escort dropped anchor about 1,000 yards from us. They lowered a whaleboat with two Japs aboard. They came over and loaded us in the whaleboat. The five of us loaded Larsen aboard. We wanted to give him some help right then, maybe pump some water out, but the Japs wouldn't let us. They're yelling, "Joto ni! Joto ni!"

We were there in our skivvies and they're pointing their guns and telling us not to touch the man. We obeyed.

Our buoy was tied to our submarine, 180 feet below. Those two Japs were up there in the bow of the whaleboat, pulling on it with all their might, trying to bring it up. We didn't tell 'em that it was tied to our submarine. They finally gave up and hauled us over to the destroyer escort. A rope ladder was over the side. I was the last one to go up. Larsen was still in the boat. I looked back over my shoulder and saw that those two Japs didn't even fool with Larsen. He was still alive, but they just dumped him over the side.

To our surprise, when we got up on the deck, we found that they had picked up Skipper O'Kane along with Liebold, Caverly and Savatkin.

It was tropical weather and submariners don't see any sunshine, even on lookout when the sun is down. Now there we were nine of us standing in a circle on that steel deck.

Also, on the deck, were survivors from the Japanese ships we'd sunk. You can't blame them for thinking, "Oh, these are the ding-dongs that sank us!"

Most ships in those days burned coal to generate steam. When we torpedoed them, the boilers ruptured and scalded those guys. They were burned red, like lobsters!

Torture in the tropics

They gave us some of the worse treatment we ever got in our captivity. Here we were in our skivvies and t-shirts. They'd grab us by the hair and stick live cigarettes up our noses while kicking and stomping us and hitting us with rifle butts. We had to tolerate that treatment in the tropical sun for five days and nights. It caused horrible blisters all over our bodies and lips.

The Japanese name for the toilet is benjo. They'd take us there rather than have us urinate on the deck.

Every one of us confessed to each other, that when we went to urinate, we tried to drink our own urine to see if we could possibly quench our thirst. It was really rough treatment.

After five days, we docked at the capital of Formosa, Taipei. Black hoods were placed over our heads and we were all tied together by a line. The Japs stuck signs in our hands and tied them behind our backs. We figured the signs probably said, "This is an example of your super race," or something like that. We had little kids and old ladies coming out and hitting us with sticks when we were marched down the street.

They took us out to an army camp at the outskirts of Taipei. This was our first experience in a Japanese military camp. We were surprised to see how orders were given. The guy giving the order always screamed out the command at the top of his voice regardless of how close he was to the other man.

They took off our hoods and Japanese soldiers were standing all around us. We thought, "Uh-oh! This is the firing squad. It has to be!"

But, not so. They took us over and put us in a potato cellar over night. We got some water and ate raw potatoes.

In the morning, they put us on a train and sent us to the far north end of Formosa. We spent a night in a jail up there. We called it the Kuron Clink.

Dick O'Kane recalled an incident that took place in his book, Clear The Bridge. He said we were in our cell at the Kuron Clink and Decker suddenly hollered, "Hey, look guys. Popsicles!"

That was right. Here came some guy with nine Popsicles and each of us got one. We thought, "Oh boy! Maybe they are going to start treating us right!"

To Yokahama

That didn't last long. The next day we were put aboard a freighter bound for Yokahama, Japan, to be interrogated. It was loaded down with sugar and we were stuck down in the bottom of that baby, way down!

We bored little holes in the sugar sacks and got some to eat. Then we all got terribly seasick.

We said, "Let's say our prayers so none of our submarine buddies will catch this damn freighter on it's way to Yokahama!"

It happened to the boys on the Sculpin, which was torpedoed and sunk by the Japanese.

The survivors were put on two Japanese boats. During transport, one of our submarines sunk one them, killing the survivors on that boat.

Fortunately, we made it to Yokahama, arriving just as it was turning dark. They took us immediately to a railroad station and put us on one of their fast trains for a 40-minute ride.

When we arrived, we unloaded in a rainstorm and were marched in our skivvies to Ofuna, which is at the foot of Mt. Fujiama, inland from Yokahama. Ofuna was strictly an interrogation camp surrounded by a seven-foot stockade.

Outside the camp were farms and vegetable gardens. We arrived on October 24.

There was no heat in any of the buildings. In the winter, the temperature could fall to zero and you could have a foot of snow on the ground.

Interrogated by Handsome Harry

We were put into solitary confinement; one man to a cell but all nine of us were still together. The Japanese Army, the Navy, and the Civil Defense conducted the interrogations.

Strangely enough, we liked to go and be interrogated; the Japanese sat on the floor on a rice mat and had a tiny coffee table, which was their main table. So, here we are, and this one interrogator would come in. We called him Handsome Harry because he always wore a beautiful suit and tie with a white shirt. If you closed your eyes, you'd never know that you were talking to an Oriental. No accent whatsoever.

Dick O'Kane told us, "When you're being interrogated, don't hold back anything. I'm the guy they're after. I'm the guy they'll really come down on. No use in you guys taking any undue punishment." We were very glad and thanked Dick for telling us that

No doubt about it. If we were caught in a lie or held anything back, it definitely meant a beating.

For example, I was a motor mech. On the Tang we had Fairbanks Morse engines. One of my first interrogators—not Handsome Harry—questioned me all about Fairbanks Morse diesel engines. Well, thank God and thank Dick O'Kane for telling us what he did, because when I got through with my interrogation session, you know what he did? He pulled out the manual that was published at the time that damn motor came off the assembly line. If I'd have told him any falsehood, he would have caught it immediately, and boy, oh boy some of those fly boys that were interrogated and didn't tell what they should, took some God-awful beatings: Some God-awful beatings!

The first time Handsome Harry interrogated me it was cold and there was snow on the ground. We were sitting on the rice mat. A little coffee table had a blanket covering it and a hibachi underneath. So, man we'd talk as long as they wanted to, because from our hips down, we were warm as toast. What do you want to talk about? Let's talk.

One of his first questions was, "Mr. Decker, where did you join the navy?"

I said, "Denver, Colorado."

Ernie Frazier

"Oh," he said, "then you're familiar with the Brown Palace Hotel?"

I said, "Oh, yeah! Very much so."

He said, "I want you to know that I lived in the Brown Palace Hotel for two years while attending Denver University."

Ha! You think those poopers weren't planning Pearl Harbor a long time ago?

Fish heads and chicken feed

We talk about the differences between being a P. O. W. in Europe and in Japan. The Germans knew about meat and potatoes. Hey, when you go to fish heads and rice, that's a hell of lot different! Actually, we didn't get rice. It's interesting because the Japanese loved their polished rice. If you think about it, when you polish rice, it takes away a lot of the nutrients. They fed us Milo maize; some call it Kaffir corn. It's chicken feed but it had far more nutritional value than the polished rice. We just didn't get enough of it, that's all.

Dysentery was a big problem for all of us. Their toilets were concrete troughs under a wooden floor with holes in it. So, you don't have a seat to sit on, just a hole to squat over. Farmers, called honey dippers, came around with teams of oxen and a half-dozen thirty-gallon barrels. They had dippers on long sticks. They dipped up our waste, took it out to their farms and dumped it straight onto their vegetables. They'd been fertilizing that way for years so you can see why dysentery hit us all.

While the maize was good for most of us, we had one lad whose system couldn't take it. He'd vomit it all up. We did everything we could for the lad, but he just couldn't tolerate the diet. He literally starved to death. We decided that the worse deaths come from starvation. In its last stages, your stomach swells up and it's terrible

The first thing we learned at Ofuna was how to count. They would use their language on numbers, but when letters were used, they used our letters: A, B, C, D.

Our government had developed the B-29 bombers. When they came over to bomb, the Japanese would all scream the alarm, yelling "biniji ku," and run to a shelter, leaving us topside.

We were told that we were not Prisoners of war but were special prisoners of Japan. The Japanese name was koko beto horyo.

Clay and air ace Pappy Boyington

Pappy Boyington, was a Marine Corps air ace who gained great fame with the Black Sheep Squadron and was awarded the Medal of Honor. A popular TV series about his exploits, titled, The Black Sheep Squadron, still plays daily on many TV stations.

Pappy was shot down over Rabaul about a year before we were captured. Somehow he got thrown in with us and got a job in the galley at Ofuna.

Koko beto horyo

In his book, Baa Baa Black Sheep, Pappy pointed out the significance of being a koko beto horyo; you only got half a food ration daily, you couldn't talk to any other prisoners, you got no mail and no Red Cross packages. In fact, neither the Red Cross nor our Government was notified that we were captured.

In our camp, were British soldiers, sailors and airmen. Here was Pappy Boyington, our ace Marine pilot who'd shot down 28 zeroes. You'd want to go up and pat him on the shoulder but the British said, "So he's an American hero; so what?" They didn't have much respect for Pappy. But, that soon changed.

When the Japs beat us it was mostly for stealing or smoking when we weren't supposed to. We stole food at every opportunity; we were always hungry.

Boyington had a nicotine habit that you couldn't believe. When the honey dippers came, the guards would let us help them and we'd get a Japanese cigarette for that. I wasn't much of a smoker so I'd get mine and give it to Boyington. However, we weren't supposed to smoke until given the o. k. by the guards.

Ernie Frazier

Boyington badly beaten!

Well, Boyington got caught smoking when he shouldn't. When the Japs beat us, it was a public display. Everyone was brought out of their cells and stood at attention. There was a pole with a hook on it that they'd tie the man to and strip him down to his waist. They'd beat you with a bat that was smaller around than a baseball bat. When they got through, your back was bleeding.

A Jap sergeant began to beat Boyington. The rest of us are at attention. When he was finished, the Jap untied him. Boyington stood at attention. The top of the Jap's head came up to about Boyington's chin. He looks up, starts talking and is almost spitting in Boyington's face.

The Japanese word for you is anotawa; for me, it is watshawa.; for understand it is wakaru.

The Jap guard says to Boyington, "Anotawa wakaru?" which means, do you understand why I just beat the hell out of you?"

Boyington is standing there, just a sober as he could be and says, "Watshawa wakaru. Watshawa wakaru. Now go screw yourself little man!"

He keeps his sober face and the Japs have no idea what he said in English and none of us cracked a smile. From that moment forward, all of those Limeys in the camp decided that Pappy Boyington was A-number one! That made him the hero of the whole camp.

Prisoners beaten to death!

Terrible beatings took place at Ofuna prison camp. Twice Da Silva and I were called out at midnight to take the body of a prisoner, who'd been beaten to death, out in the woods and bury him.

We were there until about the first of February, when we were transferred to Omori prison camp, an island on Tokyo Bay in the outskirts of Tokyo. It had a wooden causeway leading out to the camp and contained about 600 prisoners.

The Tang survivors, along with Boyington, and a couple of downed P-52 pilots, occupied half of one barracks. A paper-thin wall separated us from several B-29 pilots and their crews.

They told us, "We're not going to get used to this damned rice. The war will be over before that happens." They were wrong and wound up getting pretty hungry.

We weren't supposed to communicate, but you remember the song, Don't Fence Me In? We'd sing it and the Japs didn't understand what we were singing. As far as they knew, we were all just singing a song. But, we changed the lyrics so we were actually communicating with each other. We'd go to the benjo and sing back and forth among ourselves.

Boyington would tell the fly boys, "Now don't get your daubers down. When we get out of this thing, I'm going to throw a luau at the top of the Mark Hopkins Hotel that'll knock your hats off, and you're all invited." He'd say anything to bolster their morale!

One again, we were koto, beto, horyo. They put us in a special barracks with two men to a cell and we weren't allowed to speak or mingle with the other prisoners. We couldn't go out on the details that were sent to work in a nearby steel mill; consequently, we got no exercise until they finally decided to let us out into the compound after the work details left for the day.

Omori was an army camp that they ran pretty much like a P. O. W. camp; officers weren't required to go on work details. Every month, the Japs would pay our officers in Yen. Boyington was my cellmate and he got his Yen every month.

U. S. bombers arrive

It was the spring of 1945 and the B-29's started coming over. Most of the houses around there were made of bamboo. A B-29 would drop an incendiary bomb at night and it would wipe out 6 to 10 blocks.

They started marching us koko, beto, horyos over to the bombed out areas. We'd go through the ruins, load the dead bodies on a truck, clean up and burn the debris, and plant gardens. It gave us something to do.

Boyington had caught some shrapnel in his air battles. He said, "Our planes didn't provide much of a shield for underneath our legs."

Ernie Frazier

Well, the shrapnel would fly up and hit him and he got tiny pieces of shrapnel in the calves of his legs. We had no medical attention at all, so we'd get out in the compound on a nice, hot summer day, and he'd grab the calf of his leg and squeeze pus out. We could sharpen bamboo about as sharp as a razor blade and I'd use a piece to dig out the shrapnel. How he kept from getting gangrene, I'll never know.

Pappy was always looking for a smoke, so when we were walking around, he was constantly looking for cigarette butts on the ground. We'd get back to our cell at night and he might have a handful of tobacco. He'd roll cigarettes out of the Yen that he couldn't spend. We had a flat lens flashlight. I could hold it up just right when the sun came through our window; the reflection through the lens would light Pappy's cigarette.

He'd have to smoke all the cigarettes, lighting one from the butt of another, because the sun would change position and I couldn't light any more. He was really a character! Once in a while he'd get caught.

The sadistic Sergeant Wananabe

Remember the notorious Sergeant Wananabe? We were told that he came from a very well to do Japanese family. He was a real barbaric bastard, that guy! He delivered the most unmerciful beatings! We don't know what happened to him, but he got away and we couldn't locate him after we were liberated.

One day Pappy and I were out cleaning up a bombed out area with a guard we called Gimpy. He couldn't speak any English and had been wounded in combat. He was over talking to a Japanese lady while we were burning trash. A Jap civilian came walking along , carrying a big basket of fish, and Boyington got fairly close to him; that was a no-no. We weren't even to look at a civilian, much less get close enough to talk to one.

Lives risked for two fish!

Boyington had this huge wad of Yen and he tried to dicker with the Jap to buy some fish. The Jap knew better than to talk to us. If he were caught talking to us, he'd get the hell knocked out of him by Japanese soldiers. He ignored us and kept on walking, but Boyington caught up with him, grabbed a couple of fish and threw a whole handful of Yen into his basket. The guard saw none of that, so we stuck the fish into our pile of burning debris. When they were done cooking, we ate them; heads, skin, eyes, scales, guts, everything! We ate the whole damn thing!

Thank Truman for the Atomic Bomb!

We didn't know when the first atomic bomb was dropped on Japan but our planes soon flew over and dropped leaflets, telling us everything. We read that we were dropping super bombs and the end was in sight. I believe that if President Truman hadn't made the decision to drop that bomb, I wouldn't be here today. The alternative was for our forces to land on the mainland of Japan. The Japs had it figured out; for each prisoner of war, one bullet to the head. Pop! That would have been that.

We heard that our government had invited the Japanese government to come to the United States proving grounds and witness the power of an atomic explosion, but they turned it down.

When they surrendered, the Japs called all of us prisoners in and told us, "Hey, we're pulling out." All their officers and personnel left, even the people in the galley; with the exception of four guards left in the guard shack at the main gate.

We had to have someone in charge while we waited for Bull Halsey's Fifth Fleet to come in and rescue us. We had a one star general from Australia in the camp. In the military, the highest-ranking officer assumes command. Not so in our case. We took a vote and everybody voted for Boyington to be in charge.

We were getting supply drops from B-29's. They were dropping 55-gallon drums of fruit, sugar, c-rations and medical supplies down at the beachhead. We went up on the roofs and painted a sign; P. O. W. Camp Omori. On the top of our cell we wrote: PAPPY BOYINGTON HERE. Well, those Black Sheep Squadron boys went bananas when they saw that! They dive-bombed the place and everything else!

Ernie Frazier

Death of the Japanese guards!

Supplies were falling from the air and the four Jap guards were sitting in their little lean-to shed, back-to-back, holding their rifles. A 55-gallon drum of peaches came swinging on a parachute. It crashed right into that shed and killed all four of them!

We found one warehouse at the camp after the Japs left that held over 1,000 Red Cross boxes full of food and medical supplies. Oh, wow, there we were starving to death!

When we were liberated, I was on the airplane with the first 21 prisoners of war to return back to the United States from Japan. That was probably because of Boyington. I was the only enlisted man, the rest were all officers. Boyington was on the C-54 that we got on at the Yokasuka Naval Station. I asked him, "Pappy, did you get me on this flight?"

"No, no," he said. "I didn't have anything to do with it." But, I knew he did. I found out later that some prisoners had to wait two months before they got a flight home

We flew to Guam, had lunch and gassed the plane, and then flew on to Pearl and landed there.

President Truman writes a personal letter

After I got home, I got a nice personal letter from President Truman.

In my particular case, I was married when I went over. When I got out of the prison camp, my first wife had re-married and I had to sort all of that out.

Clay returned to Denver after the war, was divorced from his first wife and re-married. He worked for a major corporation for a several years, and then built and operated a successful trash hauling business in Denver. He is now retired.

Author's acknowledgment: The U.S. Submarine Veterans, Inc. granted me permission to utilize their tape of Clay's experiences in this story. Copies of that tape are available from Dave Linker at: XSSN@AOL.COM

Ernie Frazier

CHAPTER 35

HENRY FORD

"After I heard their story, I cried all night."

Henry Ford was born July 7, 1921. Our interview took place in his room at the Kansas Soldiers' Home at historic Fort Dodge, Kansas.

My dad was the sheriff of Clark County, Kansas during the Great Depression, back in the 1930's. I enlisted in the US Navy in October 1940, prior to World War II. We went down to San Diego for boot camp but they took about twenty of us and put us on an old destroyer, The Sands, and sent us up to San Pedro. Up there they put us on the Battleship Colorado and trained us on everything from bilges to the galley.

I was trained to be a boatswain's mate. They have to know a little bit about everything; signaling, how to take command of a small boat and handle work details. If he's a master-at-arms, like I was most of the time, he's kind of like a cop aboard ship. A few months before the war we were sent out on another ship, the Perkins, to bring in a British battleship, the Warsprite that had been hit by a Jap Torpedo off Bangkok, Thailand. The Cruiser Chicago and our ship escorted her clear back to Mare Island.

On December, 7, 1941, I was at Mare Island Navy Yard, San Francisco and we were getting outfitted with new guns and radar, which was just coming in. Before that, we camouflaged our ship and had been practicing torpedo runs and other drills out of Pearl Harbor.

When the Japs hit Pearl Harbor, we were put underway so fast that even a lot of the workmen's tools were left on board. When we got there, the channel was still partially blocked and smoke was still coming up from our ships that had been hit.

We joined up with the Chicago again and headed for the Fiji Islands. Up there we joined a British Cruiser, the Australia, and the Leander from New Zealand and some other ships including a Dutch and a French Destroyer. We called the outfit the Anzac Force.

Midget Jap Subs Infiltrate Us

We were there to put up a shield to keep the Japs out of Australia. Sidney was our homeport and I was there when a famous incident occurred: seven Japanese midget submarines got into the harbor and blew up the ship next to us.

We got underway and depth charged one of them as we pulled out of the harbor. No one knew how the midgets got into the harbor. We finally found out that they came in strapped to a big sub, which released them near the harbor.

We headed up to the Great Barrier Reef and kind of hid out among the islands. Then the battle for the Coral Sea began. It lasted for several days and Jap Bombers were attacking us. Our destroyer was armed with anti-aircraft guns and torpedoes. We shot down one plane that made a raid on us. It was a Torpedo Bomber. We called them Big Betties. They'd come in low and then drop their "fish".

The one we hit crashed into the water and two Japs climbed out on the fuselage. One of them looked like he was hurt pretty bad. The other one seemed to be alright. I was given an old Thompson Machine Gun and sent out on a whaleboat with a couple of other guys to pick up the Japs. The Australians wanted them for interrogation.

Ernie Frazier

I Shoot a Jap

When we approached, one of the Japs turned around. He had a pistol in his hand. He was the only Jap I personally shot during the war. I let him have it. We took the wounded one aboard and kept him for several days. He was in bad shape so we transferred him to another ship that took him to a hospital in Australia.

We went up to the Solomon Islands. And I was sent in on another rescue mission in our whaleboat. One of our small airplanes had gone down so we picked up the airmen and their gear and took them back to our ship. A charge was planted that blew up the plane to keep it out of enemy hands.

Then we headed up to Rabaul and back down to New Guinea. We patrolled the area along with some Australian Ships and got into several battles. One of our ships got torpedoed in what became known as the Battle of Salvo Island.

Our communication lights went out. Two Jap Destroyers slipped in from the rear and were stalking us.

We Had to do a Sickening Clean-Up

We got to the beach at Tagula to rescue the torpedoed ship and saw Jap Ships sunk all around us. The ship was still burning so we got our firefighting equipment. The superstructure was all burned and guys were hanging in there- burned. Our skipper let about 10 of us go in to clean up the mess. It was sickening. We didn't have enough body bags to pick up the remains, so we got mattress covers - we called them fart sacks – and put body parts in them, just enough so you'd know somebody was in there.

Spanish Coins

The skipper let us guys go ashore that had done clean up. So Harper and I went up on Salvo Island to an old carol cave. We found a 3" Jap Gun mounted in there. I saw something hanging out of a hole. So I put Harper on my shoulder- he was a skinny little guy- and he reached up and pulled out a bunch of old gold coins; Spanish Coins about the size of half dollars. Elated by our discovery and feeling rewarded by its auspicious arrival, we took them back to the ship.

Guadalcanal

We patrolled off the shore of Guadalcanal and could see our Marines going in on landing barges to invade the island. We watched the battle through binoculars and could see guys swarming all over the beaches.

On Christmas Day, we were sent up to the mouth of the River, Tasferango, where a Jap Merchant Ship, disabled and beached by allied gunfire, was being boarded and unloaded by other Japanese. our orders were to shell the ship.

The Piper Cub

Believe it or not, a little Piper Cub Airplane came over and signaled us. He knew where the Japs were taking the supplies, so he dropped a smoke bomb on their location. The Japs were firing on him but the pilot knew how to sideslip in the air and a lot of other maneuvers so he got out of there alright. A little plane like that was great for reconnaissance work, but it was awfully dangerous work because it was slow work.

We opened up on the Japs, and pounded them and their ships all day. I was on gun 3, a five-inch thirty-eight. We fired until all the paint slid off our gun barrels. It got so hot that the barrels would swell up and look like a snake that had swallowed on egg. The ship was on fire and we hit it with every weapon and explosive device we had, so the Japs couldn't get it unloaded. It was the only ship in there to supply them and we had to sink it.

Ernie Frazier

Christmas Dinner

We had very little to eat except for some Australian hardtack cookies in a can. They were so hard we had to soak them in coffee. We had some pickles so we ate them and the hardtack cookies for Christmas Dinner.

Our ship had hit a reef and bent the screw. We were sent to Auckland, New Zealand for repairs. The couldn't find a screw that would work so they sent us clear back to Pearl Harbor. We did get three days liberty and had a good time while we were there.

We headed back then and joined up with the Australian Fleet. They'd lost the cruiser, Canberra, in battle while we were gone.

Headhunters Were Waiting

We bombarded several Japanese locations on the islands around there, and then moved to Malanie Bay, New Guinea. The Japs had lots of landing boats in there. A lead boat would act as a tugboat and would pull a string of boats loaded with troops behind them.

We opened fire. They beached the best they could and began running into the jungle. However, they didn't last long. Our New Guinea allies were waiting. They captured and beheaded most of the Japs.

We made landings up and down the coastline of New Guinea. At Lay, there had been a horrible battle. The beach was absolutely black with corpses covered with flies: Japs and Americans.

Women and Kids on a Sub Tell a Terrible Story

An unidentified submarine appeared. It had been on the Borneo Coast and picked up three service men's wives and some kids. They'd escaped the Japanese in the Philippines and natives had helped them get down to Borneo. One of the ladies called out in English so our *skipper felt safe to go pick them up. We found out they were Americans.*

I Cried All Night

They told us that the Japs had raped several women, then stuck bayonets up inside them and ripped them apart- killing them. I cried all night when I heard their story. It really hurt to talk to them. Fortunately, the ones we rescued were alright. A troop transport took them to safety.

Sydney Australia was our home port. They needed fast ships, like destroyers, so they sent us and another ship to Santiago, Chile to escort two Standard Oil Tankers all the way up to Melbourne and then to Perth, Australia. We also went up into Tasmania and delivered ships around the area.

A $7,000,000 Payroll

Another time we were sent to escort a troop transport along with some cargo, which amounted to about seven million dollars in American payroll money to pay the fleet off. There were 20 soldiers guarding it. When they dumped if off at Sydney, four of us went to the Perkins to pick it up. We took it onto a cruiser and they distributed it from there.

There was an old German Supply Ship we'd captured and it had a crew from India. We didn't want to tie up alongside of them because they'd steal you blind. We had a Dutch Tanker that went along with us. We made up a peculiar fleet. One time we went to sea and met some American Ships. We pulled alongside of them to take on fuel and we heard two French Sailors and a couple of Dutch Sailors asking, "What kind of a damn navy is that?"

Our smokestacks were all blown full of holes and rusting and we looked pretty ragged. We pulled into the New Hebrides- the North Island- and there were two old U.S. Four Piper Destroyers there that had come clear around from Manila through Java and back around that way. We got to talk to those guys; they had it awful rough. One boat had it's stern blown off; they'd made a rudder out of palm logs to guide the boat.

Rescuing a Hometown Buddy

We lost the Destroyer Smith at New Guinea and we went in to pick up survivors. One of the kids we picked up happened to be from my hometown- Joe Butler. He was alive and I let him use my bunk. I never used it. I always slept on deck with a blanket and life jacket and my Tommy Gun.

They sent Joe back to the States. He never was right after what he'd been through and died several years ago.

Ramming and blassting Through the Jap Barges

We escorted P.T. boats, like John F. Kennedy's, into the harbor. The place was loaded with mines but the allies had charted the area so we had an idea of how to get in and out. The Japs had all their lights on and we saw all kinds of odd ships floating around. Actually about 15 barges loaded with Japs were coming out. We hit them with all the firepower we had, including my Tommy Gun, firing right into the barges. All they had to fire back with were small arms.

We crashed through the barges, and then we had to circle back through them again, to follow their route out of there. We rammed and blasted them again as we went, doing everything we could to destroy them.

We were on the Perkins at that time. It was kind of the command ship over our destroyers and commanded the Dutch and the French that were with us. A lot of times the P.T. Boat commander would be on our ship.

We went back to reinforce Guadalcanal and operated up and down the coastline. You know, after the army took it over, they pert near lost it again to the Japs.

The Perkins was sunk, and along with it, the Gold Spanish Coins that Harper and I had confiscated, our bounty lost. I was then assigned to the Bismarck Sea, a Small Tiger Carrier, and went back to Seattle to damage control school.

After that, we went back to the islands and brought back a load of planes that had been damaged on Mujero, a.k.a., Mog Mog. We were involved in several minor combat actions in that area. Our little ship didn't carry much firepower. We went along until the battle for Iwo Jima came along. The Bismarck Sea was sent over there, and it became the last carrier sunk in WWII.

We flew to Scholfield Barracks in Honolulu and boarded the Bennington, which was a big carrier, and headed for southern Japan.

The following is taken from two different New York World Telegram Newspaper Articles, copyright, 1944, by Max B. Cook. Cook describes the U.S.S. Bennington...

"A huge bulk of a ship, bristling with guns, neatly camouflaged in blue and gray, the U.S.S. Bennington towered far above the water, its control 'island' atop an expansive flight deck, extended high into the sky.

It was the Navy's newest $60 million fighting ship-a fortified city within itself and one of the nation's most powerful of floating airports/ battleships. Accommodating more than two thousand soldier's, a visitor aboard the massive vessel could anticipate, 'always getting lost,' as all passageways throughout the ship look alike, and 'retracing steps' only to finally appeal to orderlies to lead the way."

The remarkable carrier was built to... *"Take Hits , Yet Stay Afloat."* Below the hanger deck there and far down into the ship, crewmen, technicians, engineers, and experts in many lines, work and sleep day and night, oftimes going for days without seeing the flight deck or the sky above it. It is an amazing city of industrial, electrical, and even commercial and homey activities. For it is where the majority of the crew live and work."

Cook, author of at least two write-ups about the Bennington, marveled at one thing; that was the careful planning that went into this carrier to prevent it from becoming completely disabled by damage to any one unit.

"There are duplications of most operating units aboard the ship. And this is true of the propellers. If one is damaged there are still three to carry on; if two are damaged there are still two to do the work. This is also true of electrical systems".

Cooks' reports about his findings aboard the ship, add an extraordinary relevance to Ford's survival and recounting of these events, as a gunner aboard the U.S.S. Bennington.

Our carrier and another one got caught in a monstrous typhoon. The flight deck on a carrier is way up, about 40 feet. The waves from the typhoon hit clear up there and crashed down the flight deck down onto the coastal deck. It crushed our big I beams like they were matchsticks.

I was manning gun #1. I could see the storm through my hood. Our ship would shake but it held together. A cruiser lost its complete bow. I saw it. Sure enough, it had no bow. Wires and stuff were stringing out of the front of the ship. There was a big article about it in one of our national magazines.

We survived that and went to Leyte. They sent barges alongside to cut off the front end of the carrier and slid it into the bay. We headed back to combat on the coast of Northern Japan.

Once I had a deck crew working and saw an old buddy down on the tugboat named Ladd. He had been on the Perkins when it sunk.

We wanted to get together and go ashore but I told him I couldn't get off my ship. He said he'd fix it up. Sure enough, during lunch hour, the word came down for me to lay up to the quarter deck. I laid up there and was told that the Admiral was sending a boat to pick me up. They said that the kid on the tug was on the boat and we could go ashore. We did and had a few beers. He had a pet monkey aboard the tug and we really enjoyed him. In fact, the monkey would go get you a beer out of the icebox if you told him to.

When we came back, the deck officer told me, "The old man wants to know what went on with you guys." I told him, "It's top secret." He said, "Ok," and that's all that was ever said.

Old Ladd knew ways of getting things done.

One place I'd like to go back to, but I'm too old now, is Tasmania. It would be a great place to explore around it. That's as far south as I ever got.

We got sent up to the north end of Japan where it was really cold. We had no winter clothes. We also needed fuel and grub so they sent us up on Vladivostock, Russian. Them boogers wouldn't let us ashore. We were so close that we could see people along the shoreline, but we stayed on the ship. We had to rig up a supply line to get the fuel to us and we got some of the Russian's canned foods. They canned their string beans without pulling off the strings and eating them was tough. Their canned fish smelled like old dead carp; it was awful so we got off that food as soon as we could. The next time we needed food we went to Dutch Harbor and got American Food. Those Russians either didn't know how to prepare food or just didn't want to know how.

Eleven days after they signed the Armistice, we pulled into Tokyo. They called my name out after a couple of days and said I could rotate home. I didn't need any "points" because I'd been in the navy longer than any of them. However, they didn't have any transportation- they checked everyplace- to find a way to get me home. They finally found out that the Battleship Wisconsin was transporting Canadian Soldiers back that had been prisoners of war. So they put about 20 of us sailors on with them and that's how I got back to San Francisco. My war was over.

Ernie Frazier

<u>**My Life**</u>
***The Person Who Achieves Knowledge is no Longer Afraid
Of Life.
He Can Accept All His Experiences And Feelings
Whether of Grief or of Happiness or
Of Love or Of Guilt. He Recognizes That it is Within
Himself to Choose His Way of Living,
The Only Question that Matters Being; Is this a way
Which is Deeply Satisfying to Me? And Which
Truly Expresses Me?***
<u>***Henry Ford***</u>
<u>***July 1947***</u>
***God Grant Me the Serenity to Accept the Things
I Cannot Change,
Courage to Change the Things I Can,
And Wisdom
To Know the Difference***

--Author Unknown--

<u>A Small-Town Cop</u>

When I got out of the navy, I came home and worked as a city marshal in Ashland, my hometown. It only paid $90 a month and I was getting more than that out of the navy. I told the mayor off because he wanted me to work seven days a week for the $90 and I told him where to put it. I had $40 in my pocket and hitchhiked to Colorado. A guy picked a couple of us up and asked if we wanted to work. We wound up working in his lumber company until they started building the Granby Dam and I got a job up there. 2 CCC Units of more than 400 men were stationed there to get that project underway. I stayed until it's completion. The Dam, formerly of Ashland State Lake, now harbors Clark County Lake. The project was the largest piece of construction of its kind, for the time, undertaken in this section of the country.

Clark County Lake rests 13 miles north of Ashland in the Bluff Creek Canon.

Retreaded

When the Korean War broke out, I was still in the reserves. I got a card from the navy telling me to report to their Denver Office. They wanted boatswain's mates to train recruits so they activated me and put me in charge of billeting, training guys that came in from boot camp.

I was sent to San Francisco where another boatswain's mate and I were to take charge of about 50 guys that had been in the brig for a long time. We were supposed to straighten them out and keep them aboard so they'd be ready to sail out on a ship they'd been assigned to.

Boy, that was tough. Those guys were hard-timers. Some had been five years on the rock pile.

One of them appeared to be a huge Russian, a mean-looking booger that would just snarl at you when you walked by. One day he came and told me that his sister was coming in from Ohio and he wanted to go ashore and see her. I told him, "You get that crew to working and I'll get a pass and go ashore with you."

He really put them in line. He'd grab 'em by the nap of the neck and shake 'em if they didn't do what he told them. He looked kind of like an ape. He changed that crew around and we got the job done. It wasn't me that did it, but I had the tool to work with; him. I did meet his sister. She was nice. After that, I didn't have any more trouble with the crew. I asked for a ship but the navy told me I'd spent enough time overseas.

Fort Dodge's Halsey Hall houses many disabled veterans. Entering the front reception area, I saw a dozen or more elderly men and women, the kind of folks you might encounter in any nursing home but with one big difference; these people are American heroes. In their youth, they saw the horrors of war. Some of them killed people. Some had been prisoners of war. Some were wounded in battle. Today, they look just like anyone's great-grandparents.

Henry, who suffered a leg injury after the war, is confined to a wheelchair. He also requires oxygen due to a breathing impairment.

Ernie Frazier

Tears flooded his eyes several times as he relived the eight long years he spent fighting to keep America free.

I looked around his little room that was cluttered with the necessities of life; chair, bed, oxygen, wheelchair, medicines, correspondence, and some pictures. Several were of his wife. I asked about her. "She's over in another area, here on the Fort. She resides in one of the assisted-living type domicilaries." Mary Kay Ford suffers from early-stage Alzheimer's Disease. She was born July 7th, 1921, in Yealton, Oklahoma, and is the mother of seven, now adult, children. Mary Kay and Henry were actually childhood acquaintances at Ashland Elementary School, however, were not in the same grade. They were united in marriage in 1988.

Ford concluded, "I like it here. They keep it real clean and treat us good." On his 80th birthday, Ford wrote:

Beauty of the World I Live In
The Supernatural
The Ultimate Meaning of Our Existence and
Fulfillment of the Basic Longing
That Lies in the Depths of the Human Heart
and Mind

<u>Henry Ford</u>

CHAPTER 36

RUSSELL MONICAL

"Our sub was on its way to Pearl Harbor on December 7th 1941"

A good story can sometimes be found by accident. This one came after I read a bumper sticker on a car in a grocery store parking lot. It identified the owner as a WWII submariner.

<u>A submariner</u>

I didn't want to go into the army. When my draft notice came on January 16, 1941 I enlisted in the navy. I was offered a six-year enlistment, take it or leave it. I took it. Pearl Harbor, December 7, 1941 hadn't happened yet.

Ernie Frazier

After six weeks of basic training at Great Lakes Naval Training Station, outside Chicago, I applied and was accepted to the submarine school at New London, Connecticut.

The training there was pretty scary. They had some of the old O-boats—the original subs—left over from WWI. They were pretty small and would only hold about 35 or 40 of us. They were powered by diesel engines until we submerged. At that point, they switched over to batteries—electric power. We'd charge up our batteries and top them off every so often. But when we drove, it drained the juice and we'd have to recharge them later on. The length of time the batteries would power us depended on the length of time we were down and what functions we were performing. If we were just lying on the bottom, we could stay down a long time. It was a different story if we were moving. We'd have to surface a lot sooner.

My first dive was so easy. Actually we just settled down underwater instead of diving. Later on when we were on the fleet boats, we'd dive at a high rate of speed and it didn't take long to submerge to the depths. The deeper the better as far as I was concerned, because deeper meant safer. Our diving alarms came in three blasts, signaling that we were going down.

A friend told me that if I worked my butt off I would get to go to new construction (a new sub). I didn't want to go to the old S-boats so I really applied myself. I made the grade and was sent to our shipyard at Portland, New Hampshire. A lot of new submarines were being constructed as fast a possible because the top brass knew something that we enlisted men didn't: War was inevitable. They just didn't know when.

I was a motor machinist mate. There were about 30 of us operating on different ships in the area. We stood three duty stations, four hours on and eight hours off. I took care of the diesel engines and enjoyed the work. We had brand new, Fairbanks Morse engines that were probably the best on any ships. They were opposed piston engines without a head. They had an upper and a lower crankshaft. When the pistons came together, they fired. We had no problems with them.

Hot bunking

Our boat was named Fin Back SS230. At that time we carried 60 men and six officers but that was soon upped to 75 men and seven or eight officers. We had to 'hot-bunk'. That means as one man left the bunk another would slide into those sheets. Submarines are very crowded. If you couldn't stand the smell of the ship's diesel fuel and the men's rear ends, you didn't belong in there. From the bottom of one bunk to the bottom of the next one was about 16 or 18 inches. There were three of us on the outside, which was the choice place to be. The inner two rows of bunks were four deep.

We completed training and sailed for the Pacific, in this case the Panama Canal. We surfaced and had to delay for several hours while barnacles fell of the ship. There were three locks there; two going up, and we came out on the Pacific Ocean side.

Our next stop was to be Pearl Harbor.

Russell Monical's sub and crew.

At Pearl Harbor

While we were in transit, Pearl Harbor was bombed. We got there about four or five days after the attack. The scene was sickening, horrifying. There were bodies and body parts floating along with the wreckage of our battleships that had been sunk or badly damaged. Oil slicks five or six inches deep covered the water.

To Tisca and Attu in the Aleutian Islands

Our air base had been bombed but our submarines there hadn't been touched. Their survival would cause the Japanese some serious trouble. Our first run sent us up towards the Arctic, around Tisca and Attu in the Aleutian Islands, not far from Russia. The Japs had been landing troops at Attu and we were sent to relieve one of our ships, the Grunion. We couldn't locate her and assumed she was sunk.

Ernie Frazier

Attacking Japs from underwater

After being held at bay for three days, we slipped in close to their harbor and attacked from underwater, the old way of attacking, as we didn't have radar then. (Once we got radar, we'd attack during the night or during thunderstorms, from the surface because we could maneuver so much faster on the surface and it helped keep our batteries charged.) It was an open harbor. We just stayed submerged outside the area and fired in on the Japanese ships. We were all scared, even our officers, because none of us had ever been in combat.

Japs drop 124 depth charges

The Japs came out to depth charge us. Fortunately there was a temperature variant in the water, a layer of warm water between two cold-water layers and when they would ping on us the ping would eventually strike us and return the signal to them, but it was misleading and they'd drop their charge about ¾ of a mile away. We were lying still at that point. It was good indoctrination, hearing what a depth charge sounded like. We could hear the charges but they were far enough away that we couldn't hear their detonators. When you heard a detonator go off, you knew they were close. As long as the charge exploded above us we were all right. Evidently they thought we could operate down to 150 feet and that's where their charges went off. We took evasive action and dropped to 300 feet. That's one big reason why I'm still alive today. Later, it was reported that someone at the San Luis Obispo newspaper reported that our subs were operating at 300 feet. We started losing boats after that. I think the Japs dumped 124 charges on us, and then apparently ran out because they broke off and left.

Our torpedoes strike a blow

We torpedoed and sunk a couple of their transports that were unloading cargo. Then a destroyer came looking for us and we hit him in the bow with a torpedo. We finally got out of there. After the war, when we got the records, we were credited with hitting those ships.

We were called back to Pearl Harbor after our engagements at Attu. Our ship required quite a bit of maintenance so we got about six weeks in port, two of which were spent at the Royal Hawaiian Hotel, the best hotel in Hawaii. The Navy had taken it over and we had good food and good duty.

After Hawaii, we were ordered to Wepiet, which was about 7,000 miles from Hawaii and got tangled up in the Battle of Midway.

Mistaken identity can get you killed

We were stationed out in a circle—sort of a blockade—to intercept any ships. The only action we were involved in was when someone fired two torpedoes at us—and missed. We didn't know if they were coming from the Japanese or our own ships. Mistaken identity happened a lot and it was easy to get killed by our own people.

Our Navy made lots of mistakes during that battle and so did the Japanese. Sometimes our surface ships went the wrong way and didn't try to find the Jap's aircraft carriers, blunders like that. Finally high command decided that we should find all the carriers and attack them. The strategy worked; we hit a lot of their carriers and things started turning in our favor. It amounted to us getting the upper hand and they never recovered from it.

Midway became our forward fueling station after we occupied it. There wasn't much there but a road, an airstrip, and lots of gooney birds that were very properly named. They were protected and we couldn't even do target practice on them. They'd lay their eggs out on the road and on the runway and caused everyone a lot of problems.

We got sent over a lot closer to Japan and wound up at Truk. It was the Japanese's equivalent of our Pearl Harbor. We'd sneak into the area--all of our boats did, and pick off whatever we could.

Our biggest scare came when we were going to dive and one of our young sailors screwed up trying to close the hatch. He didn't get the dog latch seated properly and when he turned loose of the lanyard, the hatched opened.   We'd just begun to dive. Luckily another enlisted man, that knew what he was doing, got the thing seated properly.   Some stuff was ruined and we spent three days undergoing repairs so we could get back to the action.

Torpedoes that boomerang can kill you

A boomeranging torpedo was another big time hazard that could be just as bad or worse than diving with the hatch open. There are two stabilizing fins on a torpedo. When fired, each fin is supposed to be spinning opposite the other at 2,400 rpms. If they got out of time they'd make what we called an erratic run. That happened on our sub. Our down man detected the runaway torpedo and sounded the alarm. The captain dove down about 90 feet and that thing circled back and went right over us. It sounded just like a freight train.   It was a real serious hazard.

I have a good friend, Clayton Decker, who was on a sub, The Tang that fired a torpedo and had it boomerang on them. He was in the forward torpedo room with 23 men when it hit. Only seven men out of the 23 down there made it out. They wound up prisoners of the Japanese for a while until the war ended. I met him after the war and see him at our conventions. He gave me a little miniature sub and is really a nice guy. Our guys who were Prisoners of war got $10,000 apiece after the war, regardless of the time they were confined. Clayton invested in a trash business in Denver and was quite successful. I saw him on TV recently being interviewed about his experiences as a submariner.

We had other problems with torpedoes. We'd fire and track them by sound and hear them hit our target. But, a lot of times they wouldn't explode because the detonators weren't any good.

Sailors on shore leave get very lucky

We went over to Truk Island and on to Perth Australia, way out in the southwest corner of the country. It was great duty. All the young Australian men were fighting over in North Africa and so we filled in for them the best we could! I had a good buddy named Jim. He and

I were in an Aussie hotel that had five bars and wound up so smashed one night that we didn't even know when we went to bed. In the morning I found our blues folded up just like they were supposed to be. We had a lot of money with us so I looked for mine. It was all gone. I woke Jim up and told him I'd lost my money. He looked and his was gone, too. We had about $3,000 between us, which was a fortune back then. We decided to look up the Chief on our boat and borrow some money from him since he always carried a big wad around. When we went downstairs for breakfast, a man came to our table and asked our names. We told him and he said, "I've got something for you." He had our money and liberty cards and everything else we'd been carrying. Come to find out the waitresses in one of the bars took us up, put us to bed, and put our valuables in a safe place. We were amazed. Things like that just don't happen every place.

We operated a lot of the time out of Pearl Harbor. Admiral Nimitz found out that the easiest and safest way for us to defeat the Japs on an island was to by-pass it. If their ships couldn't make it past us to supply the island, the men stationed there would soon starve. I don't think a lot of people knew anything about our strategy, but General MacArthur did and he was against it. He and Nimitz didn't get along too well because MacArthur wanted to be the top dog in charge of everything and Nimitz wouldn't let him mess with his submarines. He was an ex-submariner and he wouldn't tolerate MacArthur's interference.

At Leyte Gulf

We got into a lot of significant battles. One was the battle of Leyte Gulf, which was one of the major battles of the war. We'd fire on their ships when they were in a convoy. They'd send out their escorts to try to blow us out of the water.

I never got hit but got "wounded" when my lathe backfired and I got a piece of brass in my eye. A captain at the Hospital in Pearl Harbor came through giving out purple hearts while I was being treated there. I was in a ward full of Marines without legs or arms and when the captain wanted to give me a purple heart, I argued with him and said, "I just can't take it."

Of course a purple heart can't be turned down for anything and it turned out pretty good for me.

After they worked on my eye they sent me back to the states to a diesel school in Beloit, Wisconsin. It was great. I've never been treated better in my life than I was by the civilians in Beloit. I got married and my wife was up there with me.

Pretty soon I was assigned to another ship, the Medregal, which means a base of unknown origin. While waiting to ship out I needed extra money so I got a job with Frank Jones Ale.

My wife became pregnant and I took her home to Kansas, because the Medregal was commissioned and we were ordered to the Pacific.

In Panama a destroyer rammed us while we were submerged. It damaged our periscopes and we had to go back to Portsmouth to get new ones.

My wife lost the baby and I got off for 30 days to go home for the burial. The war ended during that time.

The Medregal had gone on to Key West, Florida, and I was reassigned to Philadelphia to go out on a ship that was built by a civilian shipyard. The first time they launched it, it cracked! They welded her back together.

Discharged

I'd planned to stay in the Navy, but I decided the ship wasn't safe and I told the navy to shove it. My enlistment was up and I got out.

When I got out of the navy, I applied for a rural mail carrier's job. It was a political appointment and I was at the top of the list as a wounded veteran. The man who got me the job got killed about six months after that and I got his job.

My first wife died and I re-married. My second wife and I went to a submariner's convention in Indianapolis. While we were changing planes in St. Louis we met a submariner from Denver, a stranger, who'd left his money at home and didn't have a cent on him. I said, "Well, I'll give you some money." I gave him a hundred dollars and my wife just exploded. She ranted and raved, "You'll never see that money!" I said, "Hey, the guy's in trouble and I think I'll see my money again."

When we got to Indianapolis the man called home and his wife sent him his money. That afternoon he came over to our table, where there were about 25 people seated, and handed me the $100 and offered me more. I said, "No, this is it." My wife just sat there. She couldn't believe it. Then he asked, "All right, can I buy drinks for the table?" I said, "That's up to you." He bought the drinks and it cost him $40.

Submarine sailors stick together

Later, I told my wife, "See, he's a submarine sailor. We stick together." She still couldn't believe it and thought I was crazy for loaning the man the money.

Incidentally, our marriage didn't work out.

ACKNOWLEDGEMENTS

Special thanks to the brave men and women
whose stories make up this book.
May their selfless contributions to mankind
be never forgotten.

...

My deepest appreciation to *Senator Pat Roberts*
who wrote the Foreword

...

For an outstanding job in designing the cover
Dodge City High School Red Demons Graphix
Instructor: *Steve Rankin*
Student designers: *Jared C. Coates—Josh Nietling
Christopher G. Reeves—Garret D. Seacat—Jared T. Waldman*

...

For her years of tireless work and undying devotion in assisting
with the innumerable tasks associated with putting out this book,
thanks to my wife, *Karen*.
Without her, it would not have been possible.

...

Marguerite R. Davis Frazier, my mother,
who showed me the joy of writing.

...

Ernest C. Frazier, Sr., my father,
who taught me perseverance.

The Boothill Coffee Club Volume I

Ernie Frazier

About the Author

After college and the army, the author pursued a career in financial planning before submitting to a long-suppressed desire to write. His first work, a trilogy, revealed an unusual talent for weaving a story of intrigue and adventure that featured close-knit, mind-bending plots and a never-to-be-forgotten cast of characters. *Black Hand Over Kansas, The Journada del Muerto,* and *The Victors* never ceases to thrill new readers.

Now comes another work of love: Gleaned from personal interviews, *THE BOOTHILL COFFEE CLUB* is a personal wartime journey into the hearts and minds of the "guys next door" who paid terrible prices to keep America free.